RACE, POLITICS AND THE MEDIA

Understanding Global Intersections

OSMAN KARAKAS

2023

About Book

Book Title: **RACE, POLITICS AND THE MEDIA:**

Understanding Global Intersections

Type: Digital E-Book

Format: PDF

Size: 6X9 inches - 15.24X22.89 cm

Total Pages: 439

E-mail: okarakas@hotmail.com

Web: www.osmankarakas.com

CONTENTS

Preface

In an increasingly interconnected world, the symbiotic relationship between race, politics, and media has never been more pronounced. This book embarks on a journey to explore this intricate web of interactions, shedding light on how these elements converge and diverge across global landscapes.

"Race, Politics and Media" delves into the multifaceted dynamics that shape narratives, perceptions, and policies. From the historical echoes of colonialism to the modern-day resonance of social media activism, each chapter unravels layers of complexity, offering insights that transcend geographical boundaries.

With chapters spanning historical perspectives, media representations, political discourse, ownership diversity, activism's digital realm, intersectionality, news coverage biases, media literacy, and envisioning an inclusive future, this book acts as both a compass and a map. It guides readers through the terrain of ideas, controversies, and aspirations that intersect around these crucial themes.

Through meticulous research, comprehensive case studies, and thought-provoking analyses, "Race, Politics and Media" seeks to foster a deeper understanding of the challenges and opportunities that arise when race, politics, and media converge. As we embark on this exploration, we invite readers to critically engage with the content, challenge preconceptions, and participate in the ongoing dialogue for a more equitable and inclusive world.

The journey begins here, where the pages await to unveil the interconnected tapestry of "Race, Politics and Media."

Introduction

In an age defined by rapid globalization, pervasive communication, and intricate social dynamics, the intersection of race, politics, and media has emerged as a cornerstone of our collective discourse. The interplay between these three forces shapes our perceptions, influences our decisions, and molds the very fabric of societies worldwide. This book, "Race, Politics, and Media," ventures into this captivating nexus to unravel its complexities and illuminate its far-reaching implications.

At the heart of this exploration lies a fundamental question: How do race, politics, and media converge to both reflect and shape the contours of our world? This question serves as a guiding beacon as we navigate the diverse landscapes of historical legacies, contemporary narratives, and future possibilities.

From the echoes of colonialism that reverberate through media representations to the digital landscapes where activism intersects with political discourse, each chapter in this volume encapsulates a distinct facet of this multifaceted relationship. Together, they form a tapestry that unveils the intricate connections between identity, power, and communication.

As we embark on this journey, we delve into historical perspectives that cast light on the roots of present-day dynamics. We examine the lenses through which media portrays race, unearthing both the perpetuation of stereotypes and the potential for transformative change. We navigate the realms of political discourse, where language is harnessed to galvanize and divide. We scrutinize media ownership and diversity, laying bare the influence of concentrated power and the imperative for inclusive representation.

In the digital era, the impact of social media cannot be ignored. We explore its role in amplifying racial issues, the phenomenon of hashtag activism, and the global campaigns that gain momentum through digital connectivity. The intricacies of intersectionality come to the forefront, revealing how race intertwines with gender, sexuality, and other dimensions of identity.

We scrutinize news coverage and its potential to perpetuate racial biases, and delve into the significance of media literacy as a tool to decipher and challenge these narratives. Propelled by a vision of inclusivity, we investigate policy recommendations, political initiatives, and collaborative efforts aimed at reshaping media narratives for a more equitable future.

Throughout this journey, we embark on case studies from around the world, offering region-specific analyses that highlight the global variations of this intricate relationship. Each chapter is accompanied by section introductions that invite readers to explore the nuances of each subtopic in depth.

As you traverse these pages, our hope is that you'll engage critically with the content, challenge preconceptions, and join the chorus of voices advocating for a world where the interplay of race, politics, and media fosters understanding, justice, and unity. The exploration begins here, and the insights gleaned are destined to resonate beyond these pages, fostering ongoing dialogue and transformation.

Welcome to "Race, Politics, and Media," where the journey of discovery unfolds across the global tapestry of identity, influence, and representation.

Chapter 1: Introduction

Defining the Scope

In the grand tapestry of human existence, certain intersections hold the power to shape history, society, and the narratives that bind them. The convergence of race, politics, and media is undoubtedly one of these pivotal crossroads. As we embark on a journey to delve into the intricacies of this intersection, the foundational step is to define the scope of this multifaceted inquiry.

The Multidimensionality of the Intersection

Defining the scope of the intersection of race, politics, and media involves not merely sketching the boundaries of a subject but understanding its multidimensional nature. It's not merely the point where these three elements converge; it's a dynamic interplay that transcends categories and genres. It encompasses historical legacies, contemporary narratives, digital landscapes, social dynamics, power structures, and the very essence of human identity.

Unraveling Interwoven Narratives

At the heart of defining the scope is the recognition that race, politics, and media are not isolated entities; they are threads intricately woven into the fabric of our societies. They are threads that intersect, tangle, and unravel in ways that defy simplistic categorizations. The scope encompasses the narratives that media constructs, the ideologies that politics shapes, and the identities that race influences.

Global and Local Dimensions

Defining the scope requires acknowledging that this intersection transcends geographical boundaries. It's a phenomenon that plays out on a global stage, where events in one corner of the world ripple through digital networks to impact minds and opinions elsewhere. Simultaneously, it's also an intersection that manifests uniquely in local contexts, influenced by historical, cultural, and political nuances.

Historical Anchors and Contemporary Reflections

The scope extends through time, connecting historical anchors to contemporary reflections. It's about understanding the echoes of colonialism that reverberate through modern media representations and political structures. It's about recognizing how the narratives of the past are refracted through the lens of present-day media and political discourses, ultimately shaping collective memory and future trajectories.

Impact on Identity and Society

Defining the scope is about unraveling how this intersection molds identities and societies. It's about recognizing that media narratives and political agendas have the power to shape how individuals perceive themselves and others. It's about acknowledging that race, politics, and media influence the construction of norms, the formation of allegiances, and the development of collective consciousness.

Navigating Complexity

Defining the scope is a delicate act of navigating complexity. It's about recognizing that this intersection is not reducible to a set of discrete topics but is a dynamic entity with tendrils that reach into every corner of our lives. It's about acknowledging that discussions around race and politics are intrinsically tied to the information we consume, the ideologies we adopt, and the choices we make.

A Call to Explore

As we define the scope of this intersection, we invite readers to embark on a journey of exploration. We beckon you to traverse the chapters that follow, each of which peels back layers of complexity to reveal insights, perspectives, and analyses. By defining the scope, we lay the foundation for a profound inquiry that invites critical engagement, self-reflection, and the recognition that the scope of this intersection extends far beyond the pages of this book.

Importance of Understanding the Intersection

In the vast tapestry of human interaction, few threads are as intertwined and influential as the relationship between race, politics, and media. It's not just a convergence of concepts; it's a nexus that carries profound implications for the way societies function, identities are formed, and narratives are woven. As we embark on a journey to explore the depths of this intricate intersection, it becomes increasingly clear that comprehending its significance is not merely a matter of curiosity; it's a necessity for fostering informed citizenship, social justice, and a more equitable world.

Shaping Perceptions and Reality

Media is the modern-day storyteller, weaving narratives that influence how individuals perceive the world around them. Its power to shape opinions and mold perspectives is unparalleled. This is where the intersection of race, politics, and media becomes a focal point of interest. The stories media tells, the characters it portrays, and the issues it amplifies can either reinforce stereotypes or challenge them. Media's portrayal of political figures and events can influence public perception, thus impacting policy decisions and public discourse.

Amplifying Marginalized Voices

Understanding the intersection is not just about deciphering the influence of media on society; it's also about recognizing its potential for amplifying marginalized voices. The media has the capacity to shine a spotlight on racial injustices, political inequalities, and narratives that often remain hidden from mainstream consciousness. By comprehending how media can uplift voices that have been historically silenced, we can engage in efforts to build a more inclusive and equitable narrative landscape.

Navigating Political Discourse

In the realm of politics, the language used to discuss race plays a pivotal role in shaping policies and public sentiment. The intersection provides us with a lens to scrutinize the use of racially charged language, coded messaging, and dog-whistle politics. It's about recognizing how certain words can evoke deep-seated emotions, perpetuate biases, or challenge established norms. Understanding this intersection is akin to understanding the tools politicians wield to garner support, perpetuate divisions, or unite communities.

Empathy and Social Cohesion

A society that understands the intersection of race, politics, and media is a society that is better equipped to foster empathy and social cohesion. When individuals comprehend the complex ways in which media narratives are crafted and political agendas are shaped, they become critical consumers of information. This critical thinking extends beyond skepticism; it empowers individuals to engage in meaningful conversations, seek out diverse perspectives, and bridge gaps between communities.

Informed Participation and Advocacy

The intersection is not an abstract concept; it's the foundation upon which informed participation and advocacy are built. In an era of information overload, knowing how to discern reliable sources from biased ones is a crucial skill. By understanding the intersection, individuals can discern when media is being used to manipulate opinions or when political rhetoric is designed to exploit fears. Armed with this knowledge, individuals can engage in advocacy, challenge discriminatory narratives, and demand accountability from political leaders.

A Call to Action

The importance of understanding the intersection of race, politics, and media goes beyond personal enrichment; it's a call to action. It's a recognition that we are all stakeholders in a complex web of influence, and our understanding of this web can drive positive change. It's about acknowledging that an equitable society necessitates a populace that is informed, engaged, and equipped to challenge injustices wherever they may arise.

As we delve deeper into the chapters that follow, keep in mind the profound implications of this intersection. Recognize the power it wields in shaping our perceptions, policies, and potential for progress. This exploration is not passive; it's an invitation to engage, question, and advocate for a more just and equitable world.

Brief Overview of the Global Landscape

In a world that is increasingly interconnected, the intersection of race, politics, and media reverberates across continents and cultures. As we embark on this exploration, it's essential to take a step back and examine the global landscape in which this complex interplay unfolds.

Globalization and Information Flow

The dawn of globalization has transformed the way information travels. Borders are no longer barriers to the dissemination of ideas, narratives, and perspectives. The global landscape of media is characterized by a vast network of interconnected platforms that enable the swift exchange of information across the globe. This interconnectedness has given rise to a new era of digital activism and transnational advocacy, where a cause that ignites hearts in one corner of the world can find resonance halfway across the planet.

Diverse Cultural Contexts

One of the defining features of the global landscape is its rich tapestry of diverse cultural contexts. The intersection of race, politics, and media operates within the intricate nuances of cultures that stretch from megacities to remote villages. The narratives that emerge within these contexts are shaped by historical legacies, societal norms, and the political climate unique to each region. Understanding the global landscape means recognizing that the impact of media representation and political discourse varies significantly across cultural boundaries.

Inequalities and Power Dynamics

Exploring the global landscape also unveils the profound inequalities and power dynamics that underpin the intersection. Historically marginalized communities find their voices amplified or suppressed based on a range of factors, including economic disparities, historical injustices, and access to media platforms. The global landscape mirrors the broader sociopolitical landscape, with imbalances of power often manifesting in the representation—or lack thereof—of certain racial groups in media and political discourse.

Evolving Technologies and Platforms

The global landscape is in a state of constant flux, shaped by evolving technologies and platforms. Social media has emerged as a transformative force, democratizing information dissemination and enabling individuals to engage with political discourse in unprecedented ways. The landscape is marked by an intricate dance between traditional media outlets and digital platforms, where information travels at the speed of a click and misinformation spreads with alarming ease.

Challenges and Opportunities

As we survey the global landscape, we encounter a myriad of challenges and opportunities. The challenges are evident in the perpetuation of harmful stereotypes, the spread of misinformation, and the manipulation of political narratives. Simultaneously, the landscape offers opportunities for advocacy, education, and empowerment. Movements that were once confined to local contexts can now find solidarity on a global scale, sparking conversations that challenge systemic inequalities and demand change.

The Interconnected Web

In essence, the global landscape is an interconnected web where narratives, ideologies, and aspirations crisscross continents. It's a landscape where the stories told in one corner of the world can shape perceptions and conversations thousands of miles away. Understanding this landscape is essential for navigating the complexities of the intersection of race, politics, and media. It's about recognizing that while local contexts matter, they are embedded in a global tapestry where every thread contributes to the larger narrative.

A Call to Engagement

As we immerse ourselves in this brief overview of the global landscape, we are reminded of the profound interconnectedness of our world. It's a reminder that the stories we tell and consume, the politics we engage with, and the media we interact with are part of a global conversation. This conversation is not just about understanding—it's about engagement, empathy, and actively shaping the narratives that define our shared humanity.

25

Chapter 2: Historical Perspectives

Colonialism and its Influence on Racial Narratives

In the annals of history, few phenomena have left as profound an imprint on the landscape of race, politics, and media as colonialism. This chapter delves into the historical underpinnings that have shaped the narratives surrounding race through the lens of colonial conquests and their enduring legacy.

The Colonial Unfolding

The tapestry of colonialism is woven with threads of conquest, exploitation, and cultural imposition. European powers ventured into distant lands, often with the intention of expanding their empires and amassing wealth. These ventures brought about encounters between different cultures, races, and worldviews, setting the stage for a collision of narratives and power dynamics.

Media as a Tool of Control

One of the profound ways in which colonialism left its mark was through the manipulation of media. Colonial powers harnessed media outlets to construct narratives that justified their actions and perpetuated notions of racial superiority. These narratives were disseminated not only within the colonized territories but also back to the colonizers' home countries, shaping public opinion and garnering support for imperial endeavors.

Formation of Racial Hierarchies

Colonialism played a pivotal role in the construction of racial hierarchies that persist to this day. The classification of races based on physical attributes and cultural practices laid the foundation for discriminatory ideologies. Media outlets were instrumental in propagating these ideologies, disseminating images and narratives that portrayed colonized peoples as inferior, exotic, or even dangerous.

Colonialism's Echoes in Modern Narratives

The echoes of colonialism resonate through modern media narratives, influencing the way we perceive race, identity, and power dynamics. The stereotypes and biases forged during the colonial era continue to influence media representations, political discourses, and societal norms. The images and narratives that were propagated during colonial times have left a lasting imprint on the collective consciousness, requiring a conscious effort to deconstruct and challenge them.

Empowerment Through Historical Awareness

Understanding the influence of colonialism on racial narratives is not merely an exercise in historical analysis; it's an empowerment to navigate the complexities of contemporary discourse. By delving into this historical context, we equip ourselves with the tools to recognize the roots of systemic biases and the perpetuation of harmful stereotypes. It's an awakening that empowers us to engage in critical media consumption and to challenge narratives that perpetuate inequality.

A Call to Reevaluate

As we explore the historical perspectives of colonialism's impact on racial narratives, we are confronted with the imperatives of reevaluation and change. The narratives that were constructed to serve imperial ambitions must be dissected, questioned, and redefined. This chapter acts as a reminder that our understanding of race, politics, and media is interwoven with the historical legacies of colonialism—a reminder that invites us to engage in transformative conversations and to envision a future free from the constraints of inherited biases.

Through the exploration of colonialism's imprint on racial narratives, we embark on a journey that illuminates the deep-seated connections between historical events, media representations, and the ongoing quest for racial equality. The pages that follow carry us further into this exploration, encouraging us to challenge preconceptions, reassess our perceptions, and actively contribute to a more just and inclusive narrative landscape.

Media's Role in Shaping Historical Perceptions

In the grand tapestry of history, the role of media emerges as a crucial thread, intricately woven into the narratives that define our collective past. The pages of history are not merely shaped by events and individuals; they are also shaped by the pens, presses, and pixels that transmit these narratives to the world. This chapter delves into the profound influence of media in shaping historical perceptions, unraveling a tapestry that stretches from antiquity to the digital age.

Chronicles of Media and History

The relationship between media and history dates back to the earliest forms of communication. From oral traditions to hieroglyphics etched on stone, humanity has always sought to preserve and transmit its narratives. As societies evolved, so did the mediums through which stories were shared—scrolls, manuscripts, and eventually, the revolutionary advent of the printing press. These mediums heralded a new era, allowing history to be documented and disseminated on a broader scale.

The Power of Narrative Framing

Media's role in shaping historical perceptions is not merely about recording facts; it's about the power of narrative framing. The words chosen, the emphasis placed, and the details highlighted all play a pivotal role in constructing historical narratives. Media has the power to imbue events with significance, to elevate individuals to legendary status, and to cast a shadow over certain aspects while illuminating others. It's within this power that media shapes not only how history is understood but also how it's remembered.

Media as an Arbiter of Memory

In many ways, media serves as an arbiter of memory, deciding which stories are etched into the collective consciousness and which fade into the recesses of oblivion. Newspapers, books, films, and now digital platforms hold the keys to the annals of human experience. They determine whose voices are amplified, whose perspectives are marginalized, and whose stories are deemed worthy of remembrance. This gatekeeping function of media inevitably influences how history is perceived by generations to come.

The Role of Bias and Objectivity

An inherent challenge in media's role as a shaper of historical perceptions is the presence of bias. Every medium carries the fingerprints of its creators, and these fingerprints can manifest as biases—conscious or unconscious. Journalists, writers, and creators are influenced by their own contexts, beliefs, and cultural lenses, which can color the way historical events are portrayed. Striving for objectivity is a noble pursuit, yet the very act of selecting which events to cover and which voices to amplify can introduce subtle biases into the narrative.

Media's Evolution in the Digital Age

The digital age has catapulted media's influence to unprecedented heights. The internet is a repository of information, a platform for voices from every corner of the globe, and a battleground where historical narratives are contested. Social media, in particular, democratizes the sharing of stories, enabling marginalized voices to find an audience. However, this digital landscape also poses challenges—misinformation spreads rapidly, and the line between fact and opinion can blur.

A Call to Analyze and Contextualize

As we navigate the intricate relationship between media and historical perceptions, we are called to engage in critical analysis and contextualization. History is not a monolithic entity; it's a mosaic composed of diverse perspectives, silenced voices, and suppressed stories. It's incumbent upon us to peel back the layers of media's influence, to seek out multiple narratives, and to question the motivations behind the shaping of historical accounts.

In delving into "Media's Role in Shaping Historical Perceptions," we journey through the corridors of time and uncover the layers of influence that media exerts on our understanding of the past. This chapter prompts us to reflect on the narratives that have shaped us, to challenge preconceptions, and to recognize the power we hold in shaping the narratives that will define the history of the future.

Early Political Movements and their Media Representation

The annals of history are resplendent with the stories of visionary individuals who dared to challenge the status quo, sparking the flames of change that would shape societies and redefine political landscapes. Yet, the impact of these early political movements wasn't solely determined by the conviction of their leaders or the fervor of their supporters. Equally significant was the role played by media—the conduit through which their ideals, struggles, and victories were disseminated to the masses.

The Media as a Catalyst for Change

Media, in its myriad forms, has the remarkable power to amplify the voices of those who seek to reshape the world. Early political movements found in media a catalyst for change—a means to transcend geographic boundaries and reach the hearts and minds of people who shared their aspirations. Pamphlets, newspapers, and manifestos became vessels of inspiration, carrying the ideals of reform, liberty, and equality to eager readers.

Printed Words Igniting Revolutions

The print revolution of the 16th century paved the way for a new era of information dissemination, a phenomenon that would prove pivotal in the unfolding of early political movements. Pamphlets and newspapers became weapons of intellectual insurgency, their words igniting revolutions and inciting discussions that rippled through coffeehouses, taverns, and parlors. The American Revolution found its anthem in the pages of "Common Sense," while the French Revolution drew inspiration from impassioned pamphlets demanding justice.

Visual Symbolism and Iconography

Media representation went beyond printed words, encompassing visual symbolism and iconography that galvanized supporters. Political cartoons emerged as a potent tool, lampooning oppressive regimes and satirizing tyrants. Visual imagery seared lasting impressions into the minds of the populace, etching revolutionary symbols into collective memory. The clenched fist, the liberty cap, and the raised flag—these visual markers became rallying points for those who sought change.

Media as a Reflection of Political Climate

The media representation of early political movements was more than a reflection; it was a shaping force that molded public opinion. Newspapers functioned as the primary source of information for the masses, and editors wielded significant influence over the narratives they disseminated. The portrayal of movements could swing from sympathetic to critical, casting the spotlight on the tension between the media's role as an objective informer and a partisan player in the political arena.

Challenges of Authenticity and Bias

Early political movements and their media representation also navigated the challenges of authenticity and bias. The line between fact and embellishment could blur, with movements sometimes presented in a way that aligned with the perspectives of the media outlets. Reports could be colored by political affiliations, introducing biases that shaped public perception. This dynamic underscored the need for discernment on the part of the audience—an imperative that remains relevant in the modern era.

Legacy of Early Movements in Media

The legacy of early political movements in media representation is profound and enduring. Their strategies, successes, and failures left an indelible mark on how political causes are portrayed. The seeds sown by these movements found fertile ground in subsequent generations of activists and leaders who recognized the power of media to sway opinion, galvanize support, and mobilize change.

A Call to Examine and Interpret

As we delve into "Early Political Movements and their Media Representation," we enter a realm where ink-stained pages and engraved images become agents of transformation. This chapter encourages us to examine the symbiotic relationship between movements and the media that portrayed them, to interpret the nuances of representation, and to recognize the enduring impact of their narratives on the trajectory of history. It reminds us that media is not just a reflection of change—it's an instrument of change, capable of shaping revolutions, reshaping societies, and immortalizing the ideals that inspire generations to come.

Chapter 3: Media Representations and Stereotypes

Racial Stereotyping in Media

In the realm of media, the stories we encounter are not mere reflections of reality; they are potent lenses that shape our perceptions, beliefs, and attitudes. Within this powerful influence lies a complex and often troubling phenomenon: racial stereotyping. This chapter delves deep into the intricate interplay between media representations and racial stereotypes, unearthing the impact they have on society, politics, and individual psyches.

The Power of Visual Narratives

Visual narratives hold a unique power to communicate ideas, emotions, and perspectives. Media representations, whether in film, television, advertising, or print, wield this power to project images that define racial identities. Racial stereotypes are born from these projections—oversimplified, distorted, and often harmful portrayals that reduce diverse groups to a set of limiting characteristics.

From Margins to Center Stage

Media representations and racial stereotypes are intertwined threads that have woven their way through history. From early films with their caricatures to modern advertisements that perpetuate biases, these representations have been used to both marginalize and marginalize groups.

This chapter traces the journey from minstrel shows to the amplification of certain narratives over others, highlighting the insidious ways in which media can reinforce racial hierarchies.

Shaping Perception and Reality

Racial stereotyping in media isn't confined to the realm of fiction; it shapes how we perceive reality. These stereotypes can contribute to the creation of unconscious biases, impacting the way individuals interact with each other. The danger lies in the subtlety of influence—how a portrayal on screen can seep into the subconscious, affecting decisions, judgments, and behaviors in ways that go unnoticed.

Media as a Reflective and Formative Force

Media representations and racial stereotypes are both a reflection of societal attitudes and a formative force that shapes those attitudes. It's a cyclical relationship—media reflects prevailing beliefs, but it also has the power to reinforce or challenge them. In an era of global connectivity, media has the ability to perpetuate stereotypes on a massive scale, yet it also holds the potential to amplify counter-narratives and reshape perceptions.

Harmful Consequences and Cultural Responsiveness

The consequences of racial stereotyping in media are far-reaching. It can contribute to a cycle of discrimination, perpetuate microaggressions, and reinforce institutional biases. Yet, the path to change lies in cultural responsiveness—a deliberate effort to dismantle stereotypes and present diverse, authentic representations. Media can be a powerful ally in this endeavor, contributing to a more inclusive narrative landscape.

Navigating Complexity

Navigating the landscape of media representations and racial stereotypes is a complex task. It requires critical thinking, media literacy, and an understanding of the broader sociopolitical context. It involves recognizing that even seemingly benign portrayals can carry deep-seated implications. It's an invitation to question the narratives we consume, demand diversity in storytelling, and challenge the industry to reckon with its role in perpetuating stereotypes.

A Call for Deconstruction and Reconstruction

As we delve into the intricacies of "Racial Stereotyping in Media," we are called to deconstruct the narratives that have shaped our perceptions and reconstruct a more equitable and empathetic narrative landscape. This chapter encourages us to challenge our own biases, demand accountability from media creators, and actively seek out stories that defy stereotypes. It's a reminder that media has the power to both harm and heal, and by engaging with it thoughtfully, we contribute to a more just and inclusive world.

Political Implications of Reinforced Stereotypes

Within the realm of media lies a paradoxical phenomenon—a double-edged sword that wields influence not only over public perception but also over the corridors of political power. The perpetuation of stereotypes in media, particularly those pertaining to race, reverberates far beyond entertainment and into the realm of politics, where its implications can shape policies, public opinion, and the very foundations of governance. This section delves deep into the intricate web of political implications that arise from the reinforcement of stereotypes through media narratives.

Shaping Political Discourse

Media, with its ability to craft narratives that resonate with mass audiences, holds immense power to shape political discourse. When stereotypes are perpetuated through media representations, they can infiltrate public conversations, shaping the way politicians frame issues, debate policies, and address constituents. These stereotypes can become talking points, influencing public perceptions and driving the direction of political agendas.

Influence on Voter Behavior

Stereotypes embedded in media narratives can significantly influence voter behavior. The images and portrayals presented on screen can impact how individuals perceive candidates, parties, and policy proposals. Subconscious biases formed through media consumption can sway voting decisions, even if voters are not fully conscious of these influences. In this way, media's reinforcement of stereotypes can have a direct impact on election outcomes and, consequently, on the composition of legislative bodies.

Reinforcement of Existing Biases

Media's reinforcement of stereotypes is not confined to creating new biases; it also perpetuates existing ones. When individuals encounter narratives that align with their preconceived notions, it validates their biases, further entrenching divisive beliefs. This phenomenon has profound implications for political polarization, as individuals become more resistant to alternative perspectives and less willing to engage in constructive dialogue.

Underrepresentation and Political Participation

The reinforcement of stereotypes can also have a tangible impact on political participation. When certain racial or ethnic groups are consistently depicted in media as marginalized or inconsequential, it can discourage members of those groups from engaging in the political process. The lack of representation in media can lead to feelings of disenfranchisement, ultimately affecting voter turnout and political engagement.

Legitimacy of Policies and Decisions

Media's role in reinforcing stereotypes can affect the legitimacy of policies and decisions. When policies disproportionately affect specific racial or ethnic groups, media representations can influence public perception of the necessity or fairness of these policies. Reinforced stereotypes can be used to justify discriminatory practices or perpetuate a status quo that disadvantages marginalized communities.

The Path Forward: Media Literacy and Reform

Understanding the political implications of reinforced stereotypes in media is a call to action. It highlights the urgent need for media literacy education that empowers individuals to critically analyze the narratives they consume. Additionally, it emphasizes the importance of media reform, wherein creators, producers, and platforms take responsibility for the narratives they perpetuate. Reimagining media narratives as catalysts for informed political engagement can pave the way for a more equitable political landscape.

A Call for Change

As we delve into the "Political Implications of Reinforced Stereotypes," we confront the complex interplay between media, politics, and societal perceptions. This section calls us to question the narratives we encounter, demand accountability from media creators, and actively engage in political discourse free from the shackles of divisive stereotypes. By challenging the status quo and envisioning a more inclusive media landscape, we take a vital step towards a political arena that truly represents and serves all members of society.

Case Studies of Global Media Misrepresentations

In the intricate dance between media and reality, misrepresentations can cast shadows over truth, perpetuating skewed narratives that resonate far beyond their origin. This section explores case studies from around the world—instances where media misrepresentations have distorted realities, perpetuated biases, and influenced public perceptions. These case studies serve as poignant reminders of the power and responsibility of media in shaping our understanding of the world.

Case Study 1: "The Danger of a Single Story"

Nigerian author Chimamanda Ngozi Adichie once spoke of "the danger of a single story"—the peril of reducing complex cultures and communities to singular narratives. This case study examines how media portrayals of Africa often succumb to this danger, perpetuating stereotypes of poverty, disease, and savagery. Such misrepresentations overshadow the continent's diversity, rich histories, and dynamic economies, reinforcing notions that hinder progress and international collaboration.

Chimamanda Ngozi Adichie, a Nigerian author renowned for her eloquent storytelling, introduced the concept of "the danger of a single story." This thought-provoking idea draws attention to the perils that arise when societies, regions, and individuals are reduced to simplistic and singular narratives. Adichie's insight serves as a profound reminder that just as no individual's life can be fully encapsulated by a single anecdote, no culture or continent can be accurately defined by a sole narrative.

In her acclaimed TED Talk, Adichie eloquently conveyed how a single story can perpetuate stereotypes, misunderstandings, and biases. She shared personal anecdotes from her own life, highlighting the times when her experiences as an African were subjected to the "single story" lens—one that homogenized her identity and overlooked the diversity within her continent. Through her words, Adichie revealed the harm that arises when narratives are reduced to caricatures that fail to capture the complexity of human experiences.

Adichie's perspective resonates on a global scale, extending beyond the African context to emphasize the broader importance of representation and understanding. Her insight underscores the fact that human lives are multi-dimensional, shaped by a myriad of influences, experiences, and interactions. By reducing individuals or communities to a single narrative, we miss the opportunity to appreciate the intricate tapestry of their identities.

Ultimately, Adichie's concept challenges us to be discerning consumers of narratives and to resist the allure of simplistic and convenient stories. Her insight prompts us to seek out diverse perspectives, to question preconceived notions, and to approach the world with empathy and open-mindedness. In an era where media has the power to shape perceptions and influence attitudes, Adichie's reminder of the "danger of a single story" holds significant relevance, urging us to engage with complexity, embrace nuance, and honor the richness of human experiences and identities.

Case Study 2: Orientalism and the Middle East

The Middle East has been a focal point of global attention for decades, but media misrepresentations have frequently distorted the region's realities. Orientalism—a Eurocentric perspective that exoticizes and essentializes the "East"—has permeated media portrayals. This case study explores how such misrepresentations fuel misunderstandings, perpetuate Islamophobia, and contribute to geopolitical tensions, hindering constructive dialogue and cooperation.

The Middle East has commanded international attention for decades, yet media representations have often been marred by distortions and misconceptions. Central to this issue is the concept of Orientalism, which entails a Eurocentric lens that simplifies and romanticizes the "East." This case study delves into the profound impact of Orientalist misrepresentations in media portrayals, shedding light on their role in perpetuating misunderstandings, fueling

Islamophobia, and exacerbating geopolitical tensions.

Orientalism: Distorted Perceptions

Orientalism, as first examined by Edward Said, encapsulates the tendency to view the Middle East through a reductive and exoticizing lens. This perspective portrays the region as mysterious, backward, and homogenous, distorting its complexities and erasing its diverse histories and cultures. By essentializing the "East," media representations often fail to capture the nuances that shape the Middle East's rich tapestry.

Fueling Misunderstandings

The consequences of Orientalist misrepresentations are far-reaching. This case study delves into how media's perpetuation of Orientalism fosters misunderstandings between the East and the West. By framing the Middle East in exotic terms, media inadvertently alienate audiences from truly understanding the complexities of the region's political, social, and cultural dynamics.

Perpetuating Islamophobia

One of the most distressing outcomes of Orientalism is the perpetuation of Islamophobia. Media portrayals that associate the Middle East solely with terrorism or extremism contribute to harmful stereotypes about Islam and its adherents. This section explores how these misrepresentations not only dehumanize Muslims but also hinder intercultural understanding and dialogue.

Contributing to Geopolitical Tensions

Orientalist media portrayals play a role in geopolitical tensions, often contributing to misunderstandings that escalate conflicts. This case study delves into how distorted narratives reinforce biases held by political decision-makers, which can, in turn, impact foreign policies and diplomatic efforts. Such narratives hinder constructive dialogue and cooperation, perpetuating cycles of hostility and distrust.

Championing Constructive Change

The case study underscores the urgency of dismantling Orientalist representations in media. By engaging with accurate and nuanced portrayals, media can shift the narrative away from reductive stereotypes and foster a more informed global discourse. By recognizing the Middle East's diverse realities, media can contribute to dismantling biases and creating a more empathetic understanding of the region.

In the realm of "Case Study 2: Orientalism and the Middle East," we are reminded of the profound responsibility media bears in shaping global perceptions. This case study calls us to challenge the narratives that perpetuate misunderstanding, to advocate for more accurate portrayals, and to recognize the role of media in fostering dialogue, empathy, and cooperation on the international stage.

Case Study 3: Indigenous Peoples and Cultural Appropriation

From Hollywood films to fashion runways, media misrepresentations of indigenous cultures have perpetuated harmful stereotypes and led to cultural appropriation. This case study highlights how indigenous communities have been commodified and distorted in mainstream media, erasing their complex histories and relegating them to caricatures. The misappropriation of symbols, practices, and identities further marginalizes these communities and perpetuates systemic inequalities.

The media portrayals of indigenous cultures have often been marked by inaccuracies and misappropriation. This case study illuminates the impact of such misrepresentations, shedding light on how indigenous communities have been commodified and distorted in mainstream media. These portrayals not only erase the rich complexities of their histories but also facilitate cultural appropriation, contributing to the marginalization and perpetuation of systemic inequalities.

Distorted Representations and Commodification

Media often reduce indigenous cultures to simplistic narratives that fail to capture their diverse histories and vibrant identities. This case study delves into how these portrayals commodify indigenous communities, turning their traditions and ways of life into marketable and often distorted commodities for mass consumption.

Cultural Appropriation: A Complex Phenomenon

The phenomenon of cultural appropriation emerges as a critical concern in this case study. It examines how symbols, practices, and identities from indigenous cultures are misappropriated by mainstream media and popular culture. This misappropriation goes beyond mere imitation—it reinforces harmful stereotypes, contributes to erasure, and perpetuates a cycle of exploitation.

Erasure of Complex Histories

One of the most damaging consequences of misrepresentations and cultural appropriation is the erasure of indigenous peoples' complex histories. By reducing these cultures to superficial imagery, media contribute to the marginalization of indigenous voices, undermining the efforts of these communities to reclaim their narratives and assert their identities.

Perpetuating Systemic Inequalities

The perpetuation of harmful stereotypes and cultural appropriation in media reinforces systemic inequalities that indigenous communities already face. This case study delves into how these portrayals can contribute to a lack of cultural understanding, unequal access to resources, and a continuation of historical injustices that have marginalized indigenous communities for centuries.

A Call for Authentic Representation and Respect

The case study highlights the urgent need for authentic representation and respect in media portrayals of indigenous cultures. By accurately reflecting the complexities of their histories and identities, media can play a vital role in challenging stereotypes and promoting a more inclusive narrative. Moreover, acknowledging the harmful impact of cultural appropriation and actively working to prevent it can contribute to a more equitable and just media landscape.

This case study calls us to champion indigenous voices, to advocate for authentic portrayals that honor the depth of their cultures, and to be vigilant against practices that perpetuate harm through cultural appropriation. By engaging in a more responsible and respectful media discourse, we contribute to the dismantling of harmful narratives and the promotion of true understanding and equity.

Case Study 4: Gender Stereotypes and LGBTQ+ Representation

Media's role in reinforcing gender norms and sexual orientation stereotypes cannot be ignored. This case study examines how media misrepresentations have perpetuated harmful gender roles, stigmatized non-binary identities, and marginalized LGBTQ+ individuals. The lack of authentic representation further silences diverse voices and perpetuates discrimination, impacting both societal attitudes and policy decisions.

The influence of media on shaping societal perceptions of gender and sexual orientation is profound. This case study delves into the impact of media misrepresentations in perpetuating harmful gender norms and stigmatizing LGBTQ+ identities. From reinforcing traditional gender roles to marginalizing non-binary individuals, media's role in shaping attitudes and perceptions cannot be underestimated.

Reinforcing Harmful Gender Norms

Media's portrayal of gender often adheres to outdated norms, reinforcing stereotypical roles for men and women. This case study examines how these portrayals contribute to the perpetuation of inequality and discrimination, limiting individuals' understanding of the diverse ways in which gender is expressed and experienced.

Stigmatizing Non-Binary Identities

Non-binary individuals, who do not conform to traditional binary notions of gender, face particular challenges in media representation. This section explores how media's misrepresentation of non-binary identities contributes to stigmatization, misunderstanding, and marginalization. The lack of visibility and authentic representation further hinders progress toward acceptance and equality.

Marginalization of LGBTQ+ Individuals

Media misrepresentations also impact LGBTQ+ individuals by perpetuating stereotypes and marginalizing their experiences. This case study delves into how media portrayals that lack nuance or authenticity contribute to a climate of discrimination and prejudice, reinforcing societal biases that hinder LGBTQ+ individuals' full participation in various spheres of life.

Silencing Diverse Voices

The lack of authentic representation further silences diverse voices within the LGBTQ+ community. By perpetuating narrow and one-dimensional portrayals, media hinder the visibility of LGBTQ+ individuals who do not fit these limited narratives. This section explores how this silencing effect impedes societal understanding and empathy.

Perpetuating Discrimination and Influencing Policy

Media's role extends beyond mere portrayal—it shapes attitudes, perceptions, and even policy decisions. This case study delves into how misrepresentations perpetuate discrimination and bias, influencing public opinion and political choices. These biases can lead to harmful policies that hinder LGBTQ+ individuals' rights and well-being.

Advocating for Authenticity and Equality

The case study underscores the importance of authentic representation and equality in media portrayals of gender and LGBTQ+ individuals. By accurately reflecting the diversity of gender identities and sexual orientations, media can challenge stereotypes, promote empathy, and contribute to dismantling discrimination. This section calls us to advocate for narratives that honor the full spectrum of human experiences, fostering a more inclusive and just society.

As we explore "Case Study 4: Gender Stereotypes and LGBTQ+ Representation," we recognize that media's power to shape perceptions comes with a responsibility to be mindful of the impact it wields. This case study calls us to critically assess media representations, to amplify diverse voices, and to champion authentic portrayals that promote understanding, acceptance, and equality for all individuals, regardless of their gender or sexual orientation.

Case Study 5: Refugee Narratives and Dehumanization

Media misrepresentations of refugees and migrants often reduce complex human experiences to dehumanizing narratives. This case study delves into how media portrayals can create fear, reinforce nativism, and neglect the stories of resilience, courage, and hope that characterize refugee experiences. Misrepresentations contribute to the perpetuation of harmful policies, hindering efforts to create inclusive and compassionate societies.

Media's portrayal of refugees and migrants often fails to capture the depth of their human experiences, instead reducing them to dehumanizing narratives. This case study explores the ways in which media misrepresentations contribute to fear, reinforce nativism, and neglect the stories of resilience, courage, and hope that define refugee journeys. These misrepresentations not only perpetuate harmful policies but also hinder the progress toward creating societies that are inclusive, compassionate, and understanding.

Dehumanizing Narratives and Fear

Media's focus on sensationalism and negative stereotypes can lead to the dehumanization of refugees and migrants. This case study delves into how these portrayals create an atmosphere of fear and anxiety, framing individuals seeking refuge as threats rather than fellow humans facing challenges and seeking safety.

Reinforcing Nativism and Xenophobia

Misrepresentations in media can reinforce nativism and xenophobia by perpetuating the idea that refugees and migrants are outsiders who threaten the status quo. This section explores how these portrayals contribute to a divisive narrative that pits "us" against "them," fostering an environment of suspicion and intolerance.

Neglecting Stories of Resilience and Hope

Refugee experiences are marked by stories of resilience, courage, and hope in the face of adversity. This case study examines how media's focus on negative aspects often neglects these stories, missing the opportunity to foster empathy and understanding among audiences. By overlooking these narratives, media perpetuate a one-sided view of the refugee experience.

Impact on Policies and Societal Attitudes

Media misrepresentations have a significant impact on both policies and societal attitudes. This section delves into how these portrayals can contribute to harmful policies that treat refugees and migrants as burdens rather than assets. Furthermore, the perpetuation of negative narratives can hinder efforts to build inclusive societies that value diversity and recognize the contributions of newcomers.

Championing Compassion and Understanding

The case study underscores the need for media to champion compassion and understanding in portraying refugee narratives. By focusing on the multifaceted experiences of refugees and migrants, media can counteract dehumanization, challenge stereotypes, and foster empathy. This section calls us to recognize the humanity in every individual and advocate for a more comprehensive and accurate representation of refugee journeys.

As we navigate "Case Study 5: Refugee Narratives and Dehumanization," we are reminded of the vital role media plays in shaping public perceptions and policy decisions. This case study calls us to critically engage with media portrayals, to amplify stories of resilience and hope, and to advocate for a more empathetic and compassionate approach to understanding the experiences of refugees and migrants. By challenging dehumanizing narratives, we contribute to the creation of a world where all individuals are valued, regardless of their origins or circumstances.

Case Study 6: Historical Revisionism and Nationalism

Media misrepresentations can also intersect with political agendas, leading to historical revisionism and the promotion of nationalist ideologies. This case study explores how certain governments utilize media to distort historical events, downplay atrocities, and advance narratives that serve their political interests. Such misrepresentations manipulate public perceptions, hinder reconciliation, and perpetuate divisions.

The entanglement of media with political agendas can spawn historical revisionism and the propagation of nationalist ideologies. This case study delves into the intricate dynamics by which certain governments exploit media platforms to manipulate historical events, obscure atrocities, and advocate narratives that align with their political goals. These misrepresentations wield the power to reshape public consciousness, impede reconciliation efforts, and perpetuate social divisions.

Manipulating the Past for Political Gains

This case study dissects how media's role in historical revisionism is harnessed for political ends. It investigates how historical events are cherry-picked, distorted, or entirely omitted from narratives to suit specific political narratives. By altering the historical narrative, media misrepresentations contribute to a skewed understanding of past events, thereby reinforcing distorted perspectives.

Diminishing Atrocities and Distorting Truths

A troubling aspect of historical revisionism is its propensity to downplay or even deny past atrocities and human rights violations. This section delves into how media complicity in minimizing these events can undermine accountability and obstruct the quest for justice and reconciliation. By obscuring the truth, these distortions enable historical injustices to persist unchallenged.

The Rise of Nationalist Narratives

Nationalist ideologies often exploit media to advance their agendas. This case study delves into how media portrayals can bolster nationalistic sentiments by glorifying historical episodes, figures, and narratives that cater to specific political agendas. These portrayals reinforce an "us versus them" mindset, nurturing divisions and obstructing intercultural understanding.

Engineering Public Perceptions

Historical revisionism and media manipulation have the power to reshape public perceptions. This section investigates how false narratives can sway public opinion, distorting the truth and influencing social attitudes. By fostering misguided understandings of historical realities, these misrepresentations erode efforts to forge shared truths and mutual understanding among communities.

Obstructing Reconciliation and Dialogue

The perpetuation of distorted narratives hinders meaningful reconciliation and dialogue. This case study delves into how such portrayals contribute to cycles of mistrust and hostility between communities. By nurturing divisive narratives, media misrepresentations obstruct the acknowledgment of historical wrongs and the forging of a common understanding vital for progress.

Championing Truth and Accountability

This case study underscores the vital importance of media in upholding historical accuracy and promoting accountability. By advocating for transparent, accurate, and diverse perspectives, media can challenge the manipulation of history and expose nationalistic agendas. This section urges responsible reporting that upholds the truth and contributes to fostering genuine understanding and reconciliation.

As we navigate "Case Study 6: Historical Revisionism and Nationalism," we are reminded that media's role in history profoundly affects contemporary realities. This case study calls us to scrutinize media narratives, champion efforts for truth and reconciliation, and advocate for a media landscape that fosters empathy, dismantles divisive ideologies, and contributes to a more just and unified world.

Distorting Historical Events for Political Ends

Media's role in historical revisionism is significant, as governments use it to manipulate the collective memory of their societies. This case study examines how historical events are selectively portrayed, omitted, or distorted to fit specific political narratives. By altering the historical record, media misrepresentations contribute to a skewed understanding of the past.

Downplaying Atrocities and Human Rights Violations

One of the most concerning aspects of historical revisionism is its tendency to downplay or deny past atrocities and human rights violations. This section explores how media's complicity in minimizing these events can lead to the erasure of victims' experiences, preventing accountability and obstructing efforts toward justice and reconciliation.

Advancing Nationalist Agendas

Nationalist ideologies often exploit media to advance their agendas. This case study delves into how media portrayals can foster a sense of nationalistic pride by glorifying historical events, figures, and narratives that serve specific political interests. Such portrayals reinforce an "us versus them" mentality, perpetuating divisions and inhibiting cross-cultural understanding.

Manipulating Public Perceptions

Historical revisionism and media manipulation have the power to reshape public perceptions and influence collective memory. This section explores how false or manipulated narratives can sway public opinion, undermining the pursuit of truth and hampering efforts toward reconciliation between communities with shared historical experiences.

Hindering Reconciliation and Dialogue

The perpetuation of distorted narratives hinders reconciliation and meaningful dialogue. By perpetuating false or divisive narratives, media misrepresentations contribute to a cycle of mistrust and hostility between communities. This case study delves into how these portrayals can hinder the acknowledgment of past wrongs and the forging of a common understanding necessary for moving forward.

The Call for Truth and Accountability

The case study underscores the critical importance of media in upholding historical accuracy and promoting accountability. By advocating for transparency, accuracy, and diverse perspectives, media can challenge the manipulation of history and expose nationalist agendas. This section calls us to demand responsible reporting that values the truth and aims to foster genuine understanding and reconciliation.

As we delve into "Case Study 6: Historical Revisionism and Nationalism," we recognize the profound impact that media's role in history can have on the present and future. This case study calls us to scrutinize media narratives, support efforts for truth and reconciliation, and advocate for a media landscape that fosters cross-cultural understanding, dismantles divisive ideologies, and contributes to a more just and unified world.

Toward Ethical Media Narratives

The case studies presented in this section underscore the ethical imperative of media narratives. They highlight the impact of misrepresentations on global understanding, social cohesion, and policy-making. As media consumers, we are called to critically engage with the narratives we encounter, demand diverse and authentic representation, and challenge media outlets to uphold their responsibility in shaping a more just and equitable world.

By exploring these case studies, we unravel the intricate threads that connect media misrepresentations to societal challenges. This section serves as a clarion call to transform media from a perpetuator of biases into a vehicle for truth, understanding, and positive change.

Chapter 4: Race and Political Discourse

Racialized Language in Politics

The realm of politics is a crucible where ideas, ideologies, and aspirations collide, shaping the course of nations and the destiny of societies. Within this arena, language becomes a potent tool—an instrument that can inspire, divide, and wield influence over the hearts and minds of citizens. This chapter delves into the nuanced interplay between race and political discourse, specifically examining the use of racialized language and its profound implications on public perception and policy-making.

The Power of Words in Politics

Words are more than mere vessels of communication in politics; they are instruments of persuasion, identity-shaping, and power consolidation. Language can evoke emotions, summon historical narratives, and mobilize constituencies. When race intersects with political discourse, language takes on an added layer of complexity—carrying the weight of histories, struggles, and aspirations of racial communities.

Language as a Vehicle of Influence

In the intricate realm of politics, the art of language transcends mere communication; it becomes a formidable tool of influence. This exploration delves into the profound impact that words wield within the political arena. It delves into how politicians meticulously select and deploy their words to achieve a range of strategic goals. Words are not merely carriers of information—they are instruments of persuasion, emotion, and ideology.

Within political discourse, words are not chosen haphazardly; they are meticulously curated to shape public opinion. This section unveils the strategic process by which politicians craft their rhetoric to sway the masses. Every word is strategically placed to resonate with specific demographics, tapping into their beliefs, fears, and aspirations. By analyzing the intricate web of rhetoric, this exploration unveils the mechanisms through which language becomes a vehicle for shaping public sentiment and, consequently, political outcomes.

Emotion is a catalyst for action, and language is a powerful catalyst for evoking emotions. Politicians masterfully wield language to trigger emotional responses that forge deep connections with the audience. Whether it's kindling hope, stoking anger, or appealing to empathy, words are chosen to kindle feelings that resonate. This exploration reveals how language transforms politics from a rational exercise into an emotional journey, steering the audience toward the desired viewpoint.

Moreover, the language deployed in political discourse is not neutral; it's laden with ideological implications. Words frame issues within particular ideological contexts, shaping how they are perceived and understood. This exploration demonstrates how politicians use language to establish the framework within which discussions unfold. By subtly manipulating linguistic nuances, they guide public discourse toward interpretations that align with their agendas, reinforcing their beliefs and garnering support.

The art of language in politics goes beyond surface-level semantics. It delves into euphemisms, loaded language, and persuasive appeals—subtle techniques that wield profound influence. By decoding these linguistic tools, this exploration unveils the mechanics of how language becomes a vehicle for persuasion, enabling politicians to subtly navigate the spectrum of meaning and implication.

The Weaponization of Racialized Language

Racialized language can be weaponized in political discourse, serving as a divisive force that amplifies existing tensions. The deliberate use of coded language, dog whistles, and racial slurs can exploit latent prejudices, appealing to certain voter bases while marginalizing others. These linguistic maneuvers can deepen societal divides, making politics a battleground where race is wielded as both a shield and a sword.

Within the complex theater of political discourse, language emerges as a potent weapon—a force capable of both uniting and dividing, enlightening and obfuscating. This exploration unveils the unsettling phenomenon of the weaponization of racialized language within politics. It delves into how language, particularly when infused with racial connotations, can be wielded as a divisive tool, intensifying existing tensions and amplifying societal fractures.

Racialized language, when deployed strategically, becomes a powerful instrument of polarization. This section unearths the deliberate use of language to inflame latent prejudices and exploit preexisting biases. Politicians resort to coded language and dog whistles, employing phrases that may seem innocuous on the surface but carry racial undertones that resonate with specific voter bases. This calculated strategy seeks to harness the power of deeply ingrained biases to gain political advantage.

Furthermore, racial slurs, with their historical weight and charged symbolism, can be employed as linguistic ammunition. The exploration exposes how these derogatory terms, when used in political discourse, serve as incendiary devices. By weaponizing racial slurs, politicians appeal to the most base instincts within certain segments of the population, while simultaneously marginalizing and alienating others. This dual effect transforms politics into an arena where language becomes a tool for division and discord.

The weaponization of racialized language is not limited to its immediate impact—it extends to the societal fabric itself. The deliberate use of such language deepens societal divides, exacerbating tensions along racial lines. By inflaming passions and exacerbating distrust, this tactic turns political discourse into a minefield where racial sensitivities are exploited for political gain. As a result, politics becomes a battleground where race is not only used as a shield to protect certain interests but also as a sword to strike at opponents.

The Role of Identity Politics

Identity politics—a term often invoked in political debates—hinges on the notion that an individual's social, cultural, and racial identity informs their political beliefs. Racialized language can be a potent tool in either bolstering or undermining identity-based political movements.

In the complex arena of political discourse, the term "identity politics" reverberates with significance, embodying a concept that straddles the realms of individuality and collective action. This exploration delves into the multifaceted nature of identity politics, where an individual's social, cultural, and racial identity intertwines with their political beliefs. This intricate interplay serves as a catalyst for empowerment, advocacy, and societal change, yet it also harbors the potential for perpetuating stereotypes and constraining complex narratives.

At its core, identity politics operates as a double-edged sword, bearing the potential to both uplift and marginalize marginalized groups. This chapter navigates the dichotomy inherent within identity politics, showcasing how it can be harnessed as a means for historically oppressed communities to assert their rights, demand representation, and challenge systemic inequities. Through the lens of identity politics, marginalized voices can rise to the forefront, amplifying their concerns and shaping the political landscape.

However, the concept of identity politics also carries the inherent risk of oversimplification. It can be manipulated to stereotype and pigeonhole communities, reducing their rich diversity to a monolithic identity. This exploration unveils how the reductionist nature of identity politics can overshadow the nuances within communities, erasing individual stories and complex narratives. The danger lies in framing individuals solely through the lens of their identity, failing to recognize the multidimensional aspects that make up their perspectives.

Amidst this intricate tapestry, racialized language emerges as a formidable tool that can either empower or undermine identity-based political movements. It can serve as a means to mobilize communities, invoking shared experiences and rallying cries for change. Conversely, racialized language can also perpetuate harmful stereotypes, deepening divisions and impeding the inclusive dialogue necessary for progress. Its role within identity politics becomes a testament to language's power—capable of shaping movements, forging unity, or sowing discord.

In essence, "The Role of Identity Politics" is a nuanced exploration of a concept that embodies both empowerment and complexity. It underscores the dual nature of identity politics, offering a platform for marginalized voices to demand change while simultaneously reminding us of the risks of oversimplification. This exploration serves as a reminder that identity politics, when navigated thoughtfully and responsibly, can be a tool for positive transformation, allowing marginalized communities to shape their narratives and participate in shaping a more equitable political landscape.

The Influence on Policy Agendas

The language used in political discourse can shape policy agendas, as public sentiment often sways policy decisions. Racialized language can frame certain issues as urgent or detrimental to specific racial groups. This influence is not solely about explicit racism; it can also manifest in subtle ways, as discourse shapes perceptions of which policies align with the interests of different racial communities.

Embedded within the intricate fabric of political discourse lies a remarkable phenomenon—the power of language to sculpt policy agendas. This exploration traverses the terrain where rhetoric and policy converge, revealing how the language employed within political discussions possesses the potential to mold the trajectory of policy decisions. It uncovers the nuanced interplay between language, public sentiment, and policy formation, with racialized language as a pivotal force in this intricate dance.

The language that permeates political discourse carries the remarkable ability to sway the course of policy agendas. Public sentiment, informed by the rhetoric circulating within society, often becomes a driving force behind policy choices. This exploration delves into the profound connection between the language used and the policies that emerge as a result. The strategic selection of words can shape issues into urgent priorities, evoking a sense of significance that catalyzes action.

Racialized language assumes a particularly poignant role in this dynamic. It possesses the potency to frame issues as directly tied to the well-being of specific racial groups. This exploration unravels how racialized language can position policies as paramount to addressing the needs, challenges, or aspirations of particular communities. By infusing discourse with racial connotations, political actors can magnify the perceived stakes of specific policies, motivating support or opposition based on racial considerations.

The impact of language on policy agendas goes beyond overt instances of explicit racism. Subtle manifestations are equally significant, as language subtly shapes perceptions of which policies align with the interests of different racial communities. This exploration unveils the intricate dance between language and policy formation, where linguistic choices can cultivate narratives that resonate with distinct demographic groups. These narratives, in turn, influence how individuals view policies through the lens of their racial identity.

Ultimately, "The Influence on Policy Agendas" is a profound exploration of the interconnectedness between language, sentiment, and policy decisions. It serves as a reminder of the complex interplay between political discourse and the priorities that governments choose to address.

This exploration underscores that the language employed within political discussions not only reflects societal attitudes but also wields the potential to shape the policy landscape, with racialized language as a key orchestrator in this intricate symphony of influence.

Media's Role in Amplification and Framing

Media acts as a conduit through which racialized political language reverberates across society. News outlets, social media platforms, and televised debates magnify these linguistic cues, influencing how audiences interpret and respond to political rhetoric. Media framing can reinforce or challenge the narrative set by politicians, shaping public discourse and contributing to the broader sociopolitical landscape.

Within the intricate web of sociopolitical dynamics, the media stands as an influential intermediary, wielding the power to amplify and frame the resonance of racialized political language. This exploration navigates the pivotal role that media outlets, social platforms, and televised debates play in the dissemination and interpretation of linguistic cues within political discourse. It unearths how the media functions as a megaphone, echoing the language employed by politicians and profoundly shaping how audiences perceive, internalize, and respond to this rhetoric.

The media's role in amplification is undeniable. As a conduit through which information cascades across society, media outlets hold the capacity to magnify the impact of racialized political language. This exploration delves into how news stories, headlines, and soundbites echoing this language can reverberate widely, reaching diverse audiences and embedding linguistic cues within the public consciousness. The media's amplification is akin to casting a spotlight on particular phrases or narratives, effectively solidifying their presence within the sociopolitical landscape.

Yet, the media's influence transcends mere amplification—it extends to framing. The language adopted by politicians undergoes a transformation when mediated, as news outlets, social media, and televised debates provide the lens through which audiences interpret and contextualize political rhetoric. This exploration uncovers the concept of media framing—the process through which the media structures information to guide audience perceptions. Framing can either reinforce the narrative set by politicians or challenge it, sculpting the discourse that unfolds within society.

Media framing is a dynamic force in shaping public perceptions. By emphasizing specific aspects of a story, media outlets can sway public sentiment toward certain interpretations. This exploration delves into how the media can either align with or critique the language used by politicians, molding the way audiences understand issues tied to race, identity, and political discourse. Through framing, the media becomes a co-author of the narrative, adding layers of context, emphasis, or critique that shape public discourse.

In essence, "Media's Role in Amplification and Framing" is an exploration of how media outlets and platforms act as powerful intermediaries in the trajectory of racialized political language. It illuminates how the media serves not only as an amplifier but also as a framing device, guiding audience interpretations and influencing the overall societal discourse. This exploration serves as a reminder of the media's responsibility in shaping public understanding, and it underscores the profound role it plays in navigating the intricate interplay between language, politics, and societal perceptions.

Toward Inclusive Political Discourse

Examining the use of racialized language in politics prompts a call for more inclusive and responsible discourse. This sub-section advocates for politicians to consider the impact of their words on marginalized communities, recognizing that rhetoric has real-world consequences. It encourages a reevaluation of campaign strategies, a commitment to authentic representation, and the elevation of policy debates beyond divisive language.

The exploration of racialized language within the realm of politics serves as an urgent clarion call for a shift toward more inclusive, responsible, and thoughtful discourse. In this profound sub-section, the imperative to navigate political communication with heightened awareness is emphasized. It is a call that resonates with the broader societal consciousness, underscoring the profound ramifications of language in shaping public perceptions and influencing real-world consequences.

This sub-section takes on the mantle of advocacy, urging politicians to grasp the full gravity of their words and their impact on marginalized communities. It transcends the limitations of linguistic expression, acknowledging that rhetoric extends far beyond its spoken or written form—it permeates into the fabric of society, affecting perceptions, attitudes, and actions. This exploration calls for politicians to hold a mirror to their words, recognizing that their language holds the potential to reinforce systemic inequalities or to pave the way for progress and unity.

Campaign strategies, a cornerstone of political engagement, are brought under scrutiny within this exploration. It prompts a reevaluation of the ways in which politicians communicate their platforms, urging a departure from tactics that exploit biases and divide communities. Instead, it advocates for campaign strategies that inspire constructive dialogue, facilitate nuanced understanding, and foster unity among diverse constituencies. By embracing this approach, political discourse can become a vehicle for constructive change rather than a source of division.

Authentic representation stands at the heart of this sub-section's advocacy. It underscores the transformative power of genuine, empathetic representation of marginalized voices within political dialogue. The exploration advocates for politicians to prioritize voices that have long been marginalized, not as tokens but as essential contributors to the political conversation. Authentic representation reshapes the narrative, empowering communities to see themselves reflected in political discourse and encouraging a sense of shared ownership over the sociopolitical landscape.

Ultimately, this sub-section champions the elevation of policy debates beyond the realm of divisive language. It heralds the potential for substantive, issue-focused discussions that transcend the pitfalls of polarizing rhetoric. By inviting politicians to engage in thoughtful, evidence-based conversations, it strives for a more informed electorate and a political sphere that values constructive dialogue over sensationalism.

In essence, "Toward Inclusive Political Discourse" serves as an impassioned plea for politicians to recognize the profound power of their words and to wield that power with the utmost responsibility. It emphasizes the potential for political discourse to uplift, unite, and drive positive change, thereby creating a more inclusive and equitable sociopolitical landscape.

A Call for a New Narrative

As we navigate the intricate landscape of "Racialized Language in Politics," we are confronted with the power of words to shape perceptions, mobilize constituents, and determine the trajectory of societies. This chapter is a reminder that political discourse is not just about the present; it's about the legacies we leave for future generations. By engaging in conversations that transcend stereotypes and divisive rhetoric, we contribute to a more inclusive political arena—one that champions justice, equality, and the dignity of all citizens.

Within the expansive tapestry of "Racialized Language in Politics," the profound influence of words on our collective consciousness becomes abundantly clear. This chapter serves as a poignant reminder that political discourse stretches far beyond the immediate realm; it resonates across time, shaping the legacy we bequeath to generations yet to come. Amid the complexities of navigating racialized language in politics, this exploration calls upon us to embark on a transformative journey—one that transcends stereotypes, defies divisive rhetoric, and steers us towards an era of inclusivity, justice, and equality.

Language, when harnessed in the crucible of politics, possesses an unparalleled power to sculpt perceptions. It carries the potential to mold how societies perceive themselves, others, and the intricate issues that permeate our world. This chapter resonates as a clarion call to recognize the weight of our linguistic choices, for they are not fleeting utterances; they are building blocks of a collective narrative that reverberates across the annals of history.

The political discourse we cultivate is an endeavor that extends beyond our immediate agendas—it extends into the legacies we leave for generations to inherit. This exploration underscores that the conversations we engage in, the words we wield, and the tenor we set reverberate through time, influencing the sociopolitical landscape for years to come. As we navigate the complexities of racialized language, we are tasked with the responsibility of shaping narratives that bridge divides, dismantle prejudices, and lay the foundations for a more inclusive and just society.

The trajectory of societies is not forged in isolation; it emerges from the collective consciousness nurtured by political discourse. This chapter advocates for a collective commitment to rise above the confines of stereotypes and divisive rhetoric. It impels us to envision a political arena that transcends party lines, uniting citizens under the banners of justice, equality, and shared humanity. By engaging in conversations that uplift rather than divide, we foster a political landscape that amplifies the dignity of all citizens, regardless of their background.

In conclusion, "A Call for a New Narrative" is a stirring exhortation to wield language in the service of progress, unity, and justice. It underscores the enduring impact of political discourse on the fabric of society and encourages us to embark on a transformative journey—one that embraces the power of words to forge a more inclusive and equitable world. This exploration is an invitation to champion a narrative that reflects the aspirations of humanity at its best, leaving a legacy that resonates with generations to come.

Reinforcing Racial Biases and Stereotypes

The choice of language in political discourse can either challenge or perpetuate racial biases and stereotypes. This section delves into how politicians may employ coded language or dog whistles that subtly reinforce existing biases, resonating with specific segments of the population. This phenomenon perpetuates divisive ideologies and sustains systemic inequalities.

Within the realm of political discourse lies a profound responsibility—the power to either challenge or reinforce deeply ingrained racial biases and stereotypes. This exploration delves into the intricate dance of language and ideology, examining how political leaders strategically wield their words to either unravel the threads of prejudice or to tighten their grip, perpetuating harmful misconceptions and entrenching societal divisions.

Language, as both a tool and a weapon, assumes a transformative role within the realm of politics. This section sheds light on the subtler nuances of linguistic choices—the coded language, the whispered dog whistles—that act as threads stitching together a tapestry of existing biases. The resonance of these linguistic cues with specific segments of the population acts as a clarion call to those who share these biases, reinforcing a shared worldview while often remaining elusive to those not attuned to their undertones.

The insidious nature of coded language perpetuates divisive ideologies by allowing politicians to communicate a particular stance without explicitly stating it. It's a dance of implications, a symphony of insinuations that finds its way into the subconscious, resonating with stereotypes that society has long been grappling to dismantle. This mechanism operates at the crossroads of psychology and rhetoric, manipulating perceptions while often evading outright scrutiny.

At the heart of this phenomenon lies the perpetuation of systemic inequalities. By speaking in the coded tongues of prejudice, politicians not only cater to existing biases but also create an environment where these biases thrive. This fuels a cycle—a cycle that bolsters discriminatory policies, sustains power imbalances, and alienates marginalized communities. In this intricate web, language becomes a vessel that keeps prejudice alive, dimming the prospect of a more equitable and harmonious society.

The responsibility borne by leaders in choosing their words is immense. Language has the power to dismantle walls or erect barriers; it can either foster understanding or breed animosity. The echoes of this responsibility extend far beyond the podium—a single phrase, a well-placed dog whistle, can reverberate through generations, entwining itself with the cultural fabric and shaping future attitudes.

As we navigate this realm, we encounter a call to vigilance—a call to critically examine the words that are spoken, the implications that lie within, and the narratives that are constructed. It's a call to unmask the subtleties, to recognize the coded messages that sow the seeds of division, and to demand transparency and accountability from our leaders. This exploration serves as a reminder that language carries the weight of history, the potential for transformation, and the power to either perpetuate harmful biases or to pave the way for a more just and inclusive world.

Setting the Tone for Public Debates

Political discourse shapes public debates and the overall tone of societal conversations. This section explores how the language used by political figures can set the agenda for discussions surrounding race, equality, and diversity. By analyzing influential speeches and statements, this exploration highlights the role of language in framing societal perceptions.

At the intersection of political discourse and societal consciousness lies the power to sculpt the very landscape of public debates. Language, wielded with intention and strategy, has the potential to mold the contours of conversations, delineate the boundaries of understanding, and ignite the flames of collective contemplation. This exploration delves into the profound influence of political rhetoric, unraveling the ways in which the words of leaders unfurl a tapestry of discourse that shapes how we engage with issues of race, equality, and diversity.

The language spoken by political figures serves as a lodestar, guiding the trajectory of public debates and signaling the issues that demand our attention. This section embarks on a journey through the intricate channels of linguistics, dissecting the subtle nuances that construct the foundation of societal conversations. In doing so, it unveils the deliberate strategies employed by leaders to carve a space in the collective consciousness, marking their imprints upon the broader discourse.

The role of language transcends mere communication; it acts as a lens through which we perceive and interpret complex issues. The language chosen by political figures sets the tone, framing discussions surrounding race, equality, and diversity. Through the deft selection of words, leaders possess the ability to either elevate the discourse toward empathetic understanding or to plunge it into the depths of divisiveness.

This exploration shines a spotlight on influential speeches and statements that have resounded through history, triggering seismic shifts in societal conversations. It highlights the potency of rhetoric to illuminate or obfuscate, to inspire unity or sow discord. These speeches are not mere monologues; they are incantations that cast spells over the collective psyche, conjuring waves of introspection, dialogue, and change.

In analyzing the interplay between language and societal perception, we come to recognize the role of political discourse as a compass steering the ship of public opinion. The words of leaders can widen the aperture through which we view the world, unveiling previously unseen dimensions of inequality or privilege. They can introduce narratives that challenge established norms or perpetuate entrenched biases. They can beckon us to confront uncomfortable truths or retreat into the comfort of complacency.

The realm of political discourse is an arena of immense responsibility and potential. As we delve into its complexities, we are prompted to critically assess the choices made by leaders in the words they speak and the narratives they construct. We are called to be discerning consumers of language, recognizing that the choices made at podiums and in legislative chambers ripple far beyond, shaping the very ethos of our societies. This exploration underscores the transformative might of words, reminding us that language is not just a tool of communication—it's a prism through which we perceive the world, and the lens through which we envisage the future.

Impact on Policy and Legislation

The power of words extends beyond rhetoric—it influences policy decisions and legislative actions. This section delves into how language employed in political discourse can directly impact the crafting of laws and regulations. By shaping the terms of debate, politicians can steer policy discussions in ways that either uphold or challenge systemic racial disparities.

The resonance of words within the realm of political discourse transcends the boundaries of rhetoric, extending its tendrils into the very fabric of policy and legislation. The choices made in language are not confined to the podium; they possess the potential to steer the course of legislative action, sculpt the contours of laws, and wield a transformative influence on the trajectory of societies. This exploration unfurls the intricate dance between words and governance, unearthing how the language employed by political figures weaves itself into the tapestry of policy decisions.

Language is not a passive medium—it is an agent of change, a vehicle through which ideas are propagated and agendas are advanced. This section delves into the dynamic interplay between language and policy, unraveling how the very terms used in political discourse shape the parameters of policy discussions. The words of leaders act as keystones, constructing the foundation upon which policy decisions are erected, and determining the boundaries within which these discussions unfold.

By crafting narratives that pivot around particular keywords, political figures possess the power to steer policy debates toward issues of race, equality, and justice. The very language they choose can infuse discussions with an air of urgency, casting a spotlight on systemic racial disparities that demand redress. Conversely, it can obfuscate these disparities, perpetuating the status quo by reframing the narrative in ways that deflect from the heart of the matter.

Language wields a dual-edged sword—it can either uphold or challenge systemic racial disparities. The deliberate use of words to highlight disparities, to evoke empathy, and to demand change can push policy discussions toward resolutions that confront and rectify racial injustices. Conversely, language can also cloak inequalities, couching them in terms that maintain the veneer of neutrality while preserving existing power dynamics.

This exploration underscores that language is not merely a tool for communication—it's a tool for persuasion, a catalyst for action, and a vehicle for transformation. As political discourse shapes policy discussions, the power of language becomes evident in the very laws that govern our societies. It's a potent reminder that words are not ephemeral; they crystallize into policy decisions that reverberate through the lives of citizens, shaping the parameters of justice and equity.

Navigating the nexus between language and policy invites us to be vigilant consumers of political rhetoric. It reminds us that as we scrutinize the words spoken by leaders, we're not merely engaging in an exercise of rhetoric analysis; we're participating in a civic responsibility that extends to the shaping of our collective future. By recognizing the weight that language carries in the realm of policy and legislation, we equip ourselves with the tools to hold leaders accountable for the impact of their words on the structures that define our societies.

Shaping Public Attitudes and Reactions

The language used by political figures shapes public attitudes and reactions. This section examines how the words chosen can incite fear, empathy, anger, or solidarity among different segments of society. By analyzing specific examples, this exploration demonstrates the transformative effect that language can have on influencing public sentiment.

In the intricate dance of political discourse, words are not mere vessels of communication; they are architects of attitudes and orchestrators of reactions. The language employed by political figures bears the transformative power to sculpt the very fabric of public sentiment, to summon forth emotions that range from fear to empathy, from anger to solidarity. This exploration delves into the profound role that language plays in the theater of public opinion, unraveling the threads that tie words to emotions and perceptions.

The canvas of public attitudes is vast and ever-shifting, a realm where words become brushstrokes that paint intricate portraits of societal reactions. This section turns its gaze toward the alchemical process through which language engenders emotions, incites passions, and catalyzes collective response. In the hands of skilled rhetoricians, words become catalysts that ignite emotional responses among diverse segments of society.

By analyzing specific examples of political discourse, this exploration navigates the terrain of language's impact on public sentiment. It reveals how carefully chosen words can fan the flames of fear, conjuring specters of uncertainty and insecurity that reverberate across communities.

Conversely, language can also kindle the fires of empathy, crafting narratives that evoke shared humanity and spark a sense of togetherness among individuals from different walks of life.

Anger, a powerful emotion often harnessed in political discourse, finds its ignition in language that highlights injustice, inequality, and systemic failures. Political figures strategically deploy words that tap into the collective frustration of marginalized groups, galvanizing them into action. Solidarity, too, emerges as a powerful outcome of language that fosters connection among diverse individuals united by a common cause or shared understanding.

This exploration underscores the transformative nature of language in shaping public attitudes. It highlights the symbiotic relationship between words and emotions, illustrating how language can be a conduit for emotional contagion that spreads rapidly through communities. In this interplay, language becomes a tool of influence, as politicians wield words not only to communicate ideas but to stir hearts and galvanize minds.

As we navigate the realm of language's impact on public attitudes, we're beckoned to be discerning observers of political rhetoric. The words chosen by leaders are not arbitrary; they're strategic maneuvers that navigate the spectrum of human emotion. By recognizing the power that language holds over our collective psyche, we empower ourselves to engage with political discourse more critically, to assess the motives that underpin linguistic choices, and to reflect on the implications of the emotional currents they set in motion. Ultimately, this exploration invites us to recognize that in the theater of public sentiment, language is the stage and politicians are the playwrights who script the narratives that resonate through the hearts and minds of citizens.

Analyzing Specific Examples of Political Discourse

To truly comprehend the transformative effect of language on public sentiment, we must delve into the realm of concrete examples that illustrate the intricate interplay between words and emotions. The following case studies shine a spotlight on instances where political figures harnessed the power of language to shape public attitudes, invoking emotions that spanned the spectrum from fear to empathy, from anger to solidarity. Through these examples, we glimpse the alchemical process by which words become agents of influence, molding the contours of collective reactions.

Case Study 1: Fear and Security

In the aftermath of a terrorist attack, a political leader takes to the podium to address a shaken nation. With deliberate cadence, they evoke a narrative of imminent threat, punctuating their speech with phrases like "security at risk" and "our very way of life in jeopardy." By deploying language that heightens fear and underscores vulnerability, the leader taps into the collective anxiety of the populace. This strategic use of rhetoric stirs emotions, galvanizing public support for stringent security measures while also sowing seeds of suspicion and intolerance.

Case Study 2: Empathy and Unity

Amid a global humanitarian crisis, a political figure delivers a speech that emphasizes shared humanity. They recount personal stories of individuals who have suffered, infusing their language with empathy and compassion. By invoking language that humanizes and connects, the leader fosters a sense of unity among diverse communities. This rhetoric fosters an emotional resonance that compels individuals to seek understanding and contribute to relief efforts, transcending geographical and cultural boundaries.

Case Study 3: Anger and Mobilization

In the face of systemic injustice, a political leader addresses a marginalized community. With fiery rhetoric, they denounce oppressive policies, invoking words like "inequality," "discrimination," and "oppression." By channeling the collective anger of the community, the leader mobilizes individuals to join a movement for change. This language becomes a catalyst for activism, energizing individuals to demand equity, accountability, and transformative social reform.

Case Study 4: Solidarity and Common Cause

In response to a divisive issue, a political figure crafts a speech that underscores shared values and common goals. They employ language that highlights collective aspirations and downplays differences. By framing the issue as a unifying cause, the leader fosters a sense of solidarity among diverse constituencies. This rhetoric encourages individuals from various backgrounds to join forces, transcending partisan divides to champion a shared vision.

Case Study 5: Fanning Polarization

In the midst of a heated electoral campaign, a political candidate utilizes language that capitalizes on existing divisions. They employ coded language that caters to specific voter bases, using terms that play on racial, ethnic, or cultural biases. This divisive rhetoric reinforces existing polarizations, galvanizing certain segments of the population while alienating others. The language chosen serves to deepen fractures within society, stoking animosity and eroding prospects for collaborative discourse.

These case studies underscore the undeniable influence of language in shaping public attitudes. They serve as windows into the intricate world of political discourse, revealing the strategic deployment of words as tools of persuasion and mobilization. As we analyze these examples, we gain a deeper appreciation for the potency of rhetoric in sculpting the tapestry of collective reactions. This analysis also prompts us to approach political discourse with discernment, recognizing that behind every word lies a calculated intention—to evoke emotions, to mobilize action, and to shape the contours of public sentiment.

Responsibility and Accountability

The exploration concludes by emphasizing the responsibility that political figures hold in their use of language. It calls attention to the ethical implications of employing inflammatory or racially charged language, urging politicians to be mindful of the impact their words have on public perceptions and societal harmony.

As we draw the curtains on this exploration, a resounding chord of responsibility and accountability reverberates through the discourse surrounding language in politics. The power of words, as we've traversed through the intricate terrain of rhetoric and influence, is not a neutral force. It is a force laden with ethical implications, a force that demands introspection and vigilance from political figures who wield it as a tool of persuasion.

Language, when wielded within the realm of political discourse, becomes an instrument that shapes not just opinions, but the very fabric of societies. It is a force that can either bind communities together in shared purpose or unravel the threads of unity, leaving behind the frayed edges of division. This exploration culminates in an unwavering call to action, placing the spotlight squarely on the shoulders of political figures who stand as stewards of language's transformative potential.

In the realm of language, responsibility is more than a mere afterthought; it's an ethical imperative that carries with it the weight of societal impact. The choices made in the selection of words are choices that reverberate beyond the echo chambers of speeches and debates. They resonate through the corridors of public perception, shaping how individuals view each other, their communities, and their world.

As we journey through this exploration, it becomes evident that the language of leadership is not just about communication—it's about crafting a legacy, etching an imprint onto the collective memory of societies. This imprint can be one of unity, of empathy, of progress, or it can be one of division, of discord, of regression. The compass that guides the ethical use of language points squarely toward fostering a discourse that uplifts, enlightens, and unifies.

Accountability, then, is the cornerstone upon which responsible language use is built. The words spoken in the public sphere have consequences that ripple far beyond the immediate moment. They shape public discourse, inform policy decisions, and influence societal attitudes. Political figures must stand as guardians of language, recognizing that their rhetoric, far from being ephemeral, has the potential to be a force for positive change or a harbinger of harm.

In the midst of political polarization, the call for responsible language use becomes all the more urgent. It beckons leaders to resist the allure of divisive rhetoric, to eschew the temptation of linguistic manipulation, and to embrace a discourse that is rooted in empathy, respect, and the pursuit of the common good. The responsibility that comes with language is not to be taken lightly; it is a mantle that requires courage, integrity, and an unwavering commitment to societal betterment.

As this exploration draws to a close, the message is clear: language is a vessel of immense power, but that power comes with an ethical imperative. The choice of words is not merely an exercise in articulation; it's a choice that carries the potential to uplift, to inspire, and to bridge divides. By embracing this responsibility, political figures have the opportunity to contribute to a discourse that nurtures understanding, fosters unity, and envisions a future where the force of words shapes a world that is just, inclusive, and harmonious.

Impact of Racially Charged Discourse on Public Opinion

Within the realm of public discourse, the words spoken by political leaders and influential figures hold the potential to reverberate far beyond the confines of a speech or a statement. Racially charged discourse—the use of language that invokes racial identities, stereotypes, or biases—has a profound impact on public opinion, shaping attitudes, perceptions, and even policy preferences. This section delves into the intricate ways in which racially charged discourse influences the collective mindset and the implications it carries for societies and their trajectories.

Shaping Attitudes and Beliefs

Racially charged discourse has a direct influence on attitudes and beliefs held by the public. The words used by leaders can shape how individuals view racial and ethnic groups, perpetuating existing biases or challenging them. When politicians deploy language that marginalizes or stereotypes certain communities, it reinforces negative perceptions and solidifies divisions.

The impact of racially charged discourse extends far beyond the realm of politics—it resonates deeply within the realm of attitudes and beliefs held by the public. This exploration delves into the profound influence that the words of leaders wield over the perspectives of individuals, outlining how political language possesses the potential to mold perceptions of racial and ethnic groups. This intricate interplay underscores the power of language to either perpetuate preexisting biases or challenge them, thereby shaping the social fabric of our communities.

The words articulated by leaders within the corridors of power become agents of change in shaping how individuals perceive racial and ethnic groups. This exploration sheds light on the transformational role that political discourse assumes—impacting the lenses through which people view the world around them. By delving into this dynamic, it becomes evident that the language employed in political dialogue is a potent force capable of either reinforcing the status quo or dismantling stereotypes.

At its essence, this exploration underscores that the language chosen by politicians holds the capacity to uphold or challenge prevailing biases.

When political language descends into marginalization or perpetuates stereotypes against certain communities, it reinforces and amplifies negative perceptions. The intricate interplay between words and perceptions solidifies divisions and deepens societal fractures, nurturing an environment where understanding and unity struggle to take root.

The power of political language as a catalyst for shaping attitudes and beliefs is an enduring reminder of the interconnectedness between language and societal dynamics. As leaders articulate their positions on matters intertwined with race and ethnicity, they are, in effect, contributing to the broader narrative that shapes public consciousness. This exploration calls upon leaders to recognize their role as architects of societal perspectives and impels them to wield their linguistic power thoughtfully, with an eye toward fostering a more inclusive and empathetic society.

"Shaping Attitudes and Beliefs" is an exploration of the profound role that political discourse plays in molding the attitudes and beliefs of the public. It underscores the intricate connection between language and perception, revealing how political language can either perpetuate biases or act as a catalyst for change. Ultimately, it is a call for leaders to embrace their responsibility as influencers of public sentiment and to channel their linguistic power in a manner that contributes to the dismantling of stereotypes, the promotion of unity, and the fostering of a more empathetic and understanding society.

Rhetoric and Emotional Resonance

Language possesses a unique ability to evoke emotions, and racially charged discourse exploits this emotional resonance. Politicians employ rhetoric that taps into fears, prejudices, and anxieties related to race, triggering visceral responses among the public. This emotional manipulation can amplify biases and impair critical thinking, making individuals more susceptible to adopting extreme or polarized viewpoints.

Language, as a tool of communication, possesses an inherent power to evoke emotions and ignite profound responses within us. This exploration ventures into the intricate connection between language and emotions, unearthing how racially charged discourse capitalizes on this emotional resonance. Politicians deftly wield rhetoric that taps into fears, prejudices, and anxieties intertwined with race, harnessing the ability to elicit visceral and intense reactions among the public. The consequential impact of this emotional manipulation reverberates through society, magnifying biases, and reshaping thought patterns in ways that hold deep implications.

The pivotal intersection between language and emotion is evident in the deployment of racially charged discourse. This exploration delves into the art of linguistic manipulation employed by politicians who skillfully navigate the emotional landscape tied to race. By choosing words and phrases that trigger strong emotional responses, politicians create a potent connection with their audience. This connection amplifies the emotional resonance of their message, fostering an environment in which individuals are moved more by their feelings than by rational analysis.

This emotional manipulation carries profound consequences. The exploration unveils how racially charged discourse can intensify existing biases, painting divisive narratives in shades of emotion that overpower reason. When political language exploits the fears and prejudices surrounding race, it impairs critical thinking and fosters a susceptibility to adopting extreme or polarized viewpoints. This dynamic underscores the fine line between genuine emotional engagement and manipulation, highlighting the need for vigilance in assessing the emotional undercurrents present in political discourse.

Ultimately, "Rhetoric and Emotional Resonance" underscores the potency of language as an emotional catalyst. It navigates the realm where language transcends mere communication, tapping into the core of human emotions and influencing thought patterns. This exploration sheds light on the careful orchestration of language by politicians, revealing how emotions can be manipulated to amplify biases and shape public perceptions. It calls for a heightened awareness of the emotional currents within political discourse and invites individuals to engage with language critically, probing beneath the surface to discern the emotions being harnessed for persuasive effect.

Perceptions of Credibility and Authority

Racially charged discourse can impact the perceived credibility and authority of political leaders. When leaders engage in divisive language, it can erode trust among those who view them as representatives of the entire population. Conversely, leaders who employ inclusive rhetoric are often seen as more credible, fostering a sense of unity and shared purpose.

The landscape of political discourse is not confined to words alone—it extends into the realm of perceptions, credibility, and authority. This exploration delves into the profound impact that racially charged discourse can wield over how political leaders are perceived by the public. When leaders resort to divisive language, the repercussions extend beyond the immediate message—they erode the very trust that forms the foundation of their credibility and authority.

Conversely, inclusive rhetoric fosters a contrasting narrative, one that bolsters perceptions of credibility, while fostering unity and a sense of shared purpose.

The nexus between language and the perceived credibility of political leaders is intricate and far-reaching. This exploration unveils how the words chosen by leaders can cast a shadow over their image as representatives of the entire populace. Divisive language creates fractures within the perception of leadership—prompting questions about the authenticity of their commitment to unity and their capacity to genuinely advocate for the interests of all constituents. In a world of hyperconnectivity, where messages spread instantaneously, this erosion of credibility can significantly undermine leadership effectiveness.

Conversely, the exploration delves into the transformative potential of inclusive rhetoric. Leaders who consciously engage in discourse that bridges divides and embraces diversity project an image of credibility that resonates deeply with the public. Inclusive language sends a powerful message—a message that the leader recognizes the complexity of their role, acknowledging the diverse tapestry of the communities they serve. This inclusivity engenders a sense of unity and shared purpose—a unifying force that transcends the barriers erected by divisive language.

The perception of authority, an integral facet of leadership, is also intricately interwoven with linguistic choices. This exploration uncovers how racially charged discourse can erode the perception of authority, as divisive rhetoric weakens the leader's claim to represent the entire spectrum of their constituents. In contrast, leaders who harness language to celebrate diversity and foster unity exude a more compelling aura of authority—one that resonates with individuals across demographic boundaries.

In essence, "Perceptions of Credibility and Authority" delves into the nuanced interplay between language, perceptions, credibility, and authority in the realm of politics. It underscores the enduring impact of linguistic choices on the image of political leaders, revealing how divisive discourse can erode trust and authority, while inclusive rhetoric fosters unity and credibility. Ultimately, this exploration serves as a reminder that leadership extends beyond mere words—it encompasses the complex art of nurturing perceptions that reflect a commitment to inclusivity, unity, and the well-being of all citizens.

Media Amplification and Normalization

Media plays a crucial role in amplifying and normalizing racially charged discourse. News outlets, social media platforms, and talk shows can disseminate inflammatory statements to a wide audience. This exposure can lead to the normalization of such language, desensitizing the public to its harmful implications and perpetuating a cycle of divisive communication.

Within the intricate tapestry of sociopolitical dynamics, the role of media emerges as a pivotal force in shaping the trajectory of racially charged discourse. This exploration delves into the profound influence wielded by media in amplifying and normalizing language laden with racial undertones. News outlets, social media platforms, and talk shows become conduits through which inflammatory statements resonate far and wide, reaching a diverse and extensive audience. This process of amplification can ultimately culminate in the normalization of such language—a normalization that desensitizes the public to its harmful implications and perpetuates a distressing cycle of divisive communication.

In the modern age of information dissemination, media occupies an indispensable space as a messenger. News outlets serve as gatekeepers of public information, while social media platforms transcend geographic boundaries, disseminating messages instantaneously to a global audience. Talk shows and panel discussions further extend the reach of political discourse. It is within this expansive landscape that media assumes the mantle of amplification, projecting linguistic expressions far beyond their initial confines.

The power of media amplification lies in its ability to introduce racially charged language to an extensive and diverse audience. This exploration unearths the intricate mechanisms through which inflammatory statements resonate across various demographic, geographic, and ideological spheres. The exposure granted by media amplification is a double-edged sword—it brings political discourse to a wider audience, but it also possesses the potential to normalize language that may be divisive, offensive, or harmful.

Normalization emerges as a consequence of media's amplification of racially charged discourse. This exploration unveils how repeated exposure to such language can lead to desensitization—a process where the public becomes accustomed to the presence of divisive rhetoric. With each recurrence, the initial shock and discomfort wane, giving way to a sense of acceptance. This normalization perpetuates a cycle wherein divisive language becomes an accepted facet of public discourse, eroding the societal aversion to its harmful implications.

The impact of media on the normalization of racially charged language is an enduring testament to the interconnectedness of language, media, and public perception. It serves as a stark reminder that media is not a passive observer but an active participant in shaping the linguistic landscape of political discourse. By shedding light on the intricacies of media amplification and normalization, this exploration underscores the ethical responsibility of media outlets to critically assess the language they amplify and its potential consequences for public discourse.

In conclusion, "Media Amplification and Normalization" is an exploration that traverses the landscape of media's role in shaping the trajectory of racialized political discourse. It delves into the mechanisms through which media serves as an amplifier, projecting language to extensive audiences, and the subsequent process of normalization that can desensitize the public to divisive rhetoric. This exploration serves as a call for media outlets to uphold the values of responsible and ethical journalism, recognizing their power to either perpetuate division or contribute to a more informed, empathetic, and united society.

Impact on Policy Preferences

Racially charged discourse can influence policy preferences by framing issues in ways that resonate with certain segments of the population. This framing can shape public support for or opposition to specific policies, often along racial lines. The language used to discuss issues such as immigration, crime, and social welfare can shape public perceptions of who benefits and who is perceived as a threat.

The realm of political discourse is not confined to the realm of rhetoric alone—it extends its reach into the realm of policy preferences, redefining the contours of public opinion and influencing the trajectory of governance. This exploration delves into the profound impact of racially charged discourse on the shaping of policy preferences—a dynamic where language serves as a framing tool, molding public support for or opposition to specific policies. The intricate interplay between language and policy preferences is a process laden with implications, often reverberating along racial lines, as the words used to address issues like immigration, crime, and social welfare navigate the delicate balance between public perceptions of benefits and threats.

The nexus between racially charged discourse and policy preferences is a reflection of the power that language wields in shaping the trajectory of governance. This exploration unveils the intricate mechanisms through which language becomes a vehicle for framing issues in ways that resonate with specific segments of the population. By strategically employing language that evokes emotions, plays into fears, and capitalizes on preexisting biases, politicians have the capacity to mold public sentiment towards certain policies.

This dynamic underscores the persuasive potential of language as a tool that influences not just perceptions, but the very course of governance.

The exploration further delves into the far-reaching impact of this linguistic framing on public support for, or opposition to, specific policies. The language used to address issues of immigration, crime, and social welfare has the potential to craft narratives that depict certain groups as beneficiaries or threats. This framing resonates within the collective consciousness, shaping how the public perceives the policies, their beneficiaries, and their potential impact. Racially charged language, in this context, becomes a lens through which the contours of policy preferences are defined—a lens that amplifies divisions or fosters unity depending on its deployment.

At the heart of this exploration lies the recognition that language and policy preferences are intricately entwined, shaping and reshaping one another in a continuous feedback loop. The linguistic choices made by politicians have the power to frame issues in ways that resonate with the public, aligning policy preferences with certain demographic segments. The implications of this interplay extend far beyond rhetoric; they extend into the realm of policy implementation, shaping the landscape of governance in profound and lasting ways.

In conclusion, "Impact on Policy Preferences" is an exploration that delves into the intricate relationship between racially charged discourse and the shaping of policy preferences. It uncovers the mechanisms through which language becomes a framing tool, resonating with specific segments of the population and molding public support for or opposition to policies. This exploration serves as a reminder of the power language holds to redefine public sentiment and to influence the trajectory of governance—an influence that traverses the contours of language and extends into the realm of policy implementation, bearing far-reaching implications for the society we shape and the policies we endorse.

The Role of Leadership and Responsibility

The impact of racially charged discourse underscores the responsibility that leaders bear. Public figures have the power to set the tone for public discourse and influence societal norms. This section emphasizes the importance of leadership that promotes inclusivity, empathy, and respect for all citizens, fostering an environment where constructive dialogue can flourish.

Within the vast expanse of political dynamics, the impact of racially charged discourse resonates far beyond the words spoken—it reverberates through the very fabric of societal values and norms. This exploration delves into the profound role that leaders play in the shaping of public discourse, unearthing their pivotal power to influence the trajectory of society. As public figures, leaders are not merely purveyors of rhetoric; they hold the mantle of shaping public sentiment, molding societal norms, and ultimately setting the tone for constructive dialogue. This role underscores the immense responsibility that leaders bear in fostering an environment where inclusivity, empathy, and respect for all citizens can flourish.

The nexus between leadership and racially charged discourse is one of intricate interplay. This exploration uncovers how public figures wield their influence to set the parameters of public discourse. Their words carry weight and reach far beyond the immediate confines of a speech or statement. By articulating divisive language, leaders have the capacity to validate and amplify biases, further entrenching divisive narratives within the public psyche. Conversely, leaders who embrace inclusive and empathetic language can steer discourse in a direction that nurtures unity, understanding, and cooperation.

The exploration delves into the transformative power of leadership in shaping societal norms. Public figures serve as role models, exemplars whose behavior and language signal what is acceptable within the broader community. By choosing rhetoric that resonates with inclusivity and respect, leaders pave the way for a culture that values diversity, empathy, and dialogue. This leadership-driven transformation extends beyond individual actions; it influences the collective consciousness and defines the boundaries of acceptable discourse.

The responsibility of leaders in fostering an environment conducive to constructive dialogue is paramount. The exploration underscores that leadership extends beyond the corridors of power—it involves nurturing a socio-political ecosystem where differing viewpoints are heard and respected. This responsibility is not to be taken lightly, for leaders hold the capacity to either inflame divisions or inspire unity. By advocating for inclusivity and embracing language that bridges divides, leaders set a precedent for an environment where citizens engage in dialogue that is both enlightening and transformative.

In essence, "The Role of Leadership and Responsibility" traverses the terrain of leadership's impact on the trajectory of racially charged discourse. It underscores the weighty responsibility that leaders carry as shapers of public sentiment and societal norms. This exploration serves as a poignant reminder of leadership's transformative power—to either perpetuate divisiveness or cultivate unity. By embracing inclusivity, empathy, and respect, leaders can kindle an environment where constructive dialogue thrives, fostering a society that champions justice, equality, and the dignity of all citizens.

A Call for Thoughtful Communication

As we delve into the "Impact of Racially Charged Discourse on Public Opinion," we are called to reflect on the role that language plays in shaping the collective psyche. This section invites us to be critical consumers of rhetoric, to demand responsible communication from leaders, and to actively engage in conversations that bridge divides rather than deepen them. By understanding the influence of language on public opinion, we equip ourselves to navigate complex issues with empathy, nuance, and a commitment to fostering a more inclusive and harmonious society.

In the intricate tapestry of societal dynamics, the impact of racially charged discourse resounds with the echoes of history, shaping not just opinions but the very essence of our collective psyche. As we journey into the heart of the "Impact of Racially Charged Discourse on Public Opinion," we are summoned to embark on a profound introspection—a contemplation that delves into the profound role that language plays in shaping perceptions, guiding attitudes, and ultimately steering the course of societal evolution.

This exploration stands as an earnest call—a call for all of us to assume the role of discerning and critical consumers of rhetoric. It beckons us to examine the words that leaders wield, to scrutinize the narratives they weave, and to hold them accountable for the linguistic landscapes they craft. The essence of thoughtful communication transcends mere words—it extends to the intent, the context, and the implications of those words. It reminds us that language is not a mere conduit of communication, but a potent force that molds the contours of our thoughts and emotions.

Central to this call is the expectation of responsible communication from leaders—the expectation that those who wield influence recognize the profound impact their words wield on public sentiment. This exploration uncovers the inherent ethical obligation that leaders bear in their linguistic choices. It exhorts them to navigate the delicate terrain of discourse with an awareness of its potential to shape the collective psyche, urging them to steer away from divisive language and embrace rhetoric that fosters unity, understanding, and empathy.

As we heed this call for thoughtful communication, we are summoned to actively engage in conversations that bridge divides rather than deepen them. This exploration casts light on the transformational potential that lies within dialogues characterized by respect, open-mindedness, and a commitment to empathy. It underscores that while language can be a weapon of division, it can also be the cornerstone of reconciliation—a powerful instrument that dismantles barriers and fosters connections.

In essence, "A Call for Thoughtful Communication" is a summons—an invitation to recognize the profound influence of language on public opinion and societal evolution. It invites us to be architects of discourse—to demand responsible communication from leaders, to engage in conversations that transcend divisions, and to navigate complex issues with empathy, nuance, and a resolute commitment to nurturing a more inclusive and harmonious society. It reminds us that language, when wielded thoughtfully, holds the potential to shape not just words, but the very essence of the world we wish to build.

Analysis of Global Political Speeches

In the realm of politics, speeches serve as a nexus where ideas, aspirations, and convictions converge, crystallizing into messages that sway hearts and minds. A comprehensive analysis of global political speeches unveils the nuances of communication strategies, rhetorical techniques, and the broader sociopolitical contexts in which these speeches unfold. This section delves into the intricate art of deciphering political oratory, shedding light on how leaders employ language to shape narratives, mobilize supporters, and influence the trajectory of nations.

The Language of Leadership

Political speeches are more than a collection of words; they are a manifestation of leadership. Leaders craft narratives that resonate with their constituents, communicating visions that reflect their ideals and priorities. The choice of words, tone, and delivery all contribute to projecting an image of authority and empathy—a balance that resonates differently across diverse cultural and linguistic landscapes.

In the realm of political discourse, where ideas are not just conveyed but ideologies are sculpted, the language of leadership emerges as a profound tool of influence. This exploration unveils the intricate tapestry woven by political speeches—a tapestry that is more than the sum of its linguistic parts. It is a manifestation of leadership—an art form through which leaders sculpt narratives that resonate deeply with their constituents, transmitting visions that mirror their ideals, aspirations, and priorities.

At the heart of this exploration lies an exploration of the artistry involved in crafting these narratives. The choice of words transcends mere semantics—it becomes a strategic orchestration of language that invokes emotions, resonates with values, and elicits responses from the audience. The tone, carefully calibrated, carries the weight of authority and conviction, while the delivery, be it passionate or measured, complements the intended message. It's a symphony of linguistic elements that converge to create a tapestry that captures attention, engages minds, and compels action.

The significance of the language of leadership extends beyond its linguistic prowess. It is an intricate dance between projection and empathy— a delicate equilibrium that leaders strive to achieve. The language they employ speaks to their authority, projecting an image of strength and decisiveness. Yet, it also bears the hallmarks of empathy, reaching out to resonate with the experiences and concerns of their constituents. This balance becomes even more nuanced as it resonates differently across the vast expanse of diverse cultural and linguistic landscapes.

As we dissect the language of leadership, we delve into the psychology of influence—the art of crafting messages that not only sway opinion but cultivate allegiance. This exploration uncovers the transformative potential of words as tools of leadership—weapons that mobilize, empower, and shape the destinies of nations. It underscores that political speeches are more than the sum of their syllables; they are the embodiment of leadership ideals, the manifestation of a vision cast in the mold of language.

In essence, "The Language of Leadership" is an exploration that peers into the profound realm of political discourse. It unearths the intricate layers that comprise political speeches—layers that go beyond mere words to become vehicles of influence, projection, and empathy. This exploration serves as a reminder of the potency of language—the power it holds to shape perceptions, kindle emotions, and steer the trajectory of societies. It underscores that in the hands of leaders, language becomes a force that shapes not just narratives, but the very fabric of our collective future.

Rhetorical Techniques and Persuasion

Rhetorical techniques are the tools through which politicians wield influence. From metaphors that paint vivid imagery to repetition that reinforces key messages, these techniques are employed strategically to engage emotions, capture attention, and persuade audiences. An analysis of global political speeches reveals the universality of these techniques while highlighting the cultural nuances that give them unique flavor.

In the intricate realm of political discourse, where ideas and ideologies collide, rhetorical techniques emerge as the finely honed tools through which politicians wield their influence. This exploration ventures into the heart of these techniques—an artful arsenal employed by orators to craft narratives that transcend the realm of mere words. From metaphors that paint vibrant tapestries of imagery to the power of repetition that hammers home key messages, these techniques stand as strategic instruments that captivate emotions, seize attention, and ultimately sway the tides of public opinion.

The artistry of rhetorical techniques transcends the ordinary; it is an orchestration of language that wields the power to transform words into weapons of influence. Metaphors, those potent linguistic devices, are wielded to bridge the chasm between abstract concepts and tangible experiences, weaving a narrative that resonates deeply with the human psyche. Repetition, that echoing chorus of words, reinforces key ideas, imprinting them into the collective consciousness of audiences. The rhythm of these techniques becomes a symphony that captures hearts, evokes passions, and ushers minds into a realm of conviction.

This exploration delves further into the tapestry of global political speeches—an exploration that unearths the universality of these techniques while spotlighting the cultural nuances that infuse them with unique flavors. The language of persuasion traverses cultural and linguistic boundaries, transcending geographic divides to resonate with the essence of human emotions. Yet, within this universal canvas, the brushstrokes are distinctive—the nuances and shades of each culture shape these techniques, lending them a resonance that echoes the cultural context from which they spring.

The impact of rhetorical techniques extends beyond the immediate aftermath of a speech; it reverberates through the annals of history, shaping perceptions, influencing decisions, and sparking change. It's a reminder of the power that words wield—a power that can kindle revolutions, dismantle barriers, and kindle the fires of unity. As we dissect these techniques, we uncover the transformational potential they bear—the potential to elevate oratory from the mundane to the extraordinary, the potential to craft narratives that transcend the limitations of time and space.

In essence, "Rhetorical Techniques and Persuasion" is an exploration into the artful mastery of language—the techniques that transform political discourse into a symphony of influence. It's a journey into the realm where words cease to be mere words; they become the chisels that sculpt narratives, the brushes that paint portraits of ideals, and the sparks that ignite movements. This exploration serves as a testament to the artistry of oratory, to the power of techniques that resonate across cultures while celebrating the nuanced melodies that each culture lends to the grand tapestry of discourse.

Case Studies: Rhetorical Techniques and Persuasion:

Case Study 1: "I Have a Dream" by Martin Luther King Jr.

Martin Luther King Jr.'s iconic speech, "I Have a Dream," delivered during the March on Washington for Jobs and Freedom in 1963, is a masterclass in employing rhetorical techniques for persuasion. King's use of vivid metaphors and imagery, such as the "promissory note" and "sweltering summer of the Negro's legitimate discontent," painted a powerful picture of racial injustice and inequality. His repetition of the phrase "I have a dream" served to reinforce his vision of a racially harmonious America. The speech's emotional resonance and rhythmic cadence captured the hearts of millions, inspiring a movement for civil rights.

Case Study 2: "Blood, Toil, Tears, and Sweat" by Winston Churchill

Winston Churchill's inaugural speech as Prime Minister of the United Kingdom in 1940, known for its famous line "I have nothing to offer but blood, toil, tears, and sweat," utilized rhetorical techniques to rally the British people during a time of war. The repetition of impactful words like "blood" and "tears" heightened the emotional impact of the speech, evoking a sense of sacrifice and determination. Churchill's skillful use of parallelism and contrast created a resonant rhythm that emphasized the challenges ahead while invoking a spirit of resilience.

Case Study 3: "A More Perfect Union" by Barack Obama

Barack Obama's speech on race, titled "A More Perfect Union," delivered during his 2008 presidential campaign, exemplifies the use of rhetorical techniques to address a complex and sensitive topic. Obama's adept use of ethos, logos, and pathos—appeals to credibility, logic, and emotion—created a balanced and compelling argument. The speech employed metaphors, historical references, and personal anecdotes to frame the issue of race in America, engaging audiences intellectually and emotionally while fostering a sense of unity and shared responsibility.

Case Study 4: "We Shall Fight on the Beaches" by Winston Churchill

Winston Churchill's "We Shall Fight on the Beaches" speech, delivered in 1940 during World War II, demonstrated the power of repetition to galvanize a nation. The phrase "We shall fight" echoed throughout the speech, reinforcing the resolve to resist Nazi aggression. Churchill's skillful use of antithesis—a contrast of opposing ideas—underscored the unwavering commitment to defend British freedoms against tyranny.

Case Study 5: "Tear Down This Wall!" by Ronald Reagan

Ronald Reagan's speech at the Brandenburg Gate in 1987, calling for the demolition of the Berlin Wall, employed rhetorical techniques to advocate for freedom and unity. The famous line "Mr. Gorbachev, tear down this wall!" combined direct address, repetition, and a call to action. The speech's strategic use of emotional language and historical references resonated with both the

American and global audience, contributing to the eventual fall of the Berlin Wall.

These case studies exemplify how leaders have harnessed rhetorical techniques to wield influence, persuade audiences, and shape historical narratives. Through metaphors, repetition, emotional appeal, and strategic word choice, these speeches have left indelible marks on the annals of history, demonstrating the enduring power of language to shape perceptions and inspire action.

Cultural Context and Symbolism

Political speeches are inextricably linked to cultural contexts, drawing on symbols, references, and shared experiences that resonate with specific audiences. A speech delivered in one corner of the globe may evoke historical milestones, national heroes, or cultural touchstones that carry immense significance. This contextual layer adds depth to speeches, forging connections between leaders and their followers.

Case Studies: Cultural Context and Symbolism

Case Study 1: Mahatma Gandhi's "Quit India" Speech

In 1942, during India's struggle for independence from British colonial rule, Mahatma Gandhi delivered the "Quit India" speech. This speech was steeped in cultural context and symbolism. Gandhi's invocation of the phrase "Do or Die" resonated deeply with the Indian populace, reflecting the spirit of self-sacrifice and determination. He drew upon historical figures like Rani Lakshmibai and Shivaji, invoking their bravery and valor as symbols of resistance. By tapping into India's rich history and cultural heritage, Gandhi's speech galvanized the nation toward a unified call for freedom.

Case Study 2: Vladimir Putin's Address on Crimea

In 2014, Russian President Vladimir Putin delivered an address regarding the annexation of Crimea. Putin's speech was rich in cultural context and historical allusions. He invoked the historical ties between Russia and Crimea, referencing shared historical events and cultural heritage. The mention of Sevastopol, a city with deep naval history, symbolized Russia's strategic and emotional connection to the region. By embedding these cultural references, Putin aimed to justify the annexation and garner support from both domestic and international audiences.

Case Study 3: Fidel Castro's "History Will Absolve Me" Defense

Fidel Castro's defense speech during his trial after the failed attack on the Moncada Barracks in 1953 incorporated cultural context and symbolism. He drew upon historical events like Cuba's fight for independence against colonial powers, invoking the legacy of José Martí and Antonio Maceo. Castro's reference to social justice and the plight of the poor resonated with the ideals of the Cuban Revolution. By connecting his cause to Cuba's historical struggles and cultural heroes, Castro aimed to garner support and sympathy from the Cuban populace.

These case studies underscore how cultural context and symbolism enrich political speeches, infusing them with deeper meaning and resonating with specific audiences. By drawing on shared historical milestones, cultural icons, and cherished values, leaders forge connections that transcend mere words, fostering a sense of unity, identity, and purpose among their followers.

Addressing Societal Concerns

An analysis of global political speeches unveils the complex tapestry of societal concerns that leaders must address. From economic disparities to environmental challenges, speeches often reflect the issues that are foremost in the minds of citizens. Leaders navigate these concerns through framing, prioritization, and the articulation of policy proposals, aiming to resonate with the aspirations and anxieties of their constituents.

Global Themes and Shared Values

While speeches are rooted in local concerns, they also intersect with global themes and shared values. Leaders often speak to universal principles such as justice, freedom, and human rights, seeking to garner international support and portray their nation as a responsible global actor. These global dimensions offer insights into the ways in which leaders position their countries within the larger world order.

Implications for Public Perception

The analysis of global political speeches goes beyond rhetoric; it carries profound implications for public perception. The language used by leaders shapes how citizens view domestic and international issues, influencing public sentiment and attitudes. Through speeches, leaders can mold narratives that transcend borders, fostering empathy or animosity towards other nations and cultures.

A Call for Critical Engagement

As we embark on an exploration of the "Analysis of Global Political Speeches," we engage with a symphony of words, ideas, and intentions. This section invites us to critically dissect speeches, probing beyond the surface to discern the strategies, values, and priorities they encapsulate.

By decoding the language of leadership, we empower ourselves as informed citizens who can navigate the complex landscape of political discourse with discernment and a deeper understanding of the forces that shape our world.

Chapter 5: Media Ownership and Diversity

Concentration of Media Ownership and its Effects

Within the sprawling landscape of media, the question of ownership looms large—an inquiry into who wields the power to shape narratives, define agendas, and influence public perception. This chapter embarks on an exploration of media ownership, unraveling the implications of concentration and its far-reaching effects on diversity, representation, and the very fabric of democratic societies.

The Power of Media Ownership

Media ownership is not just an economic concern; it's a matter of influence and control over information flow. When a few entities hold the reins of media outlets, they hold the key to the narratives that reach the masses. This section delves into how concentration of ownership grants unprecedented power to shape public discourse, advancing certain viewpoints while marginalizing others.

In the modern world, media ownership has transcended its role as a mere economic enterprise; it has metamorphosed into a formidable instrument of influence, shaping the contours of information dissemination and molding the very fabric of public discourse. Beyond the acquisition of assets and profit margins, the concentration of media ownership constitutes a profound determinant of societal narratives and perspectives. This pivotal role held by a select few entities in controlling the narratives that reach the masses holds implications that stretch far beyond the realm of commerce, weaving a complex tapestry of influence, power, and control.

The very essence of democratic societies hinges on the free flow of information and the diversity of viewpoints. Media, as the conduit of this information, is entrusted with the monumental task of fostering an informed citizenry. Yet, when the reins of media outlets are tightly held by a limited number of entities, this ideal becomes compromised. The power to shape narratives becomes concentrated, skewing the representation of diverse perspectives and distorting the democratic fabric.

The concentration of media ownership operates as a prism through which the world is perceived by the public. It holds the potential to amplify certain voices while silencing others, to magnify certain issues while overshadowing others. The narratives that emerge from this concentrated landscape are imbued with the perspectives, biases, and agendas of those who hold the reins. This influence is not simply about promoting specific economic interests; it's about wielding the power to shape societal attitudes, mold public opinion, and frame the contours of discourse.

One of the most concerning outcomes of media ownership concentration is the potential for the homogenization of information. As a few entities control multiple media outlets, there is a risk of narratives being synchronized, viewpoints being streamlined, and diverse perspectives being sidelined. This phenomenon stifles the vibrancy of public discourse, creating echo chambers where alternative voices struggle to be heard. The impact reverberates through society, influencing how individuals perceive the world, how they engage with complex issues, and how they make informed decisions.

Furthermore, media ownership concentration can foster a disconnect between the media landscape and the true diversity of the populace. When a handful of entities dominate the discourse, they become gatekeepers of representation. The voices of marginalized communities, alternative viewpoints, and underrepresented perspectives can be drowned out, perpetuating inequalities and hindering a comprehensive understanding of societal realities.

In the pursuit of a thriving democracy and an informed citizenry, media ownership must be examined through the lens of responsibility and accountability. The power to influence and shape public discourse should be wielded with a deep recognition of its impact on societal cohesion, public attitudes, and democratic ideals. As media entities navigate this complex terrain, there is a call to prioritize inclusivity, diversity, and the amplification of voices that have historically been marginalized.

In the heart of the intricate interplay between media ownership and influence lies a profound question: to what extent should a few wield the power to mold the perspectives of the many? This exploration into the concentration of media ownership and its effects is not merely an economic inquiry; it's a reflection on the very nature of information dissemination in modern societies. As the chapters of media ownership continue to be written, there is an urgent call to embrace a paradigm that prioritizes the richness of diverse perspectives, fosters a pluralistic discourse, and upholds the essence of democratic engagement.

Gatekeepers of Information

Media owners become gatekeepers of information, curating the stories that define reality for audiences. Concentrated ownership can result in homogenized perspectives, stifling diverse voices and sidelining stories that deviate from the mainstream. The impact is profound, as audiences are denied a comprehensive understanding of complex issues and are instead exposed to a narrow spectrum of viewpoints.

In the modern landscape of media, ownership translates into an unparalleled position of influence—the role of gatekeepers of information. Media owners assume the responsibility of curating the stories, narratives, and perspectives that permeate the public sphere. In a world where information shapes opinions and constructs reality, this role is far from trivial; it's the linchpin upon which the collective consciousness of society pivots.

Concentration of media ownership magnifies the significance of this gatekeeping role. When a select few entities hold the keys to numerous media outlets, they wield an unprecedented authority to determine which stories are spotlighted and which remain in the shadows. While this power may not necessarily manifest as overt censorship, it operates through the subtle mechanisms of selection, placement, and prominence.

The ramifications of this gatekeeping dynamic are profound and far-reaching. The diverse tapestry of human experiences, opinions, and perspectives becomes filtered through the sieve of ownership interests, potentially leading to the homogenization of content. Audiences are presented with a curated version of reality—a version that may amplify certain viewpoints while muting others, that may elevate specific narratives while suppressing alternative voices.

This homogenization effect reverberates through the public discourse, and its implications are both immediate and long-lasting. It narrows the spectrum of perspectives that audiences are exposed to, potentially leaving them with a skewed understanding of complex issues. As the media landscape becomes characterized by a limited range of viewpoints, the true depth and breadth of societal realities are obscured, creating a distorted mirror that reflects only a fraction of the truth.

Moreover, the role of gatekeepers of information extends beyond the mere selection of stories. It involves the allocation of resources, the prioritization of coverage, and the allocation of airtime. In a landscape of concentrated ownership, decisions about what gets covered and what gets sidelined are influenced not just by journalistic considerations, but by a complex interplay of economic, political, and ideological factors.

This phenomenon has implications for the health of democratic societies and informed citizenry. The absence of diverse voices and perspectives erodes the vibrancy of public discourse, stifles critical thinking, and undermines the foundational principles of democratic engagement. As audiences are denied exposure to a comprehensive array of viewpoints, their ability to form well-rounded opinions and make informed decisions becomes compromised.

The concept of media owners as gatekeepers of information is a reminder that the dissemination of information is not a neutral endeavor. It's a process laden with choices, biases, and consequences. As the custodians of this process, media owners hold a profound responsibility—one that extends beyond profit margins and market share. It's a responsibility that shapes the contours of public understanding, influences the direction of societies, and ultimately impacts the democratic fabric itself.

In the face of this responsibility, there is a call for media owners to approach their role with a deep commitment to transparency, diversity, and the pursuit of the common good. The gatekeeping power they wield is a double-edged sword, capable of either enriching public discourse or narrowing its horizons. As society continues to grapple with the challenges of media ownership concentration, the role of gatekeepers underscores the urgent need for a media landscape that reflects the multifaceted mosaic of human experiences and amplifies the voices that deserve to be heard.

Effects on Pluralism and Democracy

Media diversity is a cornerstone of pluralism—the belief that multiple perspectives enrich public discourse and safeguard democratic principles. Concentrated media ownership threatens this pluralistic ideal, as it can lead to echo chambers where homogenous viewpoints reinforce themselves. This chapter explores how media monopolies can erode the foundations of democracy, depriving citizens of the informed debates necessary for meaningful participation.

At the heart of thriving democracies lies the bedrock principle of pluralism—a concept that champions the richness of diverse perspectives, encourages open debate, and safeguards against the tyranny of a single narrative. In this context, media diversity becomes a cornerstone of pluralism, ensuring that the marketplace of ideas remains vibrant, dynamic, and reflective of the multifaceted tapestry of societal experiences. However, the phenomenon of concentrated media ownership casts a shadow over this ideal, raising concerns about the erosion of pluralism and its implications for the health of democracy itself.

Media monopolies have the potential to wield a profound influence over the narratives that circulate within society. As a limited number of entities gain control over multiple media outlets, there is a risk of homogenization—an alignment of viewpoints, narratives, and perspectives that reinforces itself and contributes to the creation of echo chambers. In these echo chambers, audiences are exposed to a narrow range of opinions, limiting their exposure to the diverse array of voices that are essential for well-rounded understanding.

The consequences of this erosion of pluralism are multifaceted and extend deeply into the fabric of democratic societies. When the spectrum of viewpoints becomes constrained, the robustness of public discourse is compromised. Informed debates give way to ideological polarization, nuanced discussions yield to binary thinking, and the space for dialogue narrows as alternative voices are marginalized.

Democracy thrives on informed citizenry and the power of choice. Informed citizens require access to a variety of viewpoints, enabling them to critically assess policies, evaluate candidates, and make decisions that align with their values and interests. Concentrated media ownership disrupts this flow of information, potentially leaving citizens with a limited range of perspectives from which to draw their conclusions.

Moreover, the media plays a pivotal role in holding those in power accountable. It serves as a check on governmental authority, shedding light on issues that demand scrutiny and ensuring that public officials remain answerable to the electorate. However, when media ownership is concentrated, the capacity for robust investigative journalism may be curtailed, as the potential for conflicts of interest and self-censorship looms large.

The phenomenon of concentrated media ownership poses a fundamental question: To what extent can a society be considered democratic when its media landscape is controlled by a handful of entities? The erosion of pluralism not only tilts the balance of power in favor of these entities, but it also threatens to dismantle the very foundations of democracy itself.

As citizens, stakeholders, and participants in democratic societies, there is a collective responsibility to scrutinize the effects of concentrated media ownership and demand a media landscape that reflects the ideals of pluralism. This exploration into the effects of media monopolies on pluralism and democracy is a call to action—a call to advocate for media diversity, to support independent journalism, and to engage in discourse that transcends the boundaries of echo chambers. By safeguarding the principles of pluralism, we uphold the essence of democracy—an essence that thrives on the flourishing of diverse voices, the clash of ideas, and the relentless pursuit of truth in the public sphere.

Commercial Interests and Agenda-setting

The consolidation of media ownership can also blur the lines between journalism and commercial interests. Media outlets, when owned by conglomerates with diverse business holdings, may prioritize profit over journalistic integrity. This section examines how these conflicts of interest can shape news coverage, influencing the stories that are highlighted, suppressed, or framed in a particular way.

In the intricate dance between media and commerce, a delicate balance must be maintained to ensure the integrity of journalism and the pursuit of truth. However, as media ownership becomes increasingly concentrated within conglomerates with diversified business interests, this balance can be easily disrupted, giving rise to conflicts of interest that pose a serious threat to the impartiality and objectivity of news coverage.

The phenomenon of media consolidation places media outlets under the umbrella of larger conglomerates—entities that span diverse industries and sectors, from entertainment to technology, from telecommunications to real estate. As a result, the financial interests of these conglomerates may not be confined solely to the dissemination of accurate and unbiased news; they may extend to safeguarding profits, promoting corporate agendas, and preserving business relationships that sustain various facets of their empire.

The implications of such conflicts of interest are profound, reaching into the heart of journalistic ethics and agenda-setting. News organizations that fall under the purview of conglomerates may be pressured to prioritize stories that align with the commercial interests of the parent company, potentially sidelining stories that are critical, controversial, or at odds with the corporate agenda.

Agenda-setting—the process by which media outlets determine which stories receive attention and how they are framed—becomes a terrain of negotiation between journalistic values and commercial imperatives. Stories that generate controversy, challenge power structures, or scrutinize corporate practices may be downplayed or omitted altogether, while stories that serve as promotional vehicles for affiliated products, services, or ventures may receive disproportionate coverage.

This dynamic has far-reaching effects on public discourse and the information ecosystem. The narratives that emerge from news coverage heavily influence public perception, shaping how individuals understand and engage with the world around them. When stories that shed light on corporate wrongdoing, environmental hazards, or social injustices are suppressed or underreported due to commercial pressures, the public is denied access to critical information that is essential for informed decision-making.

Moreover, the blurring of lines between journalism and commercial interests erodes the credibility of media outlets. Audiences rely on news organizations to provide accurate, unbiased, and independent information—a role that is compromised when news coverage is influenced by corporate considerations. The erosion of trust can have a chilling effect on public engagement, leaving citizens disillusioned and disconnected from the information sources they once relied upon.

The exploration of commercial interests and agenda-setting serves as a reminder that the role of journalism in society is multifaceted and deeply consequential. It is a vanguard of democracy, an instrument of accountability, and a beacon of truth. Yet, these roles are jeopardized when media outlets are ensnared in the web of commercial interests.

As consumers of news and participants in democratic societies, the onus is on us to demand transparency, ethical journalism, and the separation of media from undue corporate influence. By advocating for independent journalism, supporting media outlets committed to impartial reporting, and engaging in critical media literacy, we contribute to the preservation of a robust information ecosystem—one that empowers citizens to make informed decisions, question authority, and actively participate in shaping the collective narrative of our times.

Impact on Representation and Marginalization

Concentration of media ownership has a direct impact on representation, particularly for marginalized communities. When ownership lacks diversity, the stories and perspectives of underrepresented groups are sidelined or distorted. This chapter delves into how concentrated ownership perpetuates systemic inequalities by limiting opportunities for authentic representation.

In the kaleidoscope of human experiences and narratives, representation matters. It is the bridge that connects diverse voices to the collective consciousness, allowing stories to be heard, experiences to be acknowledged, and identities to be validated. However, as media ownership becomes increasingly concentrated within a few hands, the tapestry of representation risks being woven with limited threads, leaving vast portions of society's stories untold, unrecognized, and marginalized.

Representation in media serves as a mirror through which individuals, communities, and cultures see themselves reflected. It shapes perceptions, cultivates empathy, and fosters a sense of belonging. Yet, the phenomenon of concentrated media ownership threatens this delicate equilibrium by limiting the diversity of voices that find space on the stage of public discourse.

When ownership lacks diversity, the stories and perspectives of underrepresented communities are often sidelined or distorted. Newsrooms and media outlets, reflective of their owners' backgrounds and experiences, may fail to adequately cover issues that impact marginalized communities. The absence of authentic representation can result in skewed narratives, missed opportunities for in-depth coverage, and the perpetuation of stereotypes that reinforce systemic inequalities.

Consider the experiences of communities that have historically been marginalized—racial and ethnic minorities, LGBTQ+ individuals, indigenous peoples, and more. These communities have unique stories, struggles, and triumphs that deserve to be shared authentically. However, when media ownership is concentrated within entities that do not reflect the diversity of society, these stories may be overlooked, sensationalized, or inadequately understood.

The implications of this underrepresentation ripple far beyond media itself. Inadequate representation in media leads to limited visibility, which in turn hampers efforts to address systemic issues, advocate for policy changes, and build solidarity among different communities. When certain voices are excluded from the public narrative, the broader society misses out on the chance to learn, empathize, and work toward more equitable and inclusive societies.

Moreover, concentrated ownership perpetuates systemic inequalities by limiting opportunities for authentic representation. As media outlets are controlled by a few entities, the gatekeepers of these platforms hold immense influence over whose stories are elevated and whose are silenced. This control over narratives can translate into a cycle of exclusion, where marginalized communities are denied the chance to shape their own narratives, challenge stereotypes, and rewrite the scripts that have confined them.

The exploration of the impact of concentrated media ownership on representation and marginalization is a reminder that media is not merely a neutral conduit of information—it is a powerful shaper of perceptions, attitudes, and social norms. As consumers of media, advocates for equity, and participants in democracy, we have a role to play in demanding diverse and authentic representation. By supporting media outlets that prioritize inclusivity, championing independent journalism, and amplifying underrepresented voices, we contribute to a media landscape that reflects the vibrant tapestry of human experiences and paves the way toward a more just and inclusive future.

Championing Media Pluralism

Amidst the challenges posed by concentrated ownership, efforts to champion media pluralism emerge as crucial. This section highlights initiatives aimed at promoting diverse ownership models, fostering independent journalism, and creating platforms that amplify underrepresented voices. By challenging the status quo, these efforts contribute to a more inclusive and vibrant media ecosystem.

In the realm of media, diversity is not just a buzzword—it's a fundamental principle that underpins the health of democratic societies and the vitality of public discourse. As concentrated media ownership tightens its grip on the flow of information, the need to champion media pluralism becomes more urgent than ever. This section sheds light on the initiatives and movements that are rising to the challenge, working tirelessly to dismantle the barriers to diverse and independent media ownership.

At the heart of these efforts lies a commitment to breaking the monopoly of voices that currently dominate the media landscape. Diverse ownership models are championed as a means to ensure that media outlets reflect the rich tapestry of society itself. These models encompass community-owned media, nonprofit journalism organizations, and cooperatives that prioritize the public interest over profit motives.

Community-owned media outlets are emerging as powerful antidotes to the homogenization that concentrated ownership breeds. By putting the reins of media in the hands of local communities, these outlets foster a sense of ownership, accountability, and relevance. They prioritize stories that resonate with the unique needs and aspirations of their audiences, moving away from the one-size-fits-all approach that characterizes conglomerate-owned media.

Nonprofit journalism initiatives stand as beacons of integrity in a landscape marred by conflicts of interest. These organizations prioritize investigative journalism, diving deep into undercovered issues, and giving voice to communities that are often marginalized. By operating independently from commercial pressures, they are able to spotlight stories that matter, challenge powerful interests, and hold institutions accountable.

Cooperative ownership models extend the principle of inclusivity to the very fabric of media operations. By involving journalists, staff, and communities in decision-making processes, cooperatives ensure that media outlets remain rooted in the interests of those they serve. This cooperative ethos not only fosters a diverse range of perspectives but also acts as a safeguard against undue corporate influence.

Independent media platforms that amplify underrepresented voices have gained momentum in the digital age. These platforms provide a space for marginalized communities to tell their own stories, share their experiences, and challenge dominant narratives. Through podcasts, social media campaigns, and online publications, these platforms contribute to a more democratic and accessible media landscape.

Efforts to champion media pluralism extend beyond ownership to encompass the very fabric of journalism itself. The focus on diversity and representation is not just a token gesture—it's an acknowledgement of the fact that a multiplicity of perspectives enriches the quality of reporting and deepens the understanding of complex issues. Initiatives that prioritize diversity in newsrooms, invest in training for underrepresented journalists, and promote a culture of inclusivity are integral to this broader vision.

In a world where information shapes opinions, where narratives drive policy decisions, and where media influences the collective consciousness, the fight for media pluralism is nothing short of a fight for democracy itself. By supporting community-owned outlets, amplifying underrepresented voices, and championing initiatives that challenge concentrated ownership, we contribute to a media ecosystem that is vibrant, diverse, and truly representative of the diverse societies we inhabit. The future of democracy depends on it.

A Call for Democratic Media Landscapes

As we delve into the complexities of "Concentration of Media Ownership and its Effects," we confront the power dynamics that shape the narratives we encounter. This chapter calls us to critically assess the information sources we rely upon, demand transparency in media ownership, and advocate for policies that uphold the principles of democracy and diverse representation. By championing media pluralism, we assert our collective right to a rich tapestry of perspectives—one that reflects the mosaic of society and safeguards the foundations of democratic discourse.

The digital age has ushered in an era of unprecedented access to information, yet it has also intensified the challenges posed by concentrated media ownership. As we navigate the complexities of "Concentration of Media Ownership and its Effects," a rallying cry emerges—one that resonates with the very essence of democracy itself. This chapter isn't just an exploration; it's a call to action—a call to transform our media landscapes into bastions of democratic values, diverse representation, and inclusive discourse.

In a world where information wields the power to shape perceptions, influence decisions, and mold public sentiment, the sources from which we derive this information matter immensely. We are urged to question, to probe, and to critically assess the media outlets we rely upon. Transparency in media ownership becomes paramount—an informed citizenry has the right to know who controls the narratives that permeate their lives. We're challenged to move beyond passive consumption, to engage actively with the media we encounter, and to become discerning consumers who demand accountability.

At the heart of this call lies a fundamental principle: the right to diverse representation. A democratic society thrives on the free exchange of ideas, on a multiplicity of perspectives, and on the vibrant clash of differing viewpoints. Concentrated media ownership threatens this foundation by elevating some voices while marginalizing others. To champion media pluralism is to champion the very essence of democracy—to ensure that the mosaic of society is reflected in the stories we hear, the news we consume, and the conversations we engage in.

This call for democratic media landscapes extends beyond individual choices—it extends to policy and advocacy. It's a plea for policymakers to recognize the profound impact of media ownership concentration on democracy itself. It's a demand for regulations and safeguards that prevent monopolization, foster diverse ownership models, and promote fair competition. It's an insistence that the media ecosystem should be a level playing field where all voices, regardless of size or influence, have the opportunity to be heard.

We're called to be informed advocates, to rally behind movements that champion media pluralism and transparency. This is a call that extends to journalists who bear the responsibility of upholding their craft with integrity and truthfulness. It's a call for media outlets to take the mantle of responsibility, to prioritize public interest over profit margins, and to recognize their role as stewards of democracy.

Ultimately, this chapter's call for action is a declaration that the power to shape narratives is not the sole domain of a select few—it's a power that belongs to the masses, to the diverse communities that make up the fabric of society. By actively engaging with media, by demanding transparency, by supporting initiatives that challenge concentrated ownership, and by amplifying underrepresented voices, we pave the way for a media landscape that is reflective of democracy's core values.

In an age where misinformation spreads like wildfire, where divisive rhetoric threatens social cohesion, and where the cacophony of voices can be overwhelming, this call becomes a beacon of hope. It's a reminder that the principles of democracy are not just ideals to be upheld; they're responsibilities to be embraced. Through the collective pursuit of democratic media landscapes, we contribute to a world where truth, diversity, and inclusivity reign—a world where the foundations of democracy stand strong.

Lack of Racial Diversity in Media Ownership

Within the vast expanse of media, the faces and voices that control the narrative have profound implications for the stories that are told, the perspectives that are shared, and the communities that are represented. This section delves into a stark reality—the lack of racial diversity in media ownership—and explores the far-reaching consequences of this imbalance on the media landscape, public discourse, and the fight for inclusive representation.

The Underrepresentation Paradox

Media, often celebrated as a platform for diverse voices, grapples with a glaring paradox. While it can amplify the stories of marginalized communities, it frequently fails to reflect that diversity in its ownership. The underrepresentation of racial and ethnic minorities among media owners stands as a stark reminder of systemic inequities that pervade both the industry and society at large.

In the dynamic landscape of media, where stories are spun, narratives are woven, and perspectives are shared, a paradox emerges—a dissonance between the promise of diverse voices and the stark underrepresentation that persists within the very structures that shape our information landscape. This chapter plunges into the depths of the "Media Ownership and Diversity" debate to unveil the complexities of the underrepresentation paradox—a phenomenon that serves as both a testament to progress and a stark reminder of the systemic inequities entrenched in our society.

Media, in its multifaceted splendor, has the power to elevate the narratives of those who have been historically marginalized, silenced, or overshadowed. It's a platform where stories can be celebrated, cultures can be shared, and underrepresented communities can find a resonating voice. Yet, this narrative-rich promise clashes with the reality that ownership of these platforms often remains concentrated within a select few.

The underrepresentation paradox is, at its core, a manifestation of the broader systemic inequalities that have shaped our society over centuries. It's a paradox that mirrors the broader social, economic, and political disparities that persist between racial and ethnic communities. Just as marginalized communities are often denied equitable access to opportunities, resources, and representation, they also find themselves sidelined in the very industries that have the potential to amplify their voices.

Diverse representation in media ownership isn't just about the numbers—it's about the stories that are told, the perspectives that are shared, and the impact that media can have on shaping perceptions and driving change. When ownership remains concentrated among a homogenous group, it stifles the full spectrum of human experiences and narratives that deserve to be told. It perpetuates a cycle where certain viewpoints are prioritized over others, where particular issues are elevated while others are left in the shadows.

As the digital age accelerates the democratization of information and empowers individuals to become content creators, the underrepresentation paradox gains new dimensions. The power to share stories has never been more accessible, yet the structures of influence and control remain largely unchanged. The paradox becomes a call to action—a call to break down barriers, to challenge norms, and to redefine the ownership landscape to be reflective of the diversity that defines our world.

This chapter dives deep into the heart of the underrepresentation paradox, exploring the historical roots that have led us to this point and the potential pathways that can guide us toward a more equitable future. It sheds light on the initiatives that are championing diverse ownership models, the success stories that remind us of the power of representation, and the collective responsibility we all bear in reshaping the media landscape.

The underrepresentation paradox, while a challenge, is also a rallying point—a catalyst for change that calls us to question and challenge the status quo. As we immerse ourselves in this exploration, we're invited to envision a media landscape where ownership reflects the richness of human diversity, where stories from all corners of the world find a platform, and where the underrepresented become the architects of their own narratives.

Gatekeeping and Narrative Control

Media ownership is a form of gatekeeping—an exercise of authority over which narratives are prioritized and which are suppressed. When ownership lacks diversity, the gatekeepers hail from a narrow demographic, perpetuating narratives that align with their experiences and perspectives. This creates a distorted mirror that reflects a fraction of reality, marginalizing stories that challenge the status quo.

In the intricate dance between information and influence, media ownership emerges as a pivotal partner—its role akin to that of a gatekeeper, deciding which stories pass through the gates and into the collective consciousness, and which remain confined in the shadows. This chapter takes us on a journey into the heart of "Media Ownership and Diversity," unraveling the threads of gatekeeping and narrative control—a phenomenon that amplifies the significance of ownership diversity and its direct impact on the stories we encounter.

Gatekeeping isn't just about the mechanics of filtering information; it's a reflection of the broader power dynamics that shape our societies. Just as gates can be swung open or shut to determine who gains entry, media ownership wields the authority to amplify certain narratives while silencing others. The gatekeepers, in this case, are those who hold the keys to media outlets—the decision-makers who shape the landscape of information that molds our perspectives.

The paradox of gatekeeping becomes all the more potent when we consider the homogeneity that often characterizes media ownership. When gatekeepers share similar backgrounds, experiences, and perspectives, the narratives that emerge are inherently biased—a reflection of their own worldview. It's a scenario where the gates unwittingly become filters that sieve out stories that challenge the status quo, relegating them to the periphery.

The narrative control exercised by media ownership doesn't merely influence the stories that are told; it profoundly impacts how society perceives itself, its challenges, and its aspirations. When gatekeepers are drawn from a narrow demographic, they mirror the stories that resonate with their own lives, effectively erasing the nuances of diverse experiences. The stories that don't conform to their narratives often struggle to find a platform, perpetuating a cycle of invisibility.

Diverse media ownership becomes the key to unlocking these gates and allowing a more comprehensive array of stories to flow freely. It offers the promise of dismantling the echo chambers that have formed, where homogenous viewpoints amplify themselves while silencing dissenting voices. Ownership diversity broadens the spectrum of perspectives that guide narrative selection, reflecting the rich tapestry of human experiences.

This chapter delves into the intricate mechanisms of gatekeeping, tracing its origins, dissecting its implications, and highlighting the pivotal role of diverse ownership in breaking down the barriers that have confined narratives. It celebrates the stories that have broken through despite the odds, reminding us that the journey toward equitable representation requires persistent effort and a collective commitment to redefine the gatekeepers' role.

Gatekeeping and narrative control are not abstract concepts; they shape the contours of our understanding, influence policy decisions, and mold our shared reality. As we delve into this exploration, we're beckoned to reflect on the narratives that have shaped us, to challenge the narratives that have been silenced, and to envision a media landscape where the gates are open wide to all stories, regardless of who they come from.

The Amplification of Stereotypes

The lack of racial diversity in media ownership reinforces the perpetuation of stereotypes. Without authentic representation at the helm, media outlets are more likely to portray racial and ethnic communities through a lens of otherness and caricature. This portrayal contributes to a cycle where stereotypes are reinforced and communities are defined by limited and often distorted characteristics.

In the intricate web of media representation, the absence of racial diversity in ownership becomes a critical thread that weaves its way into the very fabric of our collective understanding. This chapter delves deep into the heart of "Media Ownership and Diversity," uncovering how this absence reverberates through media outlets and magnifies the amplification of stereotypes—a phenomenon that not only distorts the portrayal of racial and ethnic communities but also shapes the perceptions that society holds.

Imagine a canvas painted with broad strokes—brushes guided by the hands of those who have no lived experience of the nuances, struggles, and triumphs of communities they depict. This canvas is the media landscape, and the brush wielders are the owners who dictate the narratives that flow from their outlets. Without authentic representation, these narratives often fall into the trap of simplification, reducing complex communities into one-dimensional caricatures that are perpetuated through repetition.

The amplification of stereotypes is a result of a vicious cycle—a cycle where the lack of ownership diversity leads to skewed perspectives that, in turn, mold the stories that reach the public. These stories, often shaped by uninformed lenses, contribute to the reinforcement of stereotypes. Racial and ethnic communities find themselves defined by a handful of characteristics that barely scratch the surface of their diversity and complexity.

Media outlets, acting as megaphones for these limited narratives, end up projecting a distorted image of communities that deserve to be seen in all their vibrancy. The absence of authentic representation allows for the perpetuation of narratives that paint communities as monolithic entities, disregarding the myriad experiences, histories, and aspirations that form their tapestry.

This chapter plunges into the depths of this phenomenon, tracing its origins, scrutinizing its consequences, and underscoring the urgency of diversifying ownership to dismantle its grip. It explores case studies where media outlets, free from the constraints of stereotype perpetuation, have managed to present multifaceted narratives that break down the walls of misunderstanding.

The amplification of stereotypes, born from the lack of diversity in ownership, isn't just an issue of inaccurate representation—it's a matter of social justice. It stands as a barrier to empathy, a barrier to understanding, and a barrier to the pursuit of equitable societies. As we navigate through these intricacies, we're confronted with a call to action— to demand representation that reflects the complexity of our world, to challenge narratives that reduce us to mere archetypes, and to elevate voices that have long been silenced in the echo chambers of stereotype perpetuation.

Influence on Editorial Choices

Media ownership shapes editorial choices, from story selection to framing. When ownership lacks diversity, certain issues and perspectives are often sidelined or trivialized. This section examines how this lack of diversity results in editorial decisions that prioritize the interests of the powerful while overlooking the narratives of those historically marginalized.

As we journey deeper into the heart of the media landscape, we uncover a truth that underscores the power dynamics within: media ownership shapes not only the narrative but also the very choices that editors make. In the intricate dance of selecting stories, framing issues, and deciding what occupies the spotlight, ownership diversity emerges as a defining factor. This chapter unravels the intricate interplay between "Media Ownership and Diversity" and the editorial decisions that ultimately mold the media's portrayal of our world.

Imagine a newsroom—a place buzzing with the pursuit of truth, driven by the responsibility to inform the public. Behind every headline and article lies an editorial choice—a choice influenced not just by journalistic values but by the perspectives that ownership brings to the table. When ownership lacks diversity, these choices can inadvertently lean toward prioritizing narratives that align with the interests of the powerful, while sidelining or trivializing issues and perspectives of those historically marginalized.

This chapter dives headlong into this dynamic, exposing how a homogenous ownership landscape can lead to a news agenda that mirrors the viewpoints of the few rather than reflecting the tapestry of society. The stories that get greenlit, the angles that get emphasized, and the voices that get amplified—all are subject to the lens through which ownership perceives the world.

The influence on editorial choices doesn't just extend to overt biases—it's often a subtle, nuanced dance that shapes the very contours of media discourse. The absence of diversity in ownership can result in the downplaying of issues that aren't deemed "mainstream" or that don't align with the experiences of the powerful few. Narratives that challenge the status quo, stories that demand accountability, and perspectives that bring nuance to complex issues can find themselves sidelined.

This chapter delves into real-world examples, where the impact of ownership on editorial choices becomes evident in the stories that are covered and the ones that slip through the cracks. It explores instances where diverse ownership has led to a more inclusive editorial approach, where the stories of marginalized communities receive the attention and prominence they deserve.

The influence on editorial choices isn't just about the stories that are told—it's about the stories that are silenced, the perspectives that are marginalized, and the public's right to an informed and diverse discourse. As we navigate this terrain, we're prompted to critically examine the narratives that shape our understanding, to question the motivations behind editorial decisions, and to advocate for a media landscape that holds representation as a pillar of its responsibility.

Media as an Instrument of Empowerment

Diverse media ownership isn't merely about rectifying imbalances; it's about empowering communities to tell their own stories. When media outlets are owned by members of underrepresented groups, they become platforms for authentic representation, advocacy, and social change. This section celebrates instances where diverse media ownership has led to the amplification of voices that were long silenced.

As we delve into the intricate web of "Media Ownership and Diversity," we uncover a transformative aspect that transcends numbers and statistics—it's the profound potential for media to be an instrument of empowerment. Diversity in media ownership isn't just a matter of equitable distribution; it's a catalyst for reshaping narratives, amplifying voices, and engendering positive social change. This chapter unfurls the power of media as a force that can uplift communities, embolden advocacy, and carve pathways to a more inclusive society.

Imagine a media landscape where ownership reflects the diverse mosaic of society—a landscape where narratives are spun not just by the privileged few, but by those whose stories have often been sidelined or misinterpreted. In such a landscape, media outlets cease to be just businesses; they evolve into platforms of empowerment. They become the megaphones through which marginalized communities can raise their voices, challenge stereotypes, and reshape the perceptions that have long defined them.

This chapter sheds light on real-world examples where diverse media ownership has spurred remarkable change. We explore instances where underrepresented groups have harnessed media outlets to share their stories authentically, offering a counter-narrative to prevailing stereotypes. From telling stories of resilience in the face of adversity to spotlighting the achievements and aspirations of communities long marginalized, diverse media ownership has enabled narratives that were once buried to come to the forefront.

But this empowerment isn't confined to storytelling—it's about driving social change. Media outlets with diverse ownership become platforms for advocacy, sounding the call for justice, equality, and systemic reform. These outlets have the unique ability to connect with their communities on a profound level, building trust and fostering a sense of belonging. This sense of ownership over one's narrative is empowering—it instills a sense of agency, enabling communities to challenge the status quo and advocate for their rights.

The transformative potential of media as an instrument of empowerment is both inspiring and urgent. It's a reminder that media ownership isn't just about business—it's about agency, representation, and the right to shape one's own story. This chapter urges us to recognize the power we hold as consumers, to champion media outlets that elevate diverse voices, and to support initiatives that expand the ownership landscape. It's a call to embrace media as a catalyst for positive change—a tool that can dismantle biases, bridge divides, and build a more inclusive world.

A Call for Equitable Ownership

As we confront the reality of the "Lack of Racial Diversity in Media Ownership," we are faced with a crucial question: Who holds the pen that writes history, and who holds the microphone that broadcasts it? This section urges us to demand equitable ownership structures that reflect the richness of human experience. By supporting media ventures led by racial and ethnic minorities, we not only rectify historical injustices but also nurture a media landscape that honors the tapestry of humanity.

Efforts towards Inclusive Media Ownership Models

Amidst the complex web of media ownership, glimmers of change emerge—efforts that seek to dismantle the barriers that have long restricted diverse voices from the realm of influence. This section explores the initiatives and models that are paving the way towards inclusive media ownership, fostering a landscape where underrepresented communities can wield the power to shape narratives, challenge biases, and redefine the contours of storytelling.

Community-Owned Media Ventures

Fostering Empowerment and Enriching Narratives

Community-owned media ventures stand as beacons of empowerment within a landscape dominated by conglomerates. These initiatives prioritize local voices, engaging communities in the creation and dissemination of content that reflects their unique experiences. This section examines how community ownership fosters a symbiotic relationship between media and society, enriching narratives and amplifying stories that would otherwise remain untold.

Amid the vast expanse of media conglomerates and corporate giants, community-owned media ventures emerge as dynamic forces of empowerment, encapsulating the essence of a participatory and inclusive media landscape. This section delves into the captivating realm of community-owned media, shedding light on how these ventures weave a tapestry of voices, stories, and perspectives that resonate with the heartbeat of local communities.

In a world where media outlets are often seen as distant entities, community-owned ventures bring a refreshing change. They transcend the conventional boundaries of media consumption, inviting residents to become active participants in shaping the narrative of their own lives. These initiatives are rooted in the belief that the best storytellers for a community are the very individuals who live and breathe its experiences, and this belief serves as the cornerstone of their mission.

Through in-depth analysis and illustrative case studies, this section unveils the intricate symbiosis between community-owned media and the societies they serve. We explore how these ventures engage with their audience not as mere consumers, but as co-creators, fostering a sense of ownership over the stories that unfold. This participatory approach ripples through the content, breathing life into narratives that capture the nuances, struggles, triumphs, and aspirations of local life.

Community-owned media ventures are more than platforms—they are catalysts for connection, unity, and understanding. They bridge the gap between the airwaves and the community, creating spaces where individuals can share their lived experiences, raise their concerns, and celebrate their achievements. This bridge-building role extends beyond the realm of media, as these ventures nurture a sense of belonging, empowerment, and agency within the community.

This exploration shines a spotlight on the impact of community-owned media ventures on narratives that would otherwise remain unexplored. By prioritizing local voices, these initiatives shine a light on stories that are often overshadowed by the glitz of mainstream media. They provide a counterbalance to the narratives perpetuated by larger media entities, offering a lens through which the rich tapestry of community life is brought into focus.

Ultimately, community-owned media ventures serve as vibrant illustrations of how media can be a tool for empowerment and social cohesion. This section celebrates the initiatives that have carved out spaces for diverse stories, championed the underrepresented, and elevated the authentic voices that paint the true portrait of a community. As we navigate the intricate world of media ownership and its implications, these ventures stand as inspiring examples of the power of local storytelling and the transformation that can unfold when communities take the reins of their own narratives.

Independent Platforms for Underrepresented Voices

A Symphony of Empowerment and Disruption

The digital age has ushered in an era of independent platforms that offer a stage for voices traditionally marginalized by mainstream media. From podcasts to online publications, these platforms circumvent traditional gatekeepers, enabling individuals to share their stories directly with global audiences. This section celebrates the democratizing influence of independent media and the power it holds in challenging established norms.

In the ever-evolving landscape of media, a remarkable shift has taken place—an emergence of independent platforms that serve as sanctuaries for voices that have long been overlooked by traditional gatekeepers. As we venture into the digital age, this section delves into the vibrant world of these platforms, exploring how they have become beacons of empowerment, pushing the boundaries of representation, and reshaping the very fabric of storytelling.

The power of these platforms lies in their ability to transcend the confines of established media structures. In an era where conventional outlets have been criticized for perpetuating homogenized narratives, independent platforms rise as an alternative, carving out spaces for underrepresented voices to flourish. From podcasts that amplify unheard stories to online publications that challenge prevailing paradigms, these platforms celebrate diversity and champion authenticity.

Through an in-depth examination of real-world examples and groundbreaking case studies, this section unravels the democratizing potential of independent media. We navigate the virtual corridors of platforms that have cultivated communities around shared experiences, ideologies, and identities. These platforms not only provide a voice but also construct bridges between individuals who, despite geographical distances, find commonality in their stories.

As we delve further, we explore how independent platforms have become disruptive forces in a media landscape historically dominated by giants. By sidestepping the gatekeepers, these platforms have opened doors for narratives that previously struggled to secure a place in the spotlight. They have given rise to storytellers who challenge established norms, uncover hidden truths, and inspire reflection and change.

But this section doesn't merely celebrate disruption—it underscores the inherent responsibility that comes with the liberation of voice. We dissect the ethical considerations that independent platforms navigate, particularly as they strive to offer a counterbalance to the mainstream. The exploration delves into the delicate equilibrium between celebrating diversity and avoiding tokenism, all while maintaining journalistic integrity and fostering a respectful dialogue.

In essence, independent platforms for underrepresented voices are more than just digital spaces—they are catalysts for transformation. They symbolize the power of technology to bridge divides and amplify stories that have long remained on the periphery. This section, as we traverse its intricacies, stands as a tribute to the pioneers who have harnessed the digital frontier to elevate voices that deserve to be heard, reminding us that in a world rich with perspectives, every narrative matters.

Nonprofit Journalism Initiatives

Illuminating Truth and Fostering Impact

In a media landscape often dictated by commercial interests, nonprofit journalism initiatives emerge as beacons of independent reporting and social impact. These organizations redefine the purpose of journalism, prioritizing investigative rigor, amplifying underrepresented voices, and shedding light on stories that may otherwise remain hidden. This section delves into the profound role of nonprofit media outlets in bridging gaps, challenging narratives, and empowering societies through informed engagement.

Amidst the cacophony of commercial-driven media, a refreshing paradigm emerges—nonprofit journalism initiatives that shine as bastions of integrity, social responsibility, and transformative storytelling. As we journey into the heart of media's moral compass, this section unveils the inspiring world of nonprofit journalism, where the pursuit of truth and societal betterment takes precedence over profit margins.

In an era where newsrooms can be beholden to corporate interests, nonprofit journalism rises as a counterforce—a clarion call for journalism to return to its roots of serving the public good. This exploration takes us into the inner workings of these initiatives, uncovering their dedication to investigative rigor, unbiased reporting, and amplifying marginalized voices that might otherwise be muted.

With an unflinching commitment to ethical journalism, nonprofit initiatives redefine the very purpose of media. We navigate through stories that illuminate injustices, expose corruption, and challenge the status quo. These initiatives wield their influence to empower communities, fostering informed engagement that drives social change.

Through a meticulous analysis of real-world examples and case studies, this section immerses us in the tangible impact of nonprofit journalism. We witness how these initiatives act as watchdogs, holding powerful institutions accountable and unearthing truths that shape public discourse. Their approach to storytelling transcends headlines, delving into the heart of issues, and humanizing the faces behind statistics.

Moreover, this exploration delves into the delicate balance nonprofit initiatives navigate—striving for financial sustainability while safeguarding their editorial independence. We examine how they navigate the complexities of funding, audience engagement, and maintaining credibility, all while remaining true to their mission of serving the public interest.

As we venture further, we encounter the transformative power of nonprofit journalism in action. We traverse the narratives that have been reshaped, communities that have been empowered, and injustices that have been brought to light. This section is a tribute to the journalists who embody the spirit of unearthing truth, even when the road is arduous and the path less traveled.

In a world where media is often an echo chamber of sensationalism, nonprofit journalism initiatives stand as a beacon of hope—a reminder that journalism can be a force for good, a vehicle for change, and a catalyst for informed societies. This section encapsulates the spirit of fearless reporting, transformative storytelling, and the enduring impact of media that prioritizes the people it serves.

Investigative Rigor and Social Accountability

Nonprofit journalism initiatives are guided by a commitment to the truth and the pursuit of social accountability. They allocate substantial resources and time to in-depth investigative reporting, revealing corruption, systemic injustices, and issues often overlooked by profit-driven media. By pursuing these stories, nonprofit outlets hold powerful entities accountable and contribute to a more transparent and just society.

Filling Gaps in Coverage

One of the significant shortcomings of mainstream media is its tendency to overlook stories that are deemed less sensational or financially viable. Nonprofit journalism fills these gaps, illuminating issues that might otherwise remain in the shadows. By addressing these undercovered topics, nonprofit outlets ensure that diverse perspectives are included in public discourse.

Voices from the Margins

Nonprofit journalism initiatives stand as platforms for amplifying voices from the margins of society. These outlets prioritize stories that challenge the status quo, offering a space for individuals and communities whose narratives are often overshadowed by dominant perspectives. By highlighting these voices, nonprofit media contribute to a more inclusive and equitable representation of human experiences.

Challenging Dominant Narratives

One of the essential functions of nonprofit journalism is challenging dominant narratives propagated by mainstream media. By delving into issues from various angles and perspectives, nonprofit outlets counteract one-sided viewpoints. This nuanced approach fosters a more comprehensive understanding of complex issues, allowing readers to make informed judgments and decisions.

Promoting Civic Engagement

Nonprofit journalism empowers citizens to become informed participants in their societies. In-depth reporting and diverse perspectives offered by nonprofit outlets contribute to a more informed citizenry. By shedding light on critical issues, these initiatives foster engaged individuals who are better equipped to advocate for change and contribute to the betterment of their communities.

Navigating Challenges

While nonprofit journalism initiatives offer a noble alternative, they are not without challenges. Financial sustainability is a significant concern, often relying on donations, grants, and public support to sustain their operations. Additionally, nonprofit outlets must navigate potential biases to ensure that their reporting remains objective and free from undue influence. Despite these challenges, nonprofit media continue to play a vital role in fostering an informed and democratic society.

Policy Advocacy for Diversity and Inclusion

Efforts towards inclusive media ownership extend beyond grassroots initiatives to policy advocacy. This section delves into how policies can be crafted to incentivize diversity in media ownership. By offering financial support, removing regulatory barriers, and promoting transparency, governments can encourage a more equitable media landscape that reflects the diversity of the societies they serve.

Representation Matters: Role Models in Media Ownership

Representation matters not only in front of the camera but also behind it. When individuals from underrepresented backgrounds hold positions of media ownership, they become role models that inspire others to follow suit. This section celebrates pioneers who have shattered barriers and paved the way for a new generation of diverse media owners.

In the symphony of media's influence, the conductor behind the scenes wields a powerful baton—the media owner. Yet, for far too long, this role has been confined to a homogenous few, perpetuating a narrative that does not reflect the rich tapestry of our global society. "Representation Matters" emerges as a rallying cry for change, a testament to the transformative power of individuals from underrepresented backgrounds who have risen to the helm of media ownership.

Diving into this chapter, we embark on a journey through the corridors of influence, where pioneers have defied conventions and shattered glass ceilings. These trailblazers are not merely media owners; they are beacons of inspiration, radiant proof that barriers can be surmounted, and dreams can become reality. Through meticulous research and in-depth storytelling, this section unveils the stories of those who dared to disrupt, uplift, and diversify the media landscape.

These pioneers stand as living testaments to the undeniable truth: Representation in media ownership is not just symbolic; it is transformational. As we delve into their narratives, we are transported to moments of courage, persistence, and resilience—essences that have kindled fires of change. We explore the strategies they employed, the hurdles they overcame, and the impact they have left on media and society.

Beyond their personal journeys, these pioneers become lighthouses for aspiring media leaders from underrepresented backgrounds. They not only challenge traditional notions of who can occupy these positions but also dismantle stereotypes and forge new paths. Their very existence paves the way for a more inclusive media ecosystem where diversity is not just a buzzword but a lived reality.

This exploration traverses through sectors that were once considered exclusive realms—newspapers, television networks, digital platforms, and more. We uncover the stories behind their initiatives, platforms, and endeavors that have resonated with audiences hungry for authentic representation. The ripple effect of their leadership extends far beyond media, spurring conversations, shaping policy debates, and contributing to cultural shifts.

Yet, this chapter also acknowledges the hurdles these pioneers continue to face—the uphill battle for resources, recognition, and equitable opportunities. It confronts the systemic barriers that persist and the uphill journey toward true parity. Nevertheless, it is a celebration of progress and possibility—an acknowledgment that representation matters not just in numbers but in the transformation of narratives and the amplification of silenced voices.

Ultimately, "Representation Matters" serves as a testament to the power of individuals who rewrite the script of ownership, turning the lens towards the unseen, the unheard, and the unrepresented. It's an ode to the pioneers who pave the way for a more equitable media future, inspiring generations to come and reminding us that true representation in media ownership holds the key to unlocking a world of stories, perspectives, and possibilities.

A Call for Systemic Transformation

As we explore the "Efforts towards Inclusive Media Ownership Models," we are reminded that the struggle for media equity is inseparable from the broader quest for social justice. This section calls us to champion initiatives that challenge the status quo, to uplift the voices of those who have been silenced, and to recognize that a more inclusive media landscape isn't just a goal—it's a cornerstone of a just and democratic society. By supporting diverse ownership models, we contribute to a world where storytelling becomes a force for unity, empathy, and positive change.

Within the pages of this chapter lies a rallying cry—a call that echoes beyond the confines of paper and ink. "Efforts towards Inclusive Media Ownership Models" is more than just a study of initiatives; it's a profound testament to the power of collective action and a plea for systemic transformation. As we immerse ourselves in the stories of change-makers and innovators, we find ourselves at the crossroads of history, facing a pivotal moment where the destiny of media and society intertwine.

The journey into this section transcends mere chronicles; it's an odyssey of empowerment, resilience, and hope. It unfolds stories of initiatives that have risen against the tides of adversity, dismantling entrenched structures and pioneering a new media paradigm. Through captivating narratives, we meet those who have dared to question the norms, dismantle the barriers, and break the shackles of homogeneity.

Yet, this chapter is not just a celebration of accomplishments; it's a call to action—a call to all those who believe in the transformative power of media to shape minds, foster empathy, and ignite change. It resonates with the voices of those who have long been silenced, inviting them to step into the limelight and reclaim their narratives. It urges us to be architects of a media landscape that mirrors the rich diversity of our world, where stories aren't just told but lived.

At its core, this exploration is an ode to the disruptors—the organizations, collectives, and individuals who have dared to imagine a world where media ownership is democratized, where influence is shared, and where representation is not a privilege but a right. It traverses the innovative terrain of cooperative ownership, community-driven initiatives, and platforms that empower marginalized voices. Through their stories, we learn that change isn't an abstract concept; it's a tangible reality that unfolds when vision meets action.

While celebrating these victories, this chapter does not shy away from acknowledging the challenges that lie ahead. It confronts the systemic barriers, the power imbalances, and the persistent biases that continue to shape media landscapes. It underscores that the struggle for inclusive ownership models is interconnected with the broader fight for social justice—a fight that transcends screens and headlines and extends into the very fabric of our society.

More than a chapter, this is a manifesto—a testament to the power of unity, of voices coming together to orchestrate a symphony of change. It beckons us to engage not as passive observers but as active participants in shaping the media landscape of tomorrow. It is a reminder that our choices, our advocacy, and our support have the potential to sculpt a future where media is a catalyst for unity, empathy, and positive transformation.

As we conclude our exploration, we stand on the precipice of possibility, holding in our hands the blueprint for a media world that transcends divisions and embraces unity. The call echoes, the stories resound, and the path forward beckons— an invitation to be part of a movement that ushers in a new era, one where media serves not just as a mirror but as a beacon of hope and change.

188

Chapter 6: Activism and Social Media

Role of Social Media in Amplifying Racial Issues

In the interconnected age of digital communication, social media platforms have emerged as powerful catalysts for change, enabling individuals and communities to transcend geographical boundaries and mobilize for social causes. This chapter delves into the symbiotic relationship between activism and social media, focusing on the pivotal role these platforms play in amplifying and galvanizing movements that address racial injustices, challenge systemic biases, and demand transformative change.

Unleashing the Power of Connectivity: Social Media's Role in Shaping Racial Discourse

In the vast and dynamic landscape of the digital era, where bytes and pixels hold as much sway as ink and paper, social media emerges as a seismic force—one that redefines how voices are heard, stories are told, and movements are ignited. "Role of Social Media in Amplifying Racial Issues" is a chapter that peels back the layers of this virtual revolution, exploring how the digital age has become a rallying ground for change, solidarity, and justice.

This chapter is more than a study—it's an immersion into the pulse of a global phenomenon. It unfurls the intertwined narrative of activism and social media, two forces that have converged to reshape the contours of societal dialogue. At its core, this exploration is a testament to the transformative potential of connectivity—the power to bring disparate voices together, to dismantle geographical barriers, and to create a digital agora where ideas are exchanged and alliances are forged.

As we traverse this digital realm, we encounter stories that bridge continents and cultures, uniting individuals who share a common vision for a more equitable world. We delve into the moments where hashtags become battle cries, where viral videos become agents of change, and where the virtual sphere becomes a canvas for activism. It's a journey that underscores how social media has democratized advocacy, giving individuals the tools to become agents of their own narratives.

Yet, this chapter does not shy away from the complexities that emerge in this brave new world. It delves into the dual nature of social media—an arena where narratives can be both amplified and distorted. It grapples with the tension between the rapid dissemination of information and the need for accuracy and context. It explores the challenges posed by algorithms that can inadvertently reinforce existing biases, shaping our virtual realities in ways we may not always be aware of.

Central to this exploration is the phenomenon of hashtag activism—a phenomenon that has birthed movements, ignited conversations, and pushed societal boundaries. It's a journey into the heart of hashtags that carry within them the stories of countless lives, the pain of injustice, and the resilience of communities united in their demand for change. From #BlackLivesMatter to #MeToo, these hashtags are a testament to the power of collective voices transcending screens to create a resounding chorus of transformation.

As we conclude our journey through this chapter, we emerge with a profound understanding that social media is more than just a virtual landscape—it's a canvas on which dreams of a more just world are painted, a platform where the echoes of unheard voices reverberate, and a force that challenges the very fabric of the status quo. This chapter is an invitation to recognize the impact we can wield with our keyboards and screens, to harness the potential of connectivity for meaningful change, and to forge an alliance between the digital realm and the tangible world— a partnership that holds the key to a future defined by empathy, equity, and collective action.

The Digital Megaphone for Marginalized Voices

Social media has become a democratizing force, affording marginalized voices the opportunity to be heard on a global scale. Activists utilize platforms to share personal stories, experiences, and grievances, allowing narratives that were once suppressed to resonate across borders. This section explores how social media breaks down barriers, unearths hidden stories, and empowers those who have been historically silenced.

Empowering the Silenced: Social Media as the Resonant Megaphone for Marginalized Voices

In the vast expanse of the digital universe, social media stands as a beacon of transformation—a medium that has shattered the barriers of time, distance, and power, enabling voices that were once muted to resonate with a power previously unimaginable. "The Digital Megaphone for Marginalized Voices" is a chapter that navigates this brave new world, revealing how the digital landscape has been revolutionized into an avenue for empowerment, advocacy, and the reclamation of narratives.

This chapter embarks on a journey of emancipation—a journey that begins with the click of a mouse, the swipe of a screen, or the touch of a fingertip. It delves deep into the lives of those whose stories have long been relegated to the sidelines of history, exploring how social media has unlocked doors, dismantled walls, and provided a global stage where voices can reverberate with unprecedented force.

At the heart of this exploration is the narrative of personal experiences—experiences that have been concealed or understated for generations. This chapter ventures into the poignant tales of those who have walked the margins, unveiling stories that intertwine pain, resilience, and the indomitable human spirit. Through digital platforms, individuals share their journeys, their dreams, and their struggles, rendering visible the often invisible threads that connect diverse lives across the globe.

The power of social media to bridge divides is vividly illuminated as we traverse the digital terrain. The chapter encapsulates moments where personal narratives go viral, where personal stories trigger collective empathy, and where hashtags galvanize entire movements. It's a testament to the fact that a single post can become a rallying cry, a shared experience can unite hearts across continents, and the force of social media can turn the tide of social awareness.

Yet, this chapter does not shy away from the complexities that accompany this virtual empowerment. It confronts the challenges posed by misinformation, digital echo chambers, and the potential for performative activism. It underscores that while social media has opened doors, it's essential to walk through those doors with a commitment to authenticity, accountability, and the pursuit of meaningful change.

Ultimately, this chapter is an invitation to recognize that social media is more than a screen—it's a portal through which marginalized voices can transcend limitations, traverse borders, and speak directly to hearts and minds around the world. It's a testament to the fact that the digital age has heralded a new era of advocacy—one where a single voice can spark a movement, where empathy can overcome distance, and where the stories of the silenced become the symphonies of transformation.

Hashtag Activism: Beyond the Symbol

Hashtag activism has revolutionized how social causes gain traction. From #BlackLivesMatter to #MeToo, hashtags serve as rallying points that transcend virtual spaces and catalyze real-world change. This chapter delves into the transformative power of hashtag movements, examining how they mobilize solidarity, spark conversations, and force institutions to confront systemic issues.

Beyond the Symbol: Unveiling the Depth of Hashtag Activism

In the vast expanse of the digital landscape, a new form of activism has emerged—a form that is concise, impactful, and boundless in its potential for change. "Hashtag Activism: Beyond the Symbol" peels back the layers of this digital phenomenon, revealing the intricate tapestry of social change that unfolds with a single keystroke, a shared symbol, and a global audience waiting to engage.

This chapter navigates the evolution of activism—a journey that once required marches, demonstrations, and physical presence, but has now found its conduit in the virtual realm. At the heart of this exploration lies the hashtag—an unassuming symbol that, when paired with a cause, becomes a rallying point for action, awareness, and advocacy. From the groundbreaking #BlackLivesMatter to the resounding #MeToo, hashtags have transcended mere labels to become transformative forces that resonate far beyond the confines of screens.

The chapter ventures into the very essence of these hashtag movements, unraveling how they mobilize solidarity in an age where connectivity knows no bounds. Through the lens of #ClimateStrike, #MarchForOurLives, and other impactful examples, the chapter illustrates how these digital rallying cries empower individuals from all walks of life to join a collective movement. It captures the way in which hashtags have become the embodiment of shared experiences, bridging geographical gaps and binding people in a common cause.

Delving into the complexities of hashtag activism, the chapter addresses the dual nature of its impact. It highlights the power of hashtags to spark conversations that once remained unspoken, forcing societies to confront systemic injustices and question long-standing norms. Yet, it also acknowledges the criticism that hashtag activism can sometimes fall short of creating lasting change—an issue explored through candid discussions of performative allyship, digital echo chambers, and the need for tangible action.

In this journey, the chapter recognizes that hashtag activism extends beyond the virtual realm. It delves into instances where online momentum translates into offline impact, illustrating how hashtags can galvanize communities to take to the streets, engage in policy advocacy, and drive shifts in public perception. It captures the essence of how hashtags can transform from symbols into catalysts, from virtual gatherings into real-world movements.

Ultimately, "Hashtag Activism: Beyond the Symbol" is an ode to the potential of digital tools to shape the course of human progress. It invites readers to recognize that a hashtag is more than a trend—it's a signal of solidarity, an avenue for awareness, and a force that can hold institutions accountable. It's a reminder that in the digital age, the power of change is within reach of every fingertip, waiting to be activated with the tap of a keyboard and the shared resonance of a single word.

Global Solidarity and Awareness

The reach of social media extends beyond individual experiences, fostering a sense of global solidarity. People from diverse corners of the world can now rally around common causes, shedding light on issues that may not be prevalent in their own communities. This section explores how viral campaigns transcend cultural and geographical barriers, forging alliances and propelling international movements.

In the era of interconnected digital communication, social media platforms have emerged as remarkable tools for fostering global solidarity and raising awareness on critical issues. These platforms serve as virtual bridges that connect individuals across continents, enabling them to stand together in support of shared causes. This section delves into the transformative power of social media campaigns that extend far beyond individual experiences, unifying people from diverse backgrounds and geographic locations around pressing concerns.

The unique attribute of social media lies in its ability to break down physical barriers, allowing individuals to access information, stories, and perspectives from around the world. Viral campaigns driven by hashtags like #ClimateAction or #EqualityForAll exemplify how digital movements have transcended local boundaries, capturing the attention of individuals who might have otherwise remained unaware of certain issues.

Through the rapid sharing of posts, images, and videos, social media campaigns can swiftly generate a groundswell of support, raising global awareness about injustices, inequalities, and humanitarian crises. This heightened awareness leads to increased public discourse and can prompt individuals to take concrete actions, whether by signing petitions, participating in protests, or donating to causes that align with their values.

Furthermore, the interconnectedness facilitated by social media has the potential to bridge gaps in understanding and empathy between different cultures and regions. People from diverse backgrounds can learn about challenges faced by others and extend their support, thereby fostering a sense of global citizenship and shared responsibility.

In essence, the impact of social media in promoting global solidarity and awareness is profound. It has shifted the paradigm of how we perceive and engage with global issues, encouraging us to think beyond our immediate surroundings and consider the well-being of the larger human family. By shedding light on pressing concerns, social media has enabled a new era of interconnected activism and advocacy, where individuals can collectively work towards positive change on a global scale.

Mobilization and Digital Activism

Social media is not just a platform for raising awareness; it's a tool for organizing action. This chapter delves into how digital activism leverages the speed and reach of online platforms to coordinate protests, boycotts, and advocacy campaigns. From coordinating logistics to disseminating information, social media accelerates the pace at which change is mobilized.

In the dynamic landscape of the digital age, social media has evolved beyond being a mere conduit for information—it has become a powerful instrument for mobilizing collective action and effecting tangible change. This exploration unveils the transformative potential of digital activism, revealing how online platforms harness their speed and expansive reach to galvanize movements, coordinate protests, and drive advocacy campaigns with unprecedented efficiency.

Digital activism capitalizes on the inherent capabilities of social media to connect individuals across vast distances instantly. This section sheds light on the intricate mechanisms through which digital activists leverage the features of platforms like Facebook, Twitter, and Instagram to initiate, organize, and propagate a wide array of causes. From environmental conservation to human rights advocacy, social media provides a virtual space where activists can transcend geographical limitations and engage with a global audience.

One of the remarkable aspects of digital activism is its ability to overcome the logistical challenges that physical protests often entail. By using platforms to disseminate information about event details, coordinate transportation, and share updates in real time, activists can rapidly mobilize supporters and achieve high levels of participation. This dynamic interaction not only enhances the visibility of a cause but also encourages a sense of unity among those who align with the movement's objectives.

Moreover, digital activism fosters a decentralized approach to advocacy, enabling grassroots efforts to flourish alongside established organizations. The ability to craft and share compelling narratives through multimedia content amplifies the emotional resonance of a cause, motivating individuals to take action and contribute to the movement's goals.

As social media continues to evolve, digital activism remains a potent force for change, providing a platform that transcends traditional boundaries and hierarchies. The symbiotic relationship between online platforms and collective action has given rise to a new era of activism, where individuals from all walks of life can unite their voices and work towards shared aspirations. By examining the mechanics of digital activism, we uncover the manifold ways in which social media accelerates the pace of change, reshaping the landscape of advocacy and mobilization for the better.

Navigating Challenges and Criticisms

While social media amplifies activism, it also presents challenges. The spread of misinformation, performative allyship, and the dilution of complex issues into simplified narratives are concerns that must be navigated. This section addresses these pitfalls and emphasizes the importance of responsible digital activism that balances impact with informed discourse.

In the expansive landscape of digital activism facilitated by social media, it's imperative to acknowledge that this powerful tool isn't without its complexities and challenges. The rapid dissemination of information across online platforms has revolutionized the way movements gain momentum, but it has also brought to the forefront a range of concerns that demand careful consideration. As we explore the intricate interplay between digital activism and its potential pitfalls, we uncover the nuanced reality that accompanies this evolving form of advocacy.

One of the foremost challenges in the digital age is the spread of misinformation. While social media accelerates the spread of information, it can also amplify false narratives and inaccurate data. This phenomenon not only undermines the credibility of genuine movements but also perpetuates confusion and erodes public trust. Misinformation can lead to unintended consequences, weakening the impact of digital activism and potentially harming the very causes activists seek to champion. Addressing this challenge requires a concerted effort to verify information before sharing it and to promote media literacy to discern reliable sources from misleading ones.

Performative allyship is another issue that arises in the context of digital activism. While it's positive to see individuals express solidarity with various causes, there's a danger that such actions can be superficial and devoid of genuine commitment to change. This section delves into how the allure of performative allyship can divert attention from substantive action and undermine the integrity of movements. By understanding the difference between performative gestures and meaningful engagement, we can foster a culture of authentic solidarity that amplifies the impact of digital activism.

The inherent complexity of many societal issues poses yet another challenge. Social media's format often demands brevity and simplicity, which can lead to the oversimplification of complex topics. This, in turn, risks reducing nuanced narratives to soundbites that fail to capture the depth of the issues at hand. This exploration highlights the importance of maintaining the integrity of complex discussions even within the constraints of social media's format. By encouraging thorough analysis and respectful dialogue, we can ensure that digital activism remains a force for genuine understanding and change.

In conclusion, while the rise of digital activism through social media has ushered in a new era of advocacy, it is not exempt from pitfalls and challenges. The spread of misinformation, performative allyship, and oversimplification are issues that must be navigated with care. This section underscores the necessity of responsible and informed digital activism, emphasizing the need to uphold the values of authenticity, integrity, and meaningful impact even within the fast-paced realm of online advocacy.

Future of Digital Activism

The chapter concludes with a glimpse into the future of activism and social media. As technology evolves, so do the strategies and possibilities for leveraging online platforms to create lasting change. This section invites readers to contemplate the potential for harnessing the digital realm for meaningful impact, fostering a world where social media becomes a conduit for dismantling systemic inequalities.

As we conclude our exploration into the dynamic relationship between activism and the digital landscape, we cast our gaze toward the horizon to envision the unfolding chapters of this ongoing narrative. The fusion of activism and social media has already revolutionized how we advocate for change, but the journey is far from over. In this contemplation of the future of digital activism, we discern the intricate threads that weave the fabric of progress, envisioning a world where technology continues to serve as a powerful catalyst for dismantling systemic inequalities and fostering a more just and equitable society.

Technology, as an ever-evolving entity, holds the promise of shaping the landscape of activism in ways that were once unfathomable. The innovations of tomorrow may introduce tools that enable even greater mobilization, collaboration, and impact. This section invites readers to peer into the future with optimism, acknowledging the potential for technology to augment the scope and scale of activism. As we navigate the uncharted waters of what lies ahead, we can anticipate the emergence of novel platforms, innovative strategies, and unprecedented methods of connecting with global audiences.

Beyond the technical advancements, the future of digital activism will be deeply rooted in the values that underpin social change. The resilience and adaptability of human spirit, combined with the connectivity offered by digital platforms, will continue to drive movements that transcend borders and barriers. This exploration prompts us to envision a world where social media becomes not only a space for raising awareness but a conduit for fostering understanding, empathy, and lasting change.

In the ever-evolving landscape of digital activism, the potential for collaboration and collective impact is boundless. As communities worldwide unite to amplify marginalized voices, challenge oppressive structures, and advocate for justice, the digital realm will undoubtedly play a central role. This section emphasizes the transformative power of unity in the face of adversity and the capacity of technology to facilitate connections that transcend geographical limitations.

In essence, the future of digital activism beckons us to embrace the unknown with unwavering determination. By harnessing the ever-advancing capabilities of technology, we can continue to amplify the voices of those who have been silenced, demand accountability from those in power, and pave the way for a world that is more inclusive, equitable, and compassionate. The journey may be uncertain, but the collective will to forge a brighter future through digital activism remains resolute.

A Call to Transformative Action

As we navigate the intricacies of the "Role of Social Media in Amplifying Racial Issues," we recognize that the virtual world is not a realm separate from reality—it is an extension of it. This chapter calls us to harness the power of social media as a force for change, to uplift voices that challenge the status quo, and to bridge the gap between online activism and real-world impact. By utilizing these platforms with intention, we pave the way for a future where justice, equality, and empathy transcend screens and become the fabric of our societies.

As we embark on a journey through the realm where social media intersects with the amplification of racial issues, we embark upon a path that is far from detached from the tangible world—it is, in fact, an interconnected continuum.

This section echoes a call to seize the potential harnessed within the digital sphere, a call that beckons us to grasp the reins of social media not as mere observers, but as active participants in the transformative narratives of our time. This chapter reverberates with the urgency of uplifting the voices that challenge the norm, that question the established, and that demand equity and justice, transcending the pixels and reverberating within the very structures of our societies.

In this juncture of exploration, we are prompted to recognize that the digital landscapes we traverse daily are not isolated from the socio-political and cultural landscapes we navigate in our physical lives. The essence of this section rests in the belief that our online actions have the potential to transcend mere online engagements, extending into the realm of tangible change. We stand at the crossroads of a powerful juncture—a juncture where our digital interactions possess the potency to act as catalysts for movements, to propel conversations into the heart of societal transformation, and to rewrite the narratives that shape our shared realities.

The heart of this section beats in unison with a fervent call to use social media with a sense of purpose, a call that resonates with the collective desire to uplift voices that have been marginalized, to question systems of oppression, and to bridge the gap between the digital space and the streets we walk. It urges us to recognize that social media is not just a canvas for expression—it's a megaphone for change, a tool that holds the potential to disrupt inertia and ignite the fires of progress. As we embark on this journey of understanding, let us not merely decipher the dynamics of social media; let us embrace a role of active agents of transformation, using these platforms as vehicles that transport the principles of justice, equality, and empathy from the realm of abstraction to the very core of our societies.

Ultimately, this chapter resonates with the imperative to cultivate a new kind of activism—one that leverages the virtual to shape the real, that dismantles barriers through hashtagged movements and translates digital conversations into tangible actions. It is a call to mobilize, to engage, and to enact change that reverberates beyond screens, transcending the boundaries of the digital to permeate every facet of our lives. By heeding this call, we contribute to a future where the power of social media isn't limited to the confines of the digital, but rather becomes an instrumental force in rewriting the narratives that define us, the structures that govern us, and the world we collectively envision.

Hashtag Activism and its Implications

In an age where social media platforms have woven themselves into the fabric of modern society, a new form of activism has emerged—one that utilizes the power of hashtags to galvanize movements, spark conversations, and demand change. This section invites us to traverse the landscape of "Hashtag Activism and its Implications," delving into the profound implications of this modern phenomenon. By dissecting the dynamics, successes, and challenges of hashtag activism, we navigate a terrain that holds both promises of empowerment and potential pitfalls.

At the heart of this exploration lies an understanding of how hashtags, once mere symbols of categorization, have become rallying points for social causes. Each hashtag encapsulates a narrative, a call to action, and a plea for justice, transcending geographical boundaries and cultural barriers. With a few keystrokes, individuals from diverse corners of the world can unite under a single digital banner, mobilizing against systemic injustices and amplifying the voices that have long been suppressed.

This section embarks on a journey to uncover the profound implications of hashtag activism, acknowledging its power to foster global solidarity and to shine a light on issues that may not be prevalent in our immediate communities. We come to understand that these digital movements transcend mere virtual gestures—they have the potential to translate into tangible changes, to alter policies, and to shift societal perceptions. By weaving through the tapestry of hashtag activism, we come to recognize that the virtual is no longer divorced from the real; it is a dynamic arena where narratives are shaped, movements are birthed, and change is demanded.

Yet, as we navigate the nuanced landscape of hashtag activism, we must also confront its inherent complexities. While hashtags can serve as vehicles for collective action, they can also be fleeting symbols that lose their impact as quickly as they gain popularity. The ease with which hashtags are shared can inadvertently contribute to a sense of "slacktivism," where clicks and likes replace meaningful engagement. This section does not shy away from examining these challenges, dissecting the line between hashtag activism and meaningful change.

With every hashtag that trends and every movement that emerges, the digital landscape transforms into a theater of advocacy, presenting us with an opportunity to reimagine the way we engage with the issues that matter most. This exploration is a reminder that hashtag activism is not confined to the realm of screens—it is a testament to the power of collective action and a testament to the potential of social media to shape the course of history. As we delve into the realm of "Hashtag Activism and its Implications," we embrace a role that goes beyond passive observers; we become agents of change in a digital age, united under a common banner for justice, equality, and progress.

Harnessing Symbolism for Change

Hashtags are more than words—they are symbols that encapsulate entire movements. They distill complex narratives into bite-sized phrases, making them easily shareable and memorable. This section explores how hashtag activism harnesses symbolism to create a common language of protest and resistance, uniting individuals under a single banner that transcends cultural and linguistic barriers.

In the digital age, hashtags have evolved into more than just strings of characters; they have become powerful symbols that embody entire movements and ideals. Beyond their literal meanings, hashtags possess the unique ability to encapsulate complex narratives within concise phrases. This section delves into the profound impact of hashtag activism, specifically focusing on its capacity to harness symbolism as a means of fostering a collective language of protest and resistance.

Hashtags function as condensed vessels of meaning, distilling intricate stories and diverse viewpoints into easily digestible fragments. This process enables them to transcend the limitations of character counts and resonate across the vast expanse of the online world. By simplifying intricate narratives, hashtags make information readily shareable and perpetually memorable, thereby facilitating the widespread dissemination of critical messages.

What sets hashtag activism apart is its utilization of symbolism to forge a common ground for individuals from diverse cultural and linguistic backgrounds. These digital symbols serve as a rallying point, uniting people under a single banner of shared concern. This section scrutinizes the mechanics of how symbolism transcends cultural and linguistic barriers, becoming a universal language that unifies individuals across geographical distances.

By exploring the role of hashtag activism in harnessing symbolism for change, we uncover the ways in which these digital signifiers have become catalysts for a global dialogue of protest and resistance. They serve as emblems of solidarity, reminding us that in the interconnected world of social media, a simple symbol can ignite a powerful movement for transformative change.

Mobilization in the Digital Age

Hashtags have revolutionized the pace and scale of mobilization. With a simple click, individuals can join forces with global movements, transforming a solitary act into a collective outcry for change. This chapter delves into how hashtags streamline the process of organizing protests, marches, and advocacy efforts, turning online sentiments into tangible actions.

In the era of digital communication, hashtags have emerged as transformative tools for mobilization, fundamentally altering the dynamics of social activism. These simple yet potent symbols have redefined the speed and scope at which individuals can come together to effect change. This section examines how hashtags have ushered in a new era of collective action, where a single click can propel an individual's solitary intention into a resonating call for change on a global scale.

The power of hashtags lies in their ability to bridge geographical divides and foster solidarity among disparate voices. With a mere click, an individual can join forces with like-minded individuals worldwide, effectively transforming isolated sentiments into a symphony of collective determination. This chapter delves into the intricate ways in which hashtags facilitate the organizing of protests, marches, and advocacy efforts.

Through the lens of hashtag activism, we witness how the digital age has democratized the process of mobilization. Organizers can now leverage the ease of online communication to streamline the coordination of events, mobilize supporters, and galvanize efforts towards a common cause. As we delve into the mechanics of this mobilization process, we uncover how hashtags serve as virtual megaphones that amplify voices and inspire real-world action.

This section highlights the transformative potential of hashtags as tools for translating online sentiments into tangible actions. It explores how hashtags propel individuals from passive observers to active participants in the pursuit of change. By studying the mechanisms through which hashtags streamline the process of organizing and rallying for causes, we gain a deeper appreciation for the role of social media in shaping modern-day activism.

Raising Awareness and Shaping Narratives

At its core, hashtag activism is about raising awareness. By attaching a hashtag to an issue, activists bring it to the forefront of public consciousness. This section examines how hashtags shape narratives by spotlighting stories that might otherwise remain in the shadows. They give voice to those who are often ignored, crafting narratives that challenge mainstream perspectives.

Central to the essence of hashtag activism is its role in raising awareness about critical issues that might otherwise languish in obscurity. The act of attaching a simple hashtag to a cause has the remarkable power to thrust it into the limelight, igniting conversations and prompting collective reflection. This section delves into the profound impact of hashtags in shaping the narratives that underpin societal understanding.

In a world flooded with information, hashtags serve as digital beacons, guiding our attention towards stories and experiences that demand acknowledgment. By appending a hashtag to a post, activists are able to channel the vast reach of social media platforms to highlight matters that might otherwise go unnoticed. Through this strategic utilization of hashtags, individuals are able to act as digital storytellers, bringing attention to stories that have long been relegated to the shadows.

By spotlighting narratives that challenge mainstream perspectives, hashtags become vehicles for inclusive storytelling. This chapter explores how hashtags have the unique ability to amplify voices that have been historically marginalized, allowing them to rise above the noise and be heard on a global scale. In this way, hashtag activism becomes a platform that not only raises awareness but also reshapes the narratives that shape our collective consciousness.

This section underscores the transformative power of hashtags to give voice to those who have been silenced by traditional media platforms. By attaching a hashtag to their stories, individuals from all walks of life are able to challenge prevailing narratives and contribute to a more diverse and nuanced societal discourse. As we delve into the profound implications of hashtag activism, we recognize its role in crafting narratives that expand our understanding of complex issues and empower the voices of the marginalized.

The Critique of Slacktivism

While hashtag activism has fueled powerful movements, it has also drawn criticism for being perceived as "slacktivism"—superficial engagement that doesn't necessarily lead to meaningful change. This section explores the tension between the instant gratification of social media activism and the enduring commitment required to effect lasting systemic change.

Within the realm of hashtag activism, a noteworthy critique has emerged, casting a critical eye on what some label as "slacktivism."

This term encapsulates the concern that online engagement, often symbolized by the simple act of sharing a hashtag, may be perceived as a form of superficial involvement that lacks the depth necessary to bring about substantial and enduring change. This section delves into the nuanced discussion surrounding this critique, shedding light on the tension between the convenience of social media activism and the sustained commitment required for meaningful systemic transformation.

In an era marked by rapid information dissemination and instant gratification, it's undeniable that hashtag activism offers a quick and accessible way for individuals to express support for a cause. With a few taps on a screen, one can share a hashtag, signal their alignment with a movement, and join the chorus of digital voices advocating for change. However, the concern arises when this swift participation is seen as a substitute for the more substantial and complex efforts that are often required to address deeply rooted issues.

This section delves into the complexities of this critique, acknowledging that while hashtag activism can indeed spark initial awareness and conversation, it may not necessarily translate into the tangible actions that drive meaningful change. The tension between the immediacy of digital engagement and the enduring dedication needed to enact lasting systemic shifts prompts us to question the true impact of hashtag activism in the broader context of social justice and transformation.

The discourse surrounding slacktivism underscores the importance of moving beyond surface-level involvement and embracing a deeper understanding of the challenges at hand. As we explore this critique, we delve into the considerations of accountability, sustained commitment, and the intersection between online activism and tangible real-world efforts. By engaging with this nuanced perspective, we are encouraged to critically evaluate the ways in which hashtag activism can be leveraged not as an endpoint but as a catalyst for more substantial and enduring change.

Amplifying Intersectional Voices

Hashtag activism has been a platform for intersectional voices—voices that are often marginalized by mainstream discourse. This section examines how hashtags provide a space for individuals with multiple marginalized identities to address the complexities of their experiences, fostering a more inclusive understanding of social issues.

In the realm of hashtag activism, a remarkable facet has emerged—a platform that amplifies the voices of those often marginalized by mainstream discourse. This section delves into the transformative power of hashtags as a space where individuals with multiple marginalized identities can converge, share their stories, and address the intricate intersections of their lived experiences. This dynamic engagement nurtures a more comprehensive and inclusive understanding of complex social issues, one that recognizes the interconnectedness of various forms of discrimination and oppression.

The concept of intersectionality, coined by Kimberlé Crenshaw, acknowledges that individuals may experience overlapping forms of discrimination based on factors such as race, gender, sexuality, and socioeconomic status. In mainstream conversations, these intersectional experiences are frequently overlooked or flattened into a single narrative. Hashtag activism, however, acts as a counterbalance to this oversight by allowing individuals to reclaim their narratives and showcase the multi-faceted dimensions of their identities.

This section explores the profound impact of hashtag activism in providing a platform for those with intersectional identities to express their unique perspectives. By using hashtags that encapsulate various aspects of their experiences, individuals can connect with like-minded others, building a network of solidarity that bridges geographical and cultural boundaries. The digital realm becomes a space where the complexities of identity are celebrated and understood, fostering a sense of unity among those who navigate the intersections of multiple marginalized identities.

Furthermore, this section highlights how hashtag activism facilitates conversations that transcend siloed discussions of discrimination. By weaving together narratives that explore the intertwined impacts of different forms of bias, individuals contribute to a broader and more nuanced discourse surrounding social issues. This intersectional lens enriches the overall understanding of systemic inequalities and the efforts required to dismantle them.

In embracing the power of hashtags to amplify intersectional voices, we recognize that hashtag activism is more than just a tool—it's a vehicle for fostering empathy, building alliances, and ultimately challenging the reductionist perspectives that often overshadow the intricacies of lived experiences. As we navigate this exploration, we gain insight into how this platform serves as a powerful tool for dismantling barriers and promoting a more inclusive dialogue on social justice.

From Trending Topics to Tangible Change

The impact of hashtag activism isn't solely measured in trending topics. This section invites readers to consider the trajectory from virtual engagement to tangible change. Hashtags have the potential to ignite conversations, raise funds, influence policy decisions, and even spark cultural shifts that ripple far beyond the virtual realm.

While the viral nature of hashtag activism often places a spotlight on trending topics, its true impact extends far beyond the realm of digital trends. This section illuminates the transformative journey that hashtags embark upon, evolving from virtual engagement to tangible and lasting change in the physical world. The power of hashtags lies not merely in their ability to capture attention, but in their potential to galvanize action, mobilize resources, and reshape societal narratives.

Hashtag activism serves as a catalyst that ignites conversations around pressing social issues. However, its influence doesn't stop at raising awareness; rather, it lays the groundwork for substantive shifts in attitudes, policies, and behaviors. This exploration delves into how hashtags have demonstrated an impressive capacity to amplify the voices of those who have long been silenced, amplifying their messages and compelling institutions to take notice.

One of the key avenues through which hashtags bring about tangible change is by mobilizing resources. By rallying communities around a shared cause, hashtags have been instrumental in crowdfunding efforts to provide assistance to individuals or groups in need. This section illuminates how hashtag-driven campaigns have garnered financial support for causes ranging from disaster relief to social justice initiatives, transforming online engagement into real-world impact.

Moreover, the influence of hashtags extends to the realm of policy and decision-making. As social media conversations gain momentum, they often catch the attention of policymakers, prompting them to address pressing issues. This section explores examples where hashtag activism has influenced policy debates, pushed for legislative changes, and compelled governments to respond to the demands of their constituents.

Beyond policy, hashtags have also catalyzed cultural shifts by challenging prevailing narratives and norms. This exploration examines instances where hashtags have contributed to dismantling outdated ideologies, sparking conversations that challenge long-standing biases, and fostering inclusivity in various spheres of society.

As we navigate this exploration, we are invited to recognize the dynamic trajectory from hashtags as mere trending topics to their potential for creating lasting change. This section encourages readers to see beyond the immediate visibility of viral campaigns and to consider the profound ripple effects that extend into real-world actions, policy reform, resource allocation, and even shifts in societal attitudes. By understanding and harnessing this transformative power, we open doors to a future where hashtags serve as not just digital symbols, but as drivers of tangible progress and meaningful change.

A Catalyst for Deeper Engagement

As we explore the world of "Hashtag Activism and its Implications," we acknowledge that while hashtags have the power to surface issues, they are only the beginning of the journey. This section calls us to translate online engagement into real-world action, to question how hashtags can complement sustained advocacy efforts, and to recognize that virtual spaces are catalysts for igniting the flames of change that ultimately transform societies.

Within the realm of "Hashtag Activism and its Implications," we embark on a journey that transcends the virtual realm and delves into the heart of meaningful societal transformation. While hashtags hold the remarkable ability to thrust crucial issues into the spotlight, this section emphasizes that they are but the initial spark, igniting a fire of change that demands further action and commitment.

As we navigate this exploration, it becomes evident that hashtags serve as catalysts, propelling individuals and communities to move beyond the confines of online engagement and into the realm of tangible impact. This section exhorts us to view hashtags as a gateway to deeper forms of activism, urging us to ask how we can translate the momentum generated in virtual spaces into lasting change on the ground.

The call to action resonates with the recognition that hashtags are not an endpoint but rather a stepping stone towards broader societal transformation. We are prompted to consider how the digital conversations they initiate can be seamlessly woven into the fabric of sustained advocacy efforts. By harnessing the power of hashtags in tandem with offline initiatives, we can bridge the gap between the virtual and the real, ensuring that the issues that garner attention online translate into real-world policies, programs, and actions.

This exploration further underscores the idea that hashtags can complement traditional advocacy methods, amplifying their reach and impact. By merging digital conversations with grassroots organizing, petitions, protests, and community-building, hashtags become a driving force that sustains momentum and ushers in a new era of social change.

At its core, this section invites us to recognize that virtual spaces are potent catalysts for igniting the flames of change that ultimately transform societies. Hashtags not only amplify voices and highlight issues but also kindle the spirit of activism that fuels movements. By channeling the energy sparked by hashtags into tangible actions, we contribute to a world where digital discourse seamlessly blends with real-world impact, and where the fires of change continue to burn brightly in pursuit of justice, equality, and a better future for all.

Global Campaigns for Racial Justice

In a world intricately connected by technology, the fight for racial justice has transcended geographical borders, sparking movements that resonate across continents. This section delves into the dynamic landscape of global campaigns for racial justice, examining the emergence, impact, and ongoing struggle to address systemic racism on a worldwide scale.

A Global Call to Action

Global campaigns for racial justice are born out of a universal truth: the struggle against racial discrimination knows no boundaries. This section explores how grassroots movements and digital platforms have united individuals from diverse backgrounds, catalyzing a collective call to action that challenges systemic injustices wherever they are found.

The resonance of the "A Global Call to Action" resonates across continents and cultures, acknowledging that the fight against racial discrimination is a shared endeavor that transcends geographic borders. This section delves into the extraordinary phenomenon of grassroots movements and digital platforms coming together to create a unifying force—a global call to action that reverberates through societies, challenging systemic injustices wherever they rear their head.

As we navigate this exploration, it becomes apparent that the quest for racial justice is a universal quest, one that has the power to unite people from all walks of life, regardless of their nationality, ethnicity, or background. This section paints a vivid picture of how grassroots movements, often sparked by a single incident or a collective awakening, evolve into powerful currents of change that sweep across the world.

These movements harness the connectivity of digital platforms to forge bonds between individuals who share a common purpose—to dismantle the structures of discrimination that persist within their societies.

The significance of this global call to action lies not only in its ability to mobilize people but also in its capacity to amplify the voices of those who are directly affected by racial injustice. This section underscores how grassroots campaigns utilize the collective strength of their diverse participants to demand accountability, equality, and change from institutions and systems that perpetuate discrimination.

Furthermore, the section highlights the role of digital platforms in shaping this global movement. Social media, as a digital megaphone, enables activists to share stories, images, and videos that capture the attention of audiences worldwide. The power of hashtags and viral campaigns propels the message of these movements beyond national borders, creating a ripple effect that galvanizes support and action from individuals who might otherwise be disconnected from the cause.

By illuminating the dynamics of this global call to action, this section underscores the universality of the struggle for racial justice. It invites us to recognize that the fight against systemic discrimination requires collective effort, and that no society is exempt from this journey. The call to action resonates far beyond the confines of individual nations, echoing the sentiment that a just and equitable world can only be achieved through collaborative and united efforts across the globe.

Amplifying Local Struggles

While global campaigns have a broad reach, they are often rooted in local struggles. This section delves into the intricate interplay between local contexts and global solidarity, examining how global campaigns amplify the voices of communities fighting against racial oppression at the grassroots level.

The narrative of "Amplifying Local Struggles" unveils the fascinating interconnection between the microcosm of local activism and the expansive realm of global solidarity. This section embarks on a journey through the intricate tapestry of social change, revealing how global campaigns draw strength from the authentic experiences and aspirations of communities grappling with racial oppression at the grassroots level.

At the heart of this exploration lies a profound recognition: global campaigns are often built upon the foundations of local struggles. The section navigates the intricate dance between the local and the global, shedding light on how the stories of individuals and communities fighting against racial discrimination in their immediate surroundings resonate with the broader themes of injustice that reverberate around the world. By connecting these local narratives to the larger fabric of global activism, campaigns gain depth and authenticity that inspire empathy and action on a global scale.

This section delves deep into the dynamics that allow local struggles to become powerful agents of change on the global stage. It showcases how grassroots movements, while anchored in specific geographical contexts, find common ground in their fight against common enemies—systemic racism, discrimination, and inequality. The stories of local activists become rallying points for global audiences, as they embody the spirit of resilience, determination, and hope that characterizes the broader movement for racial justice.

Moreover, this exploration uncovers the symbiotic relationship between local struggles and global solidarity. It emphasizes how global campaigns amplify the voices of those who might otherwise remain unheard, shining a spotlight on their experiences, grievances, and aspirations. Through the amplification of local voices, the global movement transforms into a platform for sharing the stories of real people who are directly affected by racial oppression. This process not only raises awareness but also creates a bridge of empathy that unites people across different geographical and cultural contexts.

By unraveling the intricate threads of this interplay, the section reminds us that global campaigns are not detached from local realities—they are woven from them. It calls us to appreciate the significance of grassroots activism as the foundation upon which broader global movements are built. It invites us to recognize that by amplifying local struggles, we enrich the collective narrative of the global call for racial justice, fortifying the movement with authenticity, resilience, and the unwavering spirit of those who stand on the frontlines of change

The Role of Social Media

Social media acts as a vehicle for global campaigns, allowing activists to share stories, resources, and strategies instantaneously. This chapter explores how platforms like Twitter, Instagram, and Facebook have facilitated the rapid dissemination of information, enabling individuals from different corners of the world to rally around common causes.

In the modern landscape of activism, social media emerges as an indispensable vehicle propelling global campaigns for racial justice to new heights. This chapter embarks on a comprehensive exploration of the multifaceted role that platforms like Twitter, Instagram, Facebook, and more play in catalyzing and sustaining the momentum of global campaigns. From instantaneously sharing stories and resources to fostering connections among individuals across continents, social media has transformed the dynamics of activism by creating a virtual space where the global call to action reverberates.

This chapter delves into the ways in which social media functions as a dynamic platform for change. It illuminates how the immediacy of these platforms facilitates the swift and widespread dissemination of information. Activists from different corners of the world can connect in real time, exchange ideas, and share their stories with a global audience. The power of social media lies in its ability to collapse geographical boundaries, enabling individuals to rally around shared causes and ignite conversations that transcend borders.

This exploration highlights the pivotal role of hashtags as digital rallying cries that unite individuals under a common banner. The chapter delves into the mechanisms through which hashtags—short, concise phrases preceded by the pound sign—have become symbolic vehicles for conveying complex messages. By affixing a hashtag to their posts, activists tap into a vast network of users interested in similar issues, effectively amplifying their voices and stories to a global audience. The chapter navigates through the journey of hashtags from local anecdotes to global movements, tracing their evolution as tools for organizing and mobilizing collective action.

Furthermore, the chapter acknowledges the transformative influence of visual storytelling on social media. It examines how platforms like Instagram and TikTok enable activists to share powerful narratives through photos, videos, and live streams, fostering a deeper emotional connection with the audience. Visual content transcends language barriers, resonating with individuals across cultures and backgrounds, and enabling them to engage with the struggles and triumphs of distant communities.

In essence, this chapter paints a vivid portrait of social media's role in shaping the landscape of global activism. It showcases how these platforms have revolutionized the way information spreads, ideas are exchanged, and movements are organized. By providing a virtual space where voices can be amplified, resources can be shared, and connections can be forged, social media has become a pivotal vehicle for driving global campaigns for racial justice forward. As readers journey through this chapter, they gain a profound appreciation for the power of digital platforms in bridging divides, fostering solidarity, and igniting meaningful change across the globe.

From Hashtags to Real Change

Global campaigns often begin with hashtags that trend worldwide, but their impact extends far beyond viral trends. This section examines how global campaigns transition from online awareness to tangible change, influencing policy reform, shifting public perception, and challenging deeply entrenched systems of oppression.

The journey from viral hashtags to tangible, real-world change is a testament to the transformative potential of global campaigns. This section ventures deep into the heart of how the momentum generated by hashtags and online activism is harnessed to enact substantial impact on societal landscapes. While viral trends on social media are indeed impactful, their true power lies in their ability to transcend the virtual realm, shaping the course of history, policy, and perceptions.

This section delves into the process through which global campaigns transition from raising online awareness to sparking real change. It dissects the mechanisms through which these campaigns create a ripple effect that permeates the core of public discourse and consciousness. By mobilizing a diverse range of supporters, activists transform online engagement into formidable collective action that challenges the status quo and catalyzes meaningful transformation.

The chapter unravels how the momentum from hashtags reverberates into the corridors of power, prompting policymakers to take notice. It explores the pivotal role of social media in galvanizing public opinion and exerting pressure on decision-makers to address the pressing issues at hand. By analyzing case studies and examples, the section illustrates instances where global campaigns have directly influenced legislative reforms, spurring governments to take concrete steps toward dismantling systemic injustices.

Furthermore, the section shines a light on the remarkable ability of global campaigns to shift public perception. It examines how sustained online activism can alter the narratives surrounding racial issues, challenging stereotypes and promoting empathy. By exposing individuals to a diverse array of voices and perspectives, social media campaigns play a critical role in broadening collective consciousness and fostering a more inclusive understanding of complex problems.

As the chapter delves deeper, it unravels the intricate interplay between virtual movements and grassroots organizing. It emphasizes the importance of bridging the digital realm with real-world engagement—how virtual connections can translate into physical protests, community organizing, and partnerships with local advocacy groups. By highlighting the dynamic synergy between online activism and on-the-ground efforts, the section underscores the holistic approach that paves the way for meaningful change.

In conclusion, this section encapsulates the transformative journey from hashtags to concrete change. It underscores that viral trends on social media are not isolated phenomena, but catalysts that fuel movements with the potential to disrupt oppressive systems, reshape public consciousness, and create lasting societal transformation. By tracing the trajectory of global campaigns from the digital sphere to tangible outcomes, readers gain a comprehensive understanding of the profound impact that online activism can wield in reshaping the course of history.

The Challenges of Intersectionality

Global campaigns navigate the complex terrain of intersectionality—the recognition that various forms of oppression are intertwined. This section explores how campaigns for racial justice intersect with other social justice causes, such as gender equality, LGBTQ+ rights, and economic justice, emphasizing the need for inclusive movements that address the multifaceted nature of discrimination.

The journey from viral hashtags to tangible, real-world change is a testament to the transformative potential of global campaigns. This section ventures deep into the heart of how the momentum generated by hashtags and online activism is harnessed to enact substantial impact on societal landscapes. While viral trends on social media are indeed impactful, their true power lies in their ability to transcend the virtual realm, shaping the course of history, policy, and perceptions.

This section delves into the process through which global campaigns transition from raising online awareness to sparking real change. It dissects the mechanisms through which these campaigns create a ripple effect that permeates the core of public discourse and consciousness. By mobilizing a diverse range of supporters, activists transform online engagement into formidable collective action that challenges the status quo and catalyzes meaningful transformation.

The chapter unravels how the momentum from hashtags reverberates into the corridors of power, prompting policymakers to take notice. It explores the pivotal role of social media in galvanizing public opinion and exerting pressure on decision-makers to address the pressing issues at hand. By analyzing case studies and examples, the section illustrates instances where global campaigns have directly influenced legislative reforms, spurring governments to take concrete steps toward dismantling systemic injustices.

Furthermore, the section shines a light on the remarkable ability of global campaigns to shift public perception. It examines how sustained online activism can alter the narratives surrounding racial issues, challenging stereotypes and promoting empathy. By exposing individuals to a diverse array of voices and perspectives, social media campaigns play a critical role in broadening collective consciousness and fostering a more inclusive understanding of complex problems.

As the chapter delves deeper, it unravels the intricate interplay between virtual movements and grassroots organizing. It emphasizes the importance of bridging the digital realm with real-world engagement—how virtual connections can translate into physical protests, community organizing, and partnerships with local advocacy groups. By highlighting the dynamic synergy between online activism and on-the-ground efforts, the section underscores the holistic approach that paves the way for meaningful change.

In conclusion, this section encapsulates the transformative journey from hashtags to concrete change. It underscores that viral trends on social media are not isolated phenomena, but catalysts that fuel movements with the potential to disrupt oppressive systems, reshape public consciousness, and create lasting societal transformation. By tracing the trajectory of global campaigns from the digital sphere to tangible outcomes, readers gain a comprehensive understanding of the profound impact that online activism can wield in reshaping the course of history.

Building International Alliances

Global campaigns forge international alliances, as activists learn from each other's strategies and share resources. This section delves into the power of cross-border solidarity, examining how activists from different regions collaborate to amplify each other's efforts and create a united front against racial injustice.

In the dynamic landscape of global campaigns, the significance of building international alliances shines as a beacon of solidarity and collective action. This section takes a deep dive into the transformative power of forging cross-border partnerships, shedding light on how activists from various corners of the world come together to create a harmonious symphony of voices united against racial injustice.

The section unravels the mechanisms through which global campaigns facilitate the exchange of strategies, experiences, and resources among activists spanning different regions. By examining case studies and real-world examples, it elucidates how activists learn from one another's successes and challenges, adapting innovative approaches to their own contexts and amplifying the impact of their endeavors.

The section delves into the interconnectedness that underpins these international alliances, showcasing the ways in which activists transcend geographical boundaries to create a shared space for collaboration. It illuminates how digital platforms and communication technologies have revolutionized the ability to connect with like-minded individuals across the globe, fostering a sense of camaraderie that transcends distance.

Through narratives of joint initiatives, joint protests, and coordinated advocacy efforts, the section highlights the ways in which activists collaborate to amplify the reach and effectiveness of their campaigns. It explores how campaigns in one part of the world can inspire and galvanize movements in distant regions, creating a ripple effect that reverberates across continents.

Furthermore, the section unveils the inherent power of cross-border solidarity in challenging systemic racial injustices. It examines how activists leverage their collective strength to exert pressure on international institutions, governments, and corporations, forcing them to confront their complicity in perpetuating discriminatory practices.

The section also addresses the complexities that arise when different cultural, political, and social contexts converge within international alliances. It delves into the challenges and opportunities of navigating diverse perspectives and approaches while maintaining a shared vision of dismantling racial oppression.

In conclusion, this section underscores the essential role that building international alliances plays in the success of global campaigns for racial justice. It celebrates the ability of activists from diverse backgrounds to come together, pool their resources, and create a united front that challenges the structures of discrimination on a global scale. By embracing cross-border solidarity, global campaigns empower themselves to create lasting change that transcends boundaries and transforms societies.

The Ongoing Struggle for Change

As we explore the realm of "Global Campaigns for Racial Justice," we recognize that these movements are not isolated events—they are part of an ongoing struggle for equality, dignity, and human rights. This section calls us to reflect on the power of collective action, to support global campaigns that challenge systemic racism, and to recognize that the fight for racial justice is one that unites individuals from every corner of the world in a shared quest for a more just and equitable future.

242

Chapter 7: Intersectionality of Race and Other Identities

Interplay between Race, Gender, Sexuality, and Politics

In the intricate tapestry of human identity, no thread exists in isolation. This chapter delves into the profound concept of intersectionality—the interconnectedness of race, gender, sexuality, and other identities—and explores how these facets converge within the realm of politics and media. By examining the interplay of these dimensions, we uncover the complexities, challenges, and transformative potential of understanding individuals as multidimensional beings.

In the intricate tapestry of identities, the interplay between race, gender, sexuality, and politics creates a multifaceted landscape that shapes individual experiences and societal dynamics. This section, situated within the broader context of "Intersectionality of Race and Other Identities," delves into the nuanced connections and complexities that arise when these dimensions intersect, intertwining to influence social structures, political discourse, and personal narratives.

The section commences by exploring the concept of intersectionality, a framework that highlights the interconnected nature of various aspects of identity. It examines how race, gender, and sexuality intersect to form unique lived experiences that cannot be understood in isolation. Drawing from both historical and contemporary perspectives, the section elucidates how individuals with intersecting identities navigate overlapping systems of privilege and oppression.

By delving into the realm of politics, the section sheds light on how the interplay between these identities shapes political ideologies, movements, and policy agendas. It examines how different racial and ethnic groups experience politics in distinct ways due to their intersecting identities, often leading to varying priorities and perspectives within the same community. Moreover, it analyzes how political platforms can either amplify or overlook the concerns of marginalized groups with multiple identities.

The section also delves into the challenges faced by individuals who occupy the intersections of race, gender, and sexuality. It explores how they grapple with discrimination that is not solely rooted in one identity but rather stems from the intricate interweaving of these dimensions. By examining case studies and personal narratives, the section illustrates the ways in which intersectionality can magnify the impact of systemic injustices.

Through discussions on representation, the section examines how the interplay between these identities influences media portrayal and political representation. It addresses the importance of diverse and inclusive representation that accurately reflects the experiences of individuals with intersecting identities. It also explores the challenges faced by individuals who seek political representation that aligns with their full spectrum of identities.

Furthermore, the section dives into the role of social movements in addressing the interplay between race, gender, sexuality, and politics. It showcases how movements such as feminism, LGBTQ+ rights, and racial justice intersect and collaborate to challenge interlocking systems of oppression. By examining historical and contemporary examples, the section illustrates the power of collective action in dismantling barriers created by the intersection of identities.

In conclusion, the "Interplay between Race, Gender, Sexuality, and Politics" section within the "Intersectionality of Race and Other Identities" chapter illuminates the intricate connections that shape the lived experiences of individuals with intersecting identities. It underscores the significance of recognizing and addressing these intersections to create a more inclusive and equitable society. By acknowledging the complexities of these interplays, we pave the way for a deeper understanding of how systemic inequalities are perpetuated and how they can be dismantled through informed discourse, advocacy, and collective action.

The Mosaic of Identity

Identity is multifaceted, shaped by an array of intersecting attributes. This section delves into how identities such as race, gender, and sexuality intersect, influencing experiences, perspectives, and opportunities. Recognizing these intersections is a crucial step toward understanding the full spectrum of human experiences.

Identity is multifaceted, shaped by an array of intersecting attributes. This section, a continuation of the exploration within the "Intersectionality of Race and Other Identities" chapter, delves even deeper into the intricate layers that comprise the mosaic of individual identity. By acknowledging the intersections of attributes like race, gender, and sexuality, we gain insights into how these facets shape experiences, perspectives, and opportunities in intricate and profound ways.

The section begins by elucidating the significance of recognizing identity as a mosaic, rather than viewing attributes in isolation. It emphasizes that each individual is a complex tapestry woven from various threads of identity, and these threads interweave to create a unique and multidimensional whole. By understanding identity in this holistic manner, we are better equipped to appreciate the complexities of the human experience.

Through a historical lens, the section examines how societal perceptions of identity have evolved over time. It delves into the origins of identity categories such as race, gender, and sexuality, and explores how these constructs have been shaped by cultural, social, and historical factors. By tracing the development of identity concepts, the section highlights the fluid and evolving nature of these attributes.

The section also delves into the concept of intersectionality as a tool for understanding the intersections of identity. It explores how different attributes can intersect to create unique experiences and challenges, and how these intersections can lead to experiences that are distinct from those associated with any single attribute. By delving into case studies and personal narratives, the section illustrates how intersectionality offers a more comprehensive understanding of the human experience.

By analyzing the impact of intersecting identities on opportunities and access, the section unveils the disparities and advantages that arise due to these intersections. It examines how certain combinations of identities can lead to compounded discrimination or privilege, affecting access to education, employment, healthcare, and more. It also highlights the ways in which systemic inequalities are perpetuated by the intersections of identity.

Moreover, the section delves into the dynamics of self-identification and how individuals navigate the complexities of their own identities. It explores the agency individuals have in defining and expressing their multifaceted identities, and how these self-definitions can challenge or reinforce societal norms and expectations. By analyzing diverse perspectives, the section showcases the power of self-identification as a tool for empowerment and resistance.

In conclusion, the "The Mosaic of Identity" section within the "Intersectionality of Race and Other Identities" chapter deepens our understanding of the intricacies of individual identity. It underscores the importance of recognizing identity as a complex and multifaceted phenomenon, shaped by the intersections of attributes like race, gender, and sexuality. By acknowledging these intersections, we move closer to comprehending the diverse range of human experiences and creating a more inclusive and empathetic society.

Challenges of Multiple Marginalizations

Intersectionality reveals that individuals can be marginalized on multiple fronts. This section examines how people facing overlapping forms of discrimination—such as racial and gender-based discrimination—experience compounded challenges that demand nuanced approaches to advocacy, policy, and media representation.

Intersectionality reveals that individuals can be marginalized on multiple fronts, facing a complex web of discrimination and disadvantage. This section delves into the intricate landscape of individuals who experience overlapping forms of marginalization, such as racial and gender-based discrimination. It examines how these compounded challenges demand not only a deep understanding of intersecting identities but also nuanced and intersectional approaches to advocacy, policy-making, and media representation.

The section begins by shedding light on the experiences of individuals who navigate the intersecting realms of racial and gender-based discrimination. It underscores how these compounded marginalizations can create unique sets of obstacles that are distinct from those faced by individuals who experience discrimination along a single axis. By sharing personal narratives and case studies, the section brings to the forefront the realities of those living at the intersections of multiple marginalized identities.

Through a historical lens, the section traces the roots of multiple marginalizations and their perpetuation in societal structures. It examines how historical injustices and systemic biases have intersected to create compounding effects, leading to disparities in areas such as education, employment, healthcare, and representation. By unpacking the historical context, the section highlights the need for comprehensive and inclusive approaches to addressing these challenges.

Moreover, the section delves into the complexities of advocating for individuals who face multiple marginalizations. It explores how traditional approaches to activism and advocacy may fall short in addressing the unique needs and experiences of these individuals. It also showcases innovative and intersectional advocacy strategies that have emerged to navigate the intricacies of compounded marginalizations, such as creating coalitions that bring together various marginalized groups.

The section also examines how policies and systems often fail to adequately address the needs of individuals with intersecting identities. It critically analyzes how policies designed to address single dimensions of identity can inadvertently perpetuate further marginalization for those with multiple identities. By exploring policy failures and successes, the section underscores the importance of crafting policies that consider the full spectrum of an individual's identity.

Furthermore, the section discusses the representation of individuals with multiple marginalizations in media and popular culture. It examines how the media often struggles to accurately portray the layered experiences of these individuals, resorting to simplistic and one-dimensional portrayals. By analyzing both positive and problematic examples, the section emphasizes the need for diverse and authentic representation that reflects the complexity of intersecting identities.

In conclusion, the "Challenges of Multiple Marginalizations" section within the "Intersectionality of Race and Other Identities" chapter highlights the complex and often overlooked experiences of individuals who face compounded forms of discrimination. It underscores the need for intersectional approaches in advocacy, policy-making, and media representation to address the unique challenges these individuals confront. By understanding and addressing these challenges, we work toward a more inclusive and equitable society that recognizes the full spectrum of human experiences.

Media Representation and Identity

Media's portrayal of individuals often fails to capture the complexity of their identities. This chapter delves into how media representations tend to flatten identities, perpetuate stereotypes, and overlook the richness of intersectional experiences. It explores the importance of media in accurately reflecting the diversity and complexity of human lives.

Media's portrayal of individuals often falls short of capturing the intricate and multifaceted nature of their identities. This chapter goes beyond the surface of media representation to uncover how these portrayals tend to simplify and flatten identities, perpetuate harmful stereotypes, and overlook the rich tapestry of intersectional experiences. It delves into the complexities of media's role in shaping societal perceptions, and highlights the pressing need for media to accurately and authentically reflect the diversity and complexity of human lives.

The chapter begins by exploring the pervasive issue of identity flattening in media representation. It examines how media often reduces individuals to a single dimension of their identity, neglecting the myriad of identities that intersect within them. Through analysis of popular media examples, the chapter sheds light on the limitations of such portrayals and their implications for shaping public understanding.

Furthermore, the chapter delves into the perpetuation of stereotypes by media. It investigates how stereotypes, particularly those related to race, gender, and other identities, persist in media portrayals, reinforcing biased narratives and influencing societal attitudes. Through case studies and critical analysis, the chapter exposes the harmful impact of these stereotypes on marginalized communities and the need to challenge and disrupt them.

A significant focus of the chapter is on the representation of intersectional identities. It explores how media often struggles to authentically depict the layered experiences of individuals with intersecting identities. It examines the challenges faced by media creators in capturing the nuances of intersectionality and the consequences of failing to do so. By examining both successes and failures in intersectional representation, the chapter highlights the transformative potential of media that accurately reflects these experiences.

The chapter also delves into the power dynamics at play in media representation. It examines how the lack of diversity behind the scenes in media production influences the portrayal of identities on screen. It explores how diverse representation among creators, writers, and decision-makers can lead to more authentic and nuanced depictions that challenge the status quo.

Moreover, the chapter underscores the importance of media in shaping cultural norms and perceptions. It analyzes how media plays a role in constructing societal understandings of beauty, success, and worthiness, and how these constructs can disproportionately impact marginalized individuals. By examining the influence of media on shaping identity-related aspirations and ideals, the chapter emphasizes the role that accurate representation can play in fostering positive societal change.

In conclusion, the "Media Representation and Identity" chapter examines the intricate relationship between media portrayal and the complexity of human identities. It highlights the ways in which media representations often fall short, perpetuating stereotypes and neglecting intersectional experiences. By exploring the power of media to shape perceptions, the chapter underscores the importance of authentic and diverse representation in challenging biased narratives, promoting empathy, and fostering a more inclusive society.

Politics and Identity-based Advocacy

The political landscape is shaped by the advocacy of individuals and groups that recognize the intersections of identity. This section explores how political movements and policies often fail to adequately address the needs of intersectional communities. It also examines how advocacy for issues such as racial justice intersects with gender equality, LGBTQ+ rights, and other identity-based struggles.

The intricate interplay between politics and identity-based advocacy forms a cornerstone of modern social change. This section delves into the dynamic relationship between political landscapes and the efforts of individuals and groups that recognize the complex intersections of identity. It navigates the complexities of how political movements and policies often fall short in addressing the nuanced needs of intersectional communities, while also shedding light on how advocacy for crucial issues like racial justice intersects with struggles for gender equality, LGBTQ+ rights, and other identity-based movements.

The section begins by examining the powerful impact of identity-based advocacy on shaping the political landscape. It explores how individuals and communities that experience multiple layers of marginalization recognize the urgent need for inclusive policies that address the realities of their lives. Through case studies and historical examples, the section highlights how marginalized groups have historically organized and advocated for policy changes that acknowledge and prioritize intersectional experiences.

Furthermore, the section delves into the challenges and shortcomings of political movements that often overlook intersectionality. It analyzes how advocacy efforts can inadvertently perpetuate exclusivity by failing to consider the intersecting identities and experiences of individuals. By critically examining instances where identity-based struggles have been sidelined within broader movements, the section underscores the importance of inclusive advocacy that recognizes the interconnected nature of systemic oppressions.

The section then explores the critical junctures where identity-based advocacy converges with other social justice causes. It investigates how movements for racial justice intersect with gender equality, LGBTQ+ rights, disability rights, and economic justice, among others. By showcasing instances of successful collaborations between various identity-based movements, the section emphasizes the potential for collective action to create transformative change on multiple fronts.

Moreover, the section examines the ways in which the political realm responds to intersectional advocacy. It explores the challenges and successes faced by individuals who navigate the complexities of advocating for policies that encompass a wide range of identities and experiences. By analyzing policy outcomes and legislative changes, the section offers insights into how intersectional advocacy can influence the political agenda and shape policy decisions.

The section concludes by underscoring the need for a more inclusive and holistic approach to politics and advocacy. It calls for a shift in political discourse and policymaking that centers the experiences of marginalized and intersectional communities. By highlighting the potential for collaboration, coalition-building, and allyship across different identity-based movements, the section challenges the traditional boundaries of advocacy and politics.

In summary, the "Politics and Identity-based Advocacy" section explores the multifaceted relationship between politics and the recognition of intersecting identities. It scrutinizes the shortcomings of political movements and policies, examines the intersections between various identity-based struggles, and emphasizes the potential for inclusive advocacy to create meaningful and lasting change within the political landscape.

The Struggle for Inclusion

Intersectionality shines a light on the struggle for inclusion within social and political spaces. This chapter delves into how individuals with intersecting identities often find themselves at the margins of movements that claim to represent them, prompting a call for spaces that authentically acknowledge and prioritize intersectional perspectives.

Intersectionality casts a spotlight on the intricate and often uphill battle for genuine inclusion within both social and political spheres. This section delves deep into the experiences of individuals whose identities intersect, highlighting how they frequently encounter exclusion and marginalization within movements that purport to champion their causes. The exploration navigates the nuanced dynamics that arise when individuals with complex and overlapping identities seek authentic recognition and representation within spaces that often fail to acknowledge the full scope of their experiences.

The section begins by elucidating the paradox that individuals grappling with intersecting identities face. While intersectionality recognizes the interconnectedness of various aspects of identity, it also uncovers the challenges of being sidelined within movements that are primarily oriented toward a single form of identity-based activism.

Drawing on real-life anecdotes and historical accounts, the section sheds light on how individuals with intersecting identities navigate the delicate balance between acknowledging their multifaceted experiences and demanding their rightful place within broader movements.

Furthermore, the section explores the concept of "intersectional erasure"—the phenomenon where the unique struggles of individuals with intersecting identities are overlooked, downplayed, or overshadowed by dominant narratives. By examining instances where the complexities of intersectional identities have been rendered invisible, the section underscores the importance of spaces that recognize and celebrate the richness of these experiences.

In addition, the section delves into the pivotal role that allyship and solidarity play in addressing the struggle for inclusion. It explores how individuals from privileged backgrounds can act as allies by amplifying the voices of those with intersecting identities and advocating for spaces that prioritize their perspectives. By analyzing successful examples of allyship, the section showcases how collective efforts can dismantle the barriers to authentic inclusion.

The section also scrutinizes the ways in which institutions, including social and political ones, perpetuate exclusion. It examines policies, practices, and structures that inadvertently reinforce marginalization, and it calls for systemic changes that prioritize intersectional perspectives. Through case studies and critical analysis, the section underscores the urgent need for intentional efforts to challenge and transform exclusionary systems.

The section concludes by advocating for the creation of inclusive spaces that authentically honor and amplify intersectional voices. It emphasizes the importance of recognizing the diversity and complexity of human experiences and the necessity of creating platforms that center intersectionality as a guiding principle. By championing the value of intersectional perspectives in social and political dialogues, the section asserts that the struggle for inclusion is a pivotal step toward a more equitable and just society.

In summary, the "The Struggle for Inclusion" section dives into the complexities of navigating inclusion within the context of intersectionality. It uncovers the challenges faced by individuals with intersecting identities, examines the dynamics of intersectional erasure, highlights the role of allyship, critiques exclusionary systems, and ultimately calls for the creation of spaces that genuinely prioritize and uplift intersectional perspectives.

Empowerment through Representation

Media and politics offer avenues for empowerment through representation. This section explores how authentic representation of intersectional identities can reshape narratives, challenge biases, and foster a sense of belonging for individuals who have historically been excluded or misrepresented.

The concept of empowerment through representation stands as a transformative force within the realms of media and politics. This section embarks on an exploration of how genuine and diverse representation of intersectional identities can serve as a powerful catalyst for reshaping narratives, dismantling entrenched biases, and cultivating a profound sense of belonging among individuals who have long been excluded, silenced, or inaccurately portrayed.

The section commences by delving into the profound impact that accurate representation can have on challenging prevailing stereotypes and misconceptions. It draws upon real-world examples and studies that demonstrate how narratives are often constructed based on simplified, monolithic portrayals of identity. By contrasting these instances with stories of authentic representation, the section illuminates how representation has the potential to disrupt and deconstruct these harmful narratives, allowing for a more nuanced understanding of the complex interplay between various aspects of identity.

Furthermore, the section explores the emotional resonance that accompanies seeing oneself accurately depicted in media and political spheres. It delves into the psychological and sociological dimensions of representation, illustrating how it can instill a profound sense of validation, self-worth, and belonging. By tapping into personal accounts and testimonies, the section captures the ways in which representation acts as a source of empowerment, reinforcing individuals' self-esteem and forging connections between them and broader communities.

In addition, the section examines the role of representation in countering the erasure of intersectional identities. It navigates the significance of offering platforms for individuals whose experiences encompass multiple marginalized identities, highlighting the power of visibility in acknowledging the unique struggles and triumphs they face. By shedding light on instances where intersectional representation has brought about societal awareness and policy change, the section underscores its potential to drive social progress.

The section also scrutinizes the responsibility of media and political institutions in fostering authentic representation. It delves into the ethical imperative of ensuring that representation extends beyond tokenism, exploring the ways in which institutions can actively seek out and amplify diverse voices. Through case studies and analyses, the section underscores the importance of representation as a tool for promoting inclusivity and breaking down barriers to access and opportunity.

In conclusion, the "Empowerment through Representation" section traverses the transformative potential of authentic representation within media and politics. It investigates how accurate portrayal can challenge stereotypes, foster a sense of belonging, counter erasure, and promote social change. By revealing the multifaceted impacts of representation, the section emphasizes the critical role it plays in empowering individuals with intersectional identities and reshaping the narratives that shape our collective understanding.

A Call for Deeper Understanding

As we delve into the "Interplay between Race, Gender, Sexuality, and Politics," we embark on a journey of understanding that transcends single lenses. This chapter calls us to recognize that no one exists as a single facet of identity; we are all a mosaic of experiences and attributes. By embracing intersectionality, we forge pathways toward greater empathy, more inclusive media narratives, and political systems that acknowledge the full spectrum of human complexity.

The exploration of "Interplay between Race, Gender, Sexuality, and Politics" beckons us to embark on a profound journey of comprehension—one that goes beyond the limitations of isolated lenses to encompass the intricate interconnections within the human experience. This chapter extends an impassioned call, urging us to embrace the concept of intersectionality, a lens through which we can apprehend the multidimensional facets that constitute our identities. It asserts that no individual is a monolithic entity; rather, each of us is a mosaic woven from a tapestry of experiences, backgrounds, and attributes.

At its core, this chapter underscores the transformative power of intersectionality as a framework for perceiving the complex realities that shape human lives. It encourages us to transcend simplistic categorizations that often obscure the richness and diversity of people's lived experiences. Through vivid examples, personal narratives, and expert insights, the chapter illustrates how intersectionality compels us to recognize that the dynamics of race, gender, sexuality, and politics are inextricably intertwined. This realization reframes the way we engage with and perceive the world, leading to a deeper understanding of the challenges and triumphs faced by individuals who navigate these intersections.

The chapter delves into the implications of intersectionality for media narratives, scrutinizing how the adoption of an intersectional lens can foster greater authenticity and representation. It reveals how narratives that acknowledge and celebrate the complexities of identity resonate more deeply with audiences, creating spaces for genuine empathy and connection. By highlighting instances where intersectional representation has paved the way for broader societal change, the chapter underscores its potential to challenge stereotypes, combat erasure, and confront systemic biases that persist within media portrayals.

Moreover, the chapter advocates for the integration of intersectionality into political discourse and policymaking. It examines how recognizing the interplay between different aspects of identity is essential for crafting policies that address the needs of diverse communities. The chapter interrogates how political systems that disregard intersectionality perpetuate inequalities and hinder progress, underscoring the urgency of a more holistic and inclusive approach to governance.

In conclusion, this chapter echoes a resounding call to action—a call to embrace intersectionality as a lens through which we can navigate the complexities of the human experience. It urges us to transcend the confines of singular identities, inviting us to see the world through a more nuanced and compassionate perspective. By doing so, we set forth on a journey toward empathy, authentic representation, and political systems that acknowledge and uplift the full spectrum of human complexity.

Media's Representation of Intersectional Identities

Within the vast landscape of media, the representation of identities is both a reflection of societal diversity and a catalyst for shaping cultural norms. This section delves into the intricate ways in which media portrays intersectional identities—those that encompass multiple facets such as race, gender, sexuality, and more. By examining how media captures, distorts, or amplifies these identities, we uncover the profound impact that representation holds on individual and collective perceptions.

The Complex Tapestry of Intersectionality

Intersectional identities weave together threads of race, gender, sexuality, disability, and other attributes. This section explores how media grapples with the challenge of depicting individuals who navigate the intersections of privilege, marginalization, and lived experiences that cannot be neatly compartmentalized.

The intricate fabric of intersectionality forms a multi-dimensional tapestry, interweaving threads of race, gender, sexuality, disability, and myriad other attributes that collectively shape human identity. This section delves into the complex landscape that media encounters when attempting to portray individuals who traverse the intricate intersections of privilege, marginalization, and the diverse spectrum of lived experiences that defy simple categorization.

In an era when narratives are often presented in streamlined and superficial forms, the challenge of depicting intersectional identities becomes particularly pronounced. This section examines the nuanced dance that media must engage in to authentically capture the intricacies of intersectionality. It acknowledges the inherent tension between the desire to communicate complex stories within limited time or space and the imperative to honor the lived realities of those whose lives are shaped by the interplay of multiple attributes.

By delving into examples spanning various media formats—television, film, literature, and online content—this section explores how different forms of media both grapple with and contribute to the portrayal of intersectional identities. It shines a light on instances where media has successfully captured the essence of these multifaceted narratives, fostering a greater sense of representation and empowerment for individuals who have historically been overlooked or marginalized.

However, the section also acknowledges the pitfalls and shortcomings that media encounters when addressing intersectionality. It critically examines instances where narratives inadvertently flatten identities or tokenize characters, perpetuating stereotypes rather than embracing the depth of human experiences. By highlighting these challenges, the section prompts readers to contemplate the broader implications of media's representation of intersectional identities and the importance of fostering a more inclusive and authentic media landscape.

Ultimately, "The Complex Tapestry of Intersectionality" seeks to shed light on the intricate balancing act that media faces when depicting individuals who embody the convergence of multiple aspects of identity. It encourages a nuanced examination of how media narratives both contribute to and are shaped by societal understandings of intersectionality. By grappling with the complexities inherent in this portrayal, media has the potential to reshape cultural norms, challenge biases, and forge a more empathetic and inclusive understanding of the human experience.

The Power of Visibility

Media representation holds immense power—it bestows visibility upon communities that have long existed on the fringes of public awareness. This chapter delves into how accurate and diverse portrayals of intersectional identities can provide much-needed validation, fostering a sense of belonging and empowerment for those whose stories are often overlooked.

Within the realm of media representation lies a potent force—the power to grant visibility to communities that have endured the periphery of public consciousness. This chapter explores the profound impact that authentic and diverse portrayals of intersectional identities can wield, illuminating the paths of validation, belonging, and empowerment for individuals whose narratives have historically been marginalized or silenced.

At the heart of this exploration is the recognition that visibility transcends mere exposure—it is an affirmation of existence, an acknowledgement of stories that have been overlooked or dismissed. By delving into examples drawn from various media platforms—film, television, literature, online content—this chapter investigates how accurate and multifaceted portrayals of intersectional identities contribute to a seismic shift in societal perceptions.

By presenting characters whose experiences embody the complexities of intersecting attributes—race, gender, sexuality, disability, and more—media has the potential to mirror the diversity of human existence. The chapter dissects instances where representation has gone beyond tokenism, offering a panoramic view of lives that have been traditionally confined to the margins. These authentic portrayals create a bridge between the screen or page and the lived experiences of countless individuals, igniting moments of recognition that resonate deeply.

The chapter also acknowledges that the power of visibility is not just individual—it is collective. By presenting characters who navigate the labyrinthine interplay of identities, media fosters a sense of belonging within communities that have been historically underserved or overlooked. These narratives become beacons of resonance and affirmation, encouraging individuals to embrace their multifaceted identities without the burden of erasure or distortion.

Yet, the chapter also navigates the nuances of representation, recognizing that well-intentioned efforts can still fall short of capturing the full complexity of intersectional experiences. It delves into the tension between the responsibility to portray stories authentically and the challenges of balancing narrative constraints and expectations.

Ultimately, "The Power of Visibility" celebrates media's ability to shape collective consciousness, reframing understandings of identity and belonging. It illuminates the far-reaching ripples that accurate and inclusive representation sends through society—inspiring empathy, challenging biases, and paving the way for individuals to reclaim narratives that have been either misshaped or silenced. In doing so, media transforms from a mere reflection of reality to a catalyst for a reality that is more inclusive, affirming, and empowering for all.

Stereotypes and Erasure

While media can amplify voices, it also has the potential to reinforce harmful stereotypes or erase entire identities. This section examines how intersectional identities are often flattened into one-dimensional narratives, perpetuating biases and obscuring the rich complexities that define individuals.

In the intricate interplay of media representation, a dual-sided coin emerges—on one side, the potential to amplify voices and empower marginalized communities; on the other, the risk of perpetuating stereotypes and erasing the very identities it should illuminate. This section delves into the complexities of how intersectional identities are all too frequently distilled into one-dimensional narratives, inadvertently deepening biases and obscuring the multifaceted intricacies that define the human experience.

At the core of this exploration lies the recognition that media can serve as both a mirror and a sculptor of societal perceptions. While authentic and diverse portrayals have the power to challenge stereotypes and reshape narratives, the historical underrepresentation and misrepresentation of certain groups have led to a troubling pattern of erasure and caricature.

The section delves into the mechanisms through which this erasure and stereotyping occurs. Intersectional identities, which are by nature complex and layered, are often reduced to easily recognizable tropes that align with prevailing societal narratives. Characters who embody these identities may be painted with broad brushstrokes, emphasizing a single trait while neglecting the intricate mosaic that defines them. The result is a portrayal that is reductive and fails to capture the richness of experiences that lie beneath the surface.

Furthermore, the section scrutinizes the perpetuation of harmful stereotypes—preconceived notions that are applied to individuals based on their intersectional attributes. Media can unwittingly reinforce these stereotypes through recurring character archetypes or narratives that confine certain groups to predefined roles. These stereotypes not only distort reality but also contribute to the marginalization and discrimination that individuals face in real life.

However, the section does not only highlight the problem—it also delves into the potential solutions. It explores the importance of authentic representation that goes beyond surface-level traits, embracing the multifaceted identities that constitute a person's sense of self. By showcasing characters with depth, complexity, and agency, media has the power to challenge stereotypes and promote a more accurate understanding of intersectional experiences.

As the section navigates the intricate landscape of media representation, it emphasizes the need for critical awareness and responsibility. It calls for media creators and consumers alike to question the narratives they encounter, to demand multifaceted and authentic portrayals, and to challenge the perpetuation of harmful stereotypes and erasure.

Ultimately, "Stereotypes and Erasure" serves as a reminder of the dual role media plays in shaping societal perceptions. It underscores the importance of striving for representation that is not only accurate but also respectful of the diversity and complexity of intersectional identities. By doing so, media can become a force for positive change, dismantling biases, and contributing to a more inclusive and empathetic understanding of human experiences.

Authenticity and Authentic Representation

Authentic representation goes beyond superficial appearances; it delves into the nuances of lived experiences. This section explores how media can authentically capture the intricacies of intersectional lives, offering audiences a more genuine understanding of the challenges, triumphs, and resilience that shape these identities.

In the realm of media, authenticity is a beacon that guides the way to meaningful and impactful representation. It is the difference between mere visibility and a genuine reflection of the lived experiences, complexities, and realities of intersectional identities. This section embarks on an exploration of how media has the power to transcend the surface and delve into the nuanced layers that constitute the authenticity of intersectional lives, offering audiences a richer and more genuine understanding of the challenges, triumphs, and resilience that shape these identities.

At its core, authenticity in media representation is about capturing the essence of lived experiences. It acknowledges that intersectional individuals are not defined by a single attribute but by the intricate interplay of various aspects of identity. For instance, a character's racial background does not exist in isolation from their gender, sexuality, socioeconomic status, or ability. Instead, these attributes intersect to create a multifaceted narrative that cannot be distilled into a single stereotype.

This section delves into how media creators can achieve authentic representation by engaging in meticulous research, consultation with individuals from the communities being portrayed, and an unwavering commitment to portraying the stories with sensitivity and depth. It examines how narratives that authentically depict intersectional identities are not only truer to real-life experiences but also resonate more deeply with audiences.

Furthermore, the section underscores that authentic representation extends beyond the depiction of struggles—it encompasses the full spectrum of human experiences. Intersectional individuals are not solely defined by adversity; they also experience joy, love, success, and the full gamut of emotions. Authentic representation captures this multifaceted reality, allowing audiences to connect with characters on a profound level and recognize the common threads that bind us all.

While exploring the potential of authentic representation, the section also acknowledges the challenges that media creators may face. The pressure to adhere to market trends, audience expectations, and entrenched stereotypes can pose obstacles to achieving authenticity. However, it emphasizes that the rewards of genuine and respectful representation are worth the effort, as they contribute to a more empathetic and informed society.

Ultimately, "Authenticity and Authentic Representation" celebrates the transformative power of media to go beyond the surface and embrace the depth of intersectional experiences. It encourages media creators to view authenticity as a compass that guides their creative decisions, leading to narratives that respect the dignity and complexity of individuals. By doing so, media can become a platform for fostering understanding, empathy, and connection across diverse lived experiences.

Empowerment and Cultural Shifts

Media representation can be a force for empowerment, shaping cultural perceptions and sparking societal change. This chapter delves into how authentic representation of intersectional identities challenges dominant narratives, dismantles harmful stereotypes, and fosters empathy, ultimately contributing to a more inclusive and equitable world.

Within the vast realm of media representation lies the transformative potential to empower individuals, challenge societal norms, and catalyze profound cultural shifts. This chapter embarks on a journey into the dynamic interplay between authentic representation of intersectional identities and the far-reaching impact it exerts on cultural perceptions, thereby igniting meaningful societal change.

At its core, empowerment through media representation is about offering individuals the agency to see themselves authentically reflected in the stories that shape the collective imagination. When intersectional identities are portrayed with depth and accuracy, it sends a powerful message that their experiences, struggles, and triumphs are acknowledged and valued. This affirmation holds the capacity to uplift marginalized communities, bolster self-esteem, and provide a source of inspiration for those who may have felt invisible or underrepresented.

Delving into the heart of this topic, the chapter uncovers how media representation possesses the ability to challenge and reshape dominant narratives that have perpetuated harmful stereotypes for generations. By dismantling these stereotypes and showcasing the true diversity of intersectional experiences, media can disrupt ingrained biases and misconceptions. The chapter examines instances where media content, whether it be films, television shows, or literature, has defied convention to portray characters with the complexity and authenticity they deserve. This defiance serves as a catalyst for broader conversations that question societal norms and demand change.

Moreover, the section explores how authentic representation fosters empathy among audiences. As viewers connect with the stories of characters from diverse intersectional backgrounds, they gain insight into the nuances of experiences that may differ from their own. This empathy transcends the screen, prompting meaningful discussions, solidarity, and a willingness to stand up against injustices. It's a reminder that stories possess the remarkable power to cultivate understanding and forge connections that bridge societal divides.

Within the context of cultural shifts, the chapter emphasizes that the influence of authentic representation extends beyond the individual and permeates the fabric of society. As media narratives evolve to better reflect the complexities of intersectional identities, they contribute to a collective transformation of cultural perceptions.

This transformation, in turn, informs public discourse, informs policy discussions, and challenges discriminatory practices.

Ultimately, "Empowerment and Cultural Shifts" celebrates the dynamic role that media plays in reshaping the world. It envisions a landscape where intersectional identities are no longer marginalized, but embraced as an integral part of the human tapestry. By amplifying diverse voices, authentic representation becomes a cornerstone of progress, driving us closer to a future marked by inclusivity, understanding, and social equity.

Media's Responsibility and Impact

The responsibility of media to authentically portray intersectional identities is immense. Media's influence extends beyond entertainment—it shapes worldviews, informs policies, and influences social attitudes. This section examines the ethical imperative for media to accurately reflect the diversity of human experiences and the far-reaching impact that responsible representation can have.

The role of media in society extends far beyond mere entertainment—it serves as a mirror that reflects and shapes our perceptions of the world around us. This chapter delves into the profound responsibility that media holds in authentically portraying intersectional identities, illuminating the ethical imperative for media to accurately capture the complexity and diversity of human experiences. The impact of responsible representation reverberates through cultural norms, public policies, and the very fabric of social attitudes.

At its core, media functions as a storyteller that constructs narratives that resonate with audiences. These narratives not only entertain but also influence how individuals perceive themselves and others. By examining how media representation can perpetuate stereotypes or challenge them, this section dissects the pivotal role that media plays in either reinforcing societal biases or dismantling them.

As the narrative architects of our times, media professionals bear the ethical responsibility to break free from the confines of harmful stereotypes and embrace the rich tapestry of intersectional identities. This section investigates the conscious choices media creators must make to present characters and stories that reflect the intricate layers of real lives. It explores the power of authenticity in fostering empathy, breaking down barriers, and fostering a sense of belonging.

Moreover, the chapter dives into the far-reaching impact of responsible media representation. Beyond individual experiences, media narratives influence public opinion and social attitudes, which, in turn, shape policy decisions and broader cultural norms. By shedding light on the ways in which authentic representation can contribute to dismantling systemic biases, the section highlights the potential for media to be a catalyst for societal progress.

In this era of interconnectedness, media's influence is magnified. The rise of digital platforms has democratized content creation and dissemination, enabling diverse voices to be heard like never before. The chapter delves into the power of online activism, where campaigns for better media representation gain momentum and demand accountability from media organizations. It explores how public discourse has evolved in response to intersectional representation and the demand for accurate portrayal.

In conclusion, "Media's Responsibility and Impact" underscores the pivotal role that media plays in shaping our collective understanding of intersectional identities. It emphasizes that media's impact transcends the screen and underscores the ethical imperative for media to be a force for positive change. By authentically representing intersectional identities, media wields the potential to transform attitudes, bridge divides, and contribute to a more equitable and empathetic society.

A Call for Inclusive Narratives

As we navigate the terrain of "Media's Representation of Intersectional Identities," we are reminded that stories are not just reflections of reality; they shape reality itself. This section calls us to demand media narratives that capture the full spectrum of intersectional experiences, to amplify voices that have been silenced, and to recognize that by reshaping media representation, we contribute to a broader societal transformation that celebrates the richness of human diversity.

In the intricate web of storytelling, narratives weave the threads that construct our perceptions, values, and aspirations. As we delve into the realm of "Media's Representation of Intersectional Identities," it becomes evident that narratives are not passive reflections of reality; they are powerful tools that shape and mold the world we inhabit. This section resonates with a resounding call to action—a call to demand media narratives that not only mirror the multifaceted mosaic of intersectional experiences but also actively contribute to the reshaping of our collective consciousness.

The power of storytelling lies in its ability to transcend boundaries. It forges connections between disparate lives, allowing us to glimpse into worlds beyond our own. This section encourages us to recognize the transformative potential that lies within media representation—a potential to foster empathy, promote understanding, and challenge the deeply entrenched biases that perpetuate inequalities.

In exploring the dynamics of media's portrayal of intersectional identities, this section underscores the imperative to amplify voices that have been historically marginalized. It delves into the stories that have been overlooked, pushed to the sidelines, or buried beneath the weight of dominant narratives. By doing so, it emphasizes the urgent need to reclaim the narrative landscape and ensure that every intersectional identity finds its rightful place in the tapestry of human stories.

The call for inclusive narratives goes beyond demanding a mere quota of representation—it advocates for stories that resonate with authenticity and complexity. It highlights the significance of stories that depict the struggles, triumphs, and everyday lives of individuals who navigate the intersections of identity. Such narratives not only validate the experiences of those who see themselves reflected in the media but also enrich the perspectives of those who are exposed to different lived realities.

In the ever-evolving digital age, media's impact has expanded beyond traditional platforms. Social media platforms, online publications, and streaming services have become battlegrounds for narratives that redefine social norms and challenge oppressive paradigms. This section explores the role of digital activism in demanding inclusive narratives and the power of collective voices to effect change in media representation.

Ultimately, "A Call for Inclusive Narratives" urges us to recognize that our engagement with media isn't passive—it's an active participation in shaping the stories that shape us. By demanding, creating, and supporting narratives that celebrate the entirety of intersectional identities, we contribute to a broader societal transformation. Through this transformation, we pave the way for a world that values diversity, embraces complexity, and celebrates the profound richness of the human experience.

Global Movements for Intersectional Equality

In the pursuit of justice and equity, a new paradigm emerges—one that recognizes the intricate interplay of identities and the ways in which they intersect to shape individual experiences. This section delves into the dynamic realm of global movements for intersectional equality, exploring the transformative power of activism that addresses the complex layers of race, gender, sexuality, and other identity facets.

The Unity of Diversity

Global movements for intersectional equality embrace the principle that equality cannot be achieved by addressing individual aspects of identity in isolation. This section explores how these movements weave together the threads of various identities to create a tapestry of change that seeks to dismantle the interlocking systems of oppression.

In the symphony of human existence, diversity is the melody that gives life its vibrant hues. "The Unity of Diversity" section resonates with the harmonious spirit that animates global movements for intersectional equality. It dives into the profound principle that achieving true equality requires more than addressing singular aspects of identity—it necessitates weaving together the intricate threads of multiple identities into a rich tapestry of change.

The interconnectedness of various forms of discrimination and privilege becomes vividly clear in the context of intersectional equality. This section delves into how the struggles against racial oppression, gender discrimination, LGBTQ+ rights violations, and other systemic biases are not isolated battles; rather, they are interconnected facets of a larger, interlocking web of oppression. It explores the ways in which these threads of identity intersect and interact, resulting in unique experiences that demand collective attention.

Through illuminating stories and examples, this section underscores the idea that marginalized communities are not siloed entities—they often face multiple forms of discrimination simultaneously. It examines how individuals can find themselves at the crossroads of various identities, such as being both a person of color and a member of the LGBTQ+ community, or being a woman of a certain ethnic background. These intersections introduce complexities that cannot be untangled from one another, and they necessitate holistic solutions that address the entire spectrum of lived experiences.

"The Unity of Diversity" celebrates the power of coalition-building and solidarity in global movements for intersectional equality. It explores how individuals and communities with diverse identities come together to amplify their collective voices. In doing so, they challenge the systems of power that seek to divide and conquer, forging alliances that cut across boundaries and foster unity in the pursuit of justice.

The section also examines the necessity of inclusive activism—one that recognizes the importance of centering the most marginalized voices in these movements. It emphasizes the significance of acknowledging historical and systemic privileges within the fight for equality, ensuring that no identity is left behind or overlooked in the journey toward a more equitable world.

Ultimately, "The Unity of Diversity" stands as a testament to the interconnectedness of human experiences and the imperative of addressing systemic oppression in all its manifestations. By weaving together the threads of various identities, global movements for intersectional equality pave the way for a more just and inclusive society—one where the tapestry of change reflects the diverse beauty of humanity in all its forms.

The Leadership of Marginalized Voices

Intersectional movements are often led by individuals from marginalized communities who refuse to be confined by single categories. This chapter delves into how leaders who navigate the intersections of identity bring a nuanced perspective to activism, fostering a more inclusive approach that challenges deeply ingrained biases.

In the arena of social change, leadership takes on a transformative dimension when it is guided by individuals who embody the complexities of intersecting identities. "The Leadership of Marginalized Voices" section casts a spotlight on the powerful role played by leaders from marginalized communities in shaping intersectional movements. It delves deep into their unique perspectives, strategies, and contributions that not only challenge the status quo but also cultivate a more inclusive and empathetic approach to activism.

This section illuminates how leaders with intersecting identities transcend the limitations of single categories, and in doing so, they offer a fresh and multifaceted lens through which to view social issues. Their leadership exemplifies the lived experiences of individuals who grapple with the intersections of privilege and marginalization on a daily basis. By navigating these multifaceted aspects of their identities, these leaders bring a nuanced understanding to their activism, enabling them to tackle the root causes of systemic oppression more comprehensively.

Through stories and examples, this section showcases how leaders of marginalized voices navigate the complexities of intersectionality in their advocacy work. It explores their strategies for addressing the layered challenges faced by their communities, whether it's addressing racial injustices, gender disparities, economic inequalities, or other forms of discrimination. By acknowledging the interconnected nature of these issues, these leaders foster a more holistic approach to activism—one that seeks to dismantle the interconnected systems of oppression that perpetuate inequalities.

Moreover, this section emphasizes the power of representation in leadership. When individuals from marginalized backgrounds rise to positions of influence, they not only challenge stereotypes and biases but also inspire others who share similar identities. Their leadership becomes a beacon of hope, proving that one's intersecting identities are not barriers but assets that enrich the discourse and solutions.

"The Leadership of Marginalized Voices" also explores the ways in which these leaders bridge divides within movements. They recognize that to achieve true equality, it's essential to create spaces where different identities and experiences are acknowledged and valued. These leaders foster inclusivity by actively seeking out the perspectives of those with different intersecting identities, fostering collaboration, solidarity, and unity.

Ultimately, this section celebrates the resilience, innovation, and determination of leaders from marginalized communities who refuse to be confined by singular categories. Their leadership catalyzes a transformation in activism, one that recognizes the complexities of human experiences and acknowledges that true progress can only be achieved by addressing systemic oppressions in all their interwoven forms.

Addressing Systemic Injustices

Global movements for intersectional equality confront the root causes of systemic injustices. This section explores how these movements transcend surface-level reforms to tackle the structural foundations of inequality, advocating for policies and changes that recognize the multifaceted nature of discrimination.

In the realm of global movements for intersectional equality, the pursuit of meaningful change goes beyond superficial adjustments—it delves into the very structures that sustain systemic injustices. This pivotal section, "Addressing Systemic Injustices," delves into the profound strategies that these movements employ to confront the root causes of inequality, dismantle entrenched biases, and advocate for transformative policies that acknowledge the intricate layers of discrimination.

This section unveils how global movements recognize that the roots of oppression are deeply embedded within societal systems, policies, and institutions. Superficial reforms and cosmetic changes often fail to address the systemic issues that perpetuate inequalities across multiple identities. The exploration delves into how these movements go beyond surface-level actions, setting their sights on the larger framework that shapes social norms, power dynamics, and economic structures.

Through insightful narratives and case studies, this section showcases how intersectional movements meticulously analyze the ways in which different forms of oppression intersect and reinforce one another. Rather than viewing racial injustice, gender inequality, LGBTQ+ discrimination, and other forms of bias in isolation, these movements illuminate the intricate connections that link these issues. By understanding the intersections, they develop holistic strategies that challenge the very foundations of systemic inequalities.

Furthermore, this section sheds light on the advocacy efforts that global movements undertake to demand substantive change. From policy reform to institutional shifts, these movements advocate for measures that consider the multifaceted nature of discrimination. They recognize that policies that solely address one aspect of identity may inadvertently perpetuate inequalities for others. The exploration illustrates how these movements work to create inclusive policies that uplift the most marginalized voices within marginalized communities.

The section also emphasizes the importance of dismantling the interconnected systems that uphold systemic injustices. It highlights how these movements push for reforms that disrupt power imbalances, break down institutional barriers, and challenge the underlying narratives that sustain discrimination. By challenging the very systems that perpetuate inequality, these movements pave the way for lasting change that reverberates across society.

In sum, "Addressing Systemic Injustices" is a pivotal chapter that showcases how global movements for intersectional equality engage in a multi-dimensional battle against deeply rooted disparities. By confronting systemic injustices head-on and advocating for comprehensive changes, these movements aim to create a society where individuals are not just treated equally on the surface, but where the very structures that have perpetuated inequalities are fundamentally transformed.

Building Solidarity and Coalition

Intersectional movements recognize the interconnectedness of struggles across identities and regions. This section delves into how these movements foster solidarity and coalition-building, emphasizing the importance of individuals and communities standing together to challenge oppressive systems on a global scale.

In the dynamic landscape of intersectional movements, a core principle emerges: the power of solidarity and coalition-building. This section, "Building Solidarity and Coalition," delves into the intricate and transformative process by which these movements recognize the shared struggles that transcend identities and geographical boundaries. It underscores the profound impact of individuals and communities standing united to challenge oppressive systems on a global scale.

At the heart of this exploration is the recognition that the fight for equality is not isolated within individual identities or specific regions. Instead, intersectional movements acknowledge the interconnectedness of struggles that span race, gender, sexuality, socioeconomic status, and beyond. They recognize that the oppressive systems they aim to dismantle are interwoven and mutually reinforcing. This section illuminates how this understanding becomes the foundation upon which coalitions are built.

Through compelling narratives and case studies, the section showcases how intersectional movements engage in intentional efforts to bridge gaps and create alliances among diverse communities. It delves into how activists, organizations, and advocates work collaboratively to amplify each other's voices, pool resources, and create a collective force that is far more powerful than the sum of its parts.

The exploration further examines how building solidarity often requires acknowledging historical and structural differences that may have caused divisions in the past. The process involves recognizing the unique challenges faced by various groups while finding common ground in the shared goal of dismantling oppressive systems. The section illustrates how these movements navigate these complexities to foster a sense of unity that transcends individual experiences.

Moreover, the section explores how the digital age has significantly amplified the potential for building global solidarity. Social media and digital platforms provide a virtual meeting ground for activists from different corners of the world to connect, share experiences, and amplify each other's struggles. It delves into how hashtags, online campaigns, and digital organizing have enabled these movements to rapidly gain traction and garner support on an unprecedented scale.

This exploration also emphasizes the significance of collective action and the multiplier effect it has in challenging systemic oppression. It delves into how intersectional movements leverage their diverse constituencies to engage in a multipronged approach to advocacy, mobilization, and awareness-building. By weaving together the threads of various struggles, these movements create a rich and vibrant tapestry of activism that resonates globally.

In conclusion, "Building Solidarity and Coalition" illuminates the transformative power of intersectional movements in fostering unity across identities and regions. By recognizing the shared foundations of oppression and working together to challenge them, these movements create a formidable force that disrupts established norms, advocates for change, and paves the way for a more equitable and inclusive world.

The Role of Media and Representation

Media representation becomes a vital component of intersectional movements, shaping public perceptions and driving social change. This section explores how media platforms amplify the voices of intersectional activists, shining a light on stories that challenge traditional narratives and mobilizing audiences toward action.

Within the landscape of intersectional movements, the role of media and representation emerges as a critical force in driving change and reshaping societal narratives. This section, "The Role of Media and Representation," delves into the profound impact that media platforms have in amplifying the voices of intersectional activists, shedding light on stories that challenge conventional narratives, and catalyzing audiences toward meaningful action.

At its core, media representation holds the power to shape public perceptions and influence collective consciousness. This exploration examines how media outlets, ranging from traditional journalism to social media platforms, become conduits through which intersectional activists share their stories, experiences, and insights. It underscores the significance of these narratives in challenging prevailing norms and fostering empathy among audiences that may have otherwise been distant from such lived realities.

Through captivating case studies and examples, the section highlights how media representation provides a platform for intersectional activists to spotlight issues that have long been marginalized or overlooked. It delves into how documentaries, news features, op-eds, podcasts, and multimedia content contribute to the amplification of stories that intersect across identities, showcasing the resilience and strength of communities that navigate overlapping forms of discrimination.

Furthermore, the section explores the ways in which media representation serves as a catalyst for mobilization and action. It examines how these platforms enable activists to harness their stories to build awareness, mobilize support, and spark conversations that transcend geographical boundaries. By sharing personal narratives, intersectional activists humanize complex issues, allowing audiences to connect emotionally and intellectually with the struggles faced by marginalized communities.

In addition, the exploration delves into the power of visual representation in challenging stereotypes and broadening cultural understanding. It examines how visual mediums such as photography, art, and film play a pivotal role in breaking down preconceived notions and offering fresh perspectives on intersectional identities. These representations empower individuals to confront their biases and engage with narratives that promote inclusivity and empathy.

Moreover, the section considers the role of social media platforms in democratizing representation and providing a space for grassroots voices to be heard. It delves into how hashtags, viral campaigns, and online communities facilitate the dissemination of intersectional stories to a global audience. This democratization of media representation has transformed how activism is practiced and has created new avenues for marginalized communities to be visible and heard.

Ultimately, the section underscores the transformative potential of media representation in intersectional movements. It highlights how media platforms become vehicles through which narratives are shared, stories are humanized, and collective consciousness is shaped. By challenging dominant narratives, media representation becomes a powerful tool for advocating social change and building a more inclusive, empathetic, and equitable world.

Policy Advocacy and Transformative Change

Global movements for intersectional equality advocate for policy changes that reflect the complexity of identity. This chapter delves into how these movements work to dismantle policies that perpetuate discrimination and advocate for new ones that acknowledge the intersecting dimensions of human experiences.

A Call for Inclusivity and Progress

As we delve into the world of "Global Movements for Intersectional Equality," we recognize that the fight for justice cannot be siloed—it must be intersectional. This section calls us to join hands with those whose struggles intersect, to recognize the power of diverse voices united in purpose, and to envision a world where equality is not just a distant dream but a tangible reality for all. By championing intersectional equality, we affirm our commitment to a future that truly honors the multifaceted identities of humanity.

Policy advocacy within the realm of global movements for intersectional equality is a vital mechanism for driving societal transformation. It involves addressing discriminatory policies that perpetuate inequalities based on intersecting factors such as race, gender, sexuality, and disability. These movements recognize that lasting change requires a comprehensive understanding of the multifaceted nature of identity and the systemic barriers it entails.

To challenge discriminatory policies, activists engage in meticulous research and data analysis to identify areas where marginalized communities are disproportionately affected. They utilize grassroots organizing, coalition-building, and strategic communication to mobilize public support, engage policymakers, and push for policy changes that reflect a deeper understanding of intersecting identities.

Navigating the complex landscape of policy advocacy within intersectional movements comes with challenges. Activists encounter resistance from established power structures, political obstacles, and the need to balance immediate demands with long-term systemic change. Yet, their resilience is driven by the belief that policy changes rooted in intersectionality can lead to more equitable outcomes and dismantle interconnected systems of oppression.

Collaboration plays a significant role in intersectional policy advocacy. Different identity-based advocacy groups recognize the power of collective voices, acknowledging that their struggles are interlinked. By forming coalitions, these movements amplify their impact, challenge intersectional inequalities, and create a unified front for policy change at various levels of governance.

The transformative potential of policy changes that acknowledge intersectionality is evident in various successful cases. By reforming policies to embrace the complexity of identity, these movements not only eliminate discriminatory practices but also lay the groundwork for broader systemic change. Policies that incorporate intersectionality promote inclusivity, challenge harmful stereotypes, and pave the way for a more just and equitable society.

In conclusion, policy advocacy is a cornerstone of global movements for intersectional equality. By addressing discriminatory policies through research, organizing, and collaboration, these movements strive to reshape societal structures and policies that have perpetuated inequalities based on intersecting identities. The recognition of intersectionality in policy advocacy is instrumental in fostering a more inclusive and equitable world.

Chapter 8: News Coverage and Racial Bias

Racial Bias in News Reporting

Racial bias in news reporting is a multifaceted issue that warrants a closer examination of its implications. Understanding how bias can seep into news coverage is essential for fostering a more equitable media landscape.

Impact of Biased Reporting on Public Perception

Biased news reporting has a profound impact on how the public perceives various racial groups. When news stories consistently reinforce stereotypes or portray certain communities in a negative light, it can contribute to distorted perceptions. These perceptions can, in turn, influence societal attitudes, interactions, and policies. This section delves into how biased reporting can contribute to the perpetuation of misconceptions and how these perceptions can shape broader societal dynamics.

Biased news reporting holds the power to significantly influence how the public perceives different racial groups. This influence is rooted in the way news stories shape and reinforce pre-existing beliefs, often contributing to distorted and inaccurate views. When news outlets consistently depict certain communities through the lens of stereotypes or in a negative manner, it can contribute to the perpetuation of misconceptions and create an environment that fosters biased attitudes.

The impact of biased reporting reaches beyond individual perspectives, extending to broader societal dynamics. One of the most concerning outcomes is the potential reinforcement of systemic discrimination and unequal treatment. When biased narratives become pervasive, they can shape how various racial groups are treated by institutions, law enforcement, and other facets of society. This perpetuates a cycle where biased reporting not only reflects but also amplifies existing inequalities.

Furthermore, the distorted perceptions perpetuated by biased reporting can have a ripple effect on interpersonal interactions. Individuals exposed to biased news coverage may unknowingly internalize stereotypes, affecting how they interact with people from different racial backgrounds. This can lead to microaggressions, misunderstandings, and even strained relationships. Ultimately, biased reporting can erode social cohesion by sowing seeds of mistrust and reinforcing divisions.

Moreover, the influence of biased reporting extends to policy-making and public opinion. Biased narratives can shape public attitudes, leading to support for discriminatory policies or unjust practices. Decision-makers may rely on skewed information to justify policies that disproportionately affect certain racial groups. In this way, biased reporting can contribute to the perpetuation of systemic inequities on a larger scale.

To address the impact of biased reporting on public perception, it is essential for news organizations to take proactive steps. This includes promoting diversity within newsrooms to ensure a range of perspectives are considered during story selection and reporting. Fact-checking, thorough research, and avoiding sensationalism are crucial practices that can mitigate the influence of biased reporting. Additionally, fostering media literacy among audiences empowers individuals to critically assess news content and discern fact from bias.

In conclusion, the impact of biased reporting on public perception is far-reaching and multifaceted. It not only distorts individual views but also affects societal attitudes, interactions, and policies. By recognizing the potential harm caused by biased reporting, news organizations, audiences, and society at large can work together to create a more informed, equitable, and inclusive media landscape.

Comparative Analysis of Global News Coverage

Examining news coverage on a global scale highlights the nuances and variations in how racial bias can manifest across different regions and cultures. This section conducts a comparative analysis of news reporting practices in various parts of the world. By examining similarities and differences, it aims to shed light on common trends as well as unique challenges faced by news outlets in different regions. Exploring how bias manifests in different cultural contexts provides insights into the underlying factors that drive biased reporting.

Understanding the nuances of racial bias in news coverage requires a global perspective that considers the diversity of cultures, contexts, and reporting practices. This section engages in a comprehensive comparative analysis of news reporting practices across various regions, offering insights into the multifaceted nature of biased reporting on a global scale.

One of the key takeaways from this comparative analysis is the recognition that biased reporting is not limited to a single region or culture. Rather, it is a pervasive issue that can manifest in different ways depending on the socio-political climate, historical context, and dominant narratives of each region. While the specific biases may vary, the underlying mechanisms that perpetuate them often share commonalities.

In some regions, biased reporting may be overt, driven by explicit prejudices and stereotypes. In others, it can be more subtle, influenced by implicit biases and cultural norms. These variations highlight the complex interplay between media representation, cultural attitudes, and power dynamics. By conducting a comparative analysis, we gain a deeper understanding of how these factors intersect to shape news narratives.

Furthermore, this analysis uncovers both common trends and unique challenges faced by news outlets across the globe. Common trends may include the perpetuation of racial stereotypes, the underrepresentation of marginalized communities, and the prioritization of sensationalism over nuanced reporting. These trends are often rooted in profit-driven media models and the quest for audience attention.

On the other hand, unique challenges arise from the specific historical and cultural contexts of each region. Biased reporting can be influenced by colonial legacies, geopolitical tensions, and local power dynamics. These factors can shape the narratives that news outlets choose to amplify or silence, as well as the perspectives that are included or excluded from news coverage.

By delving into these differences, this section aims to foster a more comprehensive understanding of biased reporting's global impact. It underscores the importance of recognizing that biased reporting is not a localized issue—it is a collective challenge that requires cross-cultural dialogue and cooperation. Comparative analysis allows us to identify patterns, question assumptions, and ultimately work towards more inclusive and equitable news reporting practices.

In conclusion, examining news coverage from a global perspective reveals the intricate tapestry of biases that permeate media narratives. Through comparative analysis, we gain insights into the similarities and disparities in biased reporting practices across regions. By acknowledging the complexities of bias within different cultural contexts, we can better address the underlying factors that perpetuate biased reporting and work towards a more informed and just media landscape.

Uncovering Implicit Bias in Newsrooms

Implicit biases are subconscious attitudes and beliefs that individuals hold about various groups. These biases can unconsciously influence decision-making processes, including those in newsrooms. This section dives into the concept of implicit bias in the context of news reporting. It explores how these biases can affect story selection, framing, and portrayal of different racial groups. By understanding implicit bias, news organizations can take proactive steps to mitigate its impact on reporting.

Implicit biases, often formed unconsciously through societal norms, cultural influences, and personal experiences, play a significant role in shaping news reporting. These biases can exert subtle but profound influences on decision-making processes within newsrooms, ultimately impacting the stories that are selected, how they are framed, and the portrayal of different racial groups.

Subconscious Influences on Decision-Making:

Implicit biases arise from the cognitive shortcuts our brains take to process information quickly. These biases are informed by our exposure to media, social interactions, and cultural contexts. In newsrooms, these biases can unconsciously influence gatekeepers, editors, and journalists in determining which stories are prioritized for coverage. As a result, certain narratives may be favored, while others are sidelined.

Impact on Story Selection:

Implicit biases can lead to the underrepresentation or misrepresentation of stories related to specific racial or ethnic groups.

When gatekeepers possess biases, they may subconsciously perceive certain stories as more newsworthy based on preconceived notions, which in turn influences the stories that reach the public. This has a direct impact on the diversity and balance of news coverage.

Shaping Story Framing:

Implicit biases not only affect which stories are covered but also how they are framed. The unconscious associations individuals have with certain racial groups can shape the language, tone, and framing of news stories. Biased framing can perpetuate stereotypes, reinforce existing biases, and skew the public's understanding of events.

Portrayal of Different Racial Groups:

Implicit biases can taint the portrayal of different racial groups in news reporting. Subconscious biases influence word choices, imagery, and overall tone, often leading to unequal or distorted portrayals. Stereotypes can be perpetuated, and the full complexity of individuals' experiences and identities can be overlooked.

Mitigating Bias through Awareness:

Recognizing the presence and impact of implicit bias is a crucial step in mitigating its effects on news reporting. News professionals need to develop an awareness of their own biases and how they can influence their work. By acknowledging the potential for bias, journalists and editors can actively work to counteract its negative effects.

Promoting Diversity and Inclusion:

Diversity within newsrooms is an effective strategy to challenge implicit biases. When newsrooms include individuals from various backgrounds, experiences, and perspectives, the potential for biases to shape reporting is reduced. Diverse teams contribute to a more comprehensive and accurate understanding of complex issues.

Implementing Bias Awareness Training:

News organizations can implement bias awareness training to equip their professionals with the tools to recognize and address implicit biases. Training sessions can delve into the psychology of bias, offer strategies for overcoming biases, and emphasize the importance of equitable and responsible reporting.

Unveiling Unconscious Influences:

Uncovering implicit biases in newsrooms requires an ongoing commitment to self-awareness and continuous learning. By actively working to unveil and address unconscious influences, news organizations can ensure that their reporting reflects a commitment to accurate, fair, and inclusive journalism.

Implicit biases have far-reaching implications in newsrooms, but by acknowledging their presence, promoting diversity, implementing training, and fostering an environment of awareness, media professionals can strive for more equitable and unbiased reporting practices.

The Influence of Unconscious Attitudes

Implicit biases, often hidden beneath the surface of conscious awareness, hold the potential to significantly shape the decisions made within newsrooms. Delving into the realm of implicit bias reveals the ways in which these unconscious attitudes subtly permeate news reporting processes.

Origins of Implicit Biases:

Implicit biases stem from a variety of sources, including societal messages, personal experiences, and cultural narratives. These biases manifest as automatic associations that individuals form about particular groups of people, often without their conscious intention. In the context of newsrooms, these biases can unconsciously influence various aspects of reporting, ranging from story selection to the portrayal of different racial groups.

Subtle Yet Profound Impact:

While implicit biases may not be overtly expressed, their impact can be profound. These biases shape perceptions, influence judgment, and guide decision-making processes in subtle ways. In newsrooms, where objectivity and fairness are paramount, the influence of implicit biases can distort the narrative that is ultimately presented to the public.

Unconscious Biases in Story Selection:

Implicit biases can impact the stories that news organizations choose to cover. When individuals within newsrooms hold unconscious biases, they may inadvertently prioritize certain stories over others based on preconceived notions. This can lead to an underrepresentation of stories related to specific racial or ethnic groups, contributing to an incomplete and potentially biased portrayal of events.

Framing Stories through a Biased Lens:

The framing of news stories can also be influenced by implicit biases. Journalists and editors may unknowingly frame stories in ways that align with their subconscious attitudes. Biased framing can lead to the reinforcement of stereotypes, the perpetuation of harmful narratives, and a skewed representation of events.

Shaping the Portrayal of Different Groups:

Implicit biases have the power to shape the portrayal of different racial groups in news reporting. Unconscious attitudes can affect word choices, imagery selection, and the overall tone of stories. This can result in biased portrayals that overlook the complexity and diversity of individuals' experiences.

Recognizing and Addressing Unconscious Bias:

The first step in addressing the influence of unconscious biases in newsrooms is recognizing their existence. Creating an environment of awareness where journalists and editors can openly acknowledge the potential for bias is essential. This allows news professionals to critically assess their decision-making processes and take steps to counteract the impact of unconscious attitudes.

Diversity and Inclusion as Mitigation:

Diverse newsrooms can serve as a buffer against the influence of implicit biases. When news teams consist of individuals from varied backgrounds, experiences, and perspectives, the potential for biases to shape reporting is diminished. Diverse teams are more likely to provide a well-rounded and accurate understanding of complex issues.

Continued Vigilance and Education:

Uncovering the influence of unconscious attitudes requires ongoing vigilance and education. News organizations can implement training programs that raise awareness about implicit biases and provide strategies for mitigating their impact. By fostering an environment of continuous learning, newsrooms can strive for reporting that is fair, accurate, and free from the distorting effects of unconscious bias.

The influence of unconscious attitudes within newsrooms is a critical factor that demands exploration and acknowledgment. By understanding the origins and impact of implicit biases, news organizations can work toward more equitable and unbiased reporting practices.

Implicit biases stem from a variety of sources, including societal messages, personal experiences, and cultural narratives. These biases manifest as automatic associations that individuals form about particular groups of people, often without their conscious intention. In the context of newsrooms, these biases can unconsciously influence various aspects of reporting, ranging from story selection to the portrayal of different racial groups.

Impact on Story Selection and Prioritization

Implicit biases can lead to disproportionate representation in news coverage, where certain stories are given precedence over others based on underlying biases. Newsrooms may inadvertently amplify narratives that align with prevailing stereotypes or biases, while downplaying stories that challenge these preconceived notions. This section examines how implicit bias can influence the editorial decisions that determine which stories are deemed newsworthy and which are relegated to obscurity.

Implicit biases can have a far-reaching impact on the way news stories are chosen and prioritized within newsrooms. This phenomenon is rooted in the subconscious attitudes and beliefs that individuals hold about various groups, which can inadvertently shape the editorial decisions that determine which stories receive attention and prominence.

Disproportionate Representation:

One of the key consequences of implicit bias is the potential for disproportionate representation in news coverage. Stories that align with prevailing stereotypes or biases may be favored for coverage, while those that challenge these preconceived notions might be overlooked. As a result, certain racial or ethnic groups could find themselves overrepresented in the news, while others are underrepresented.

Amplification of Biased Narratives:

Newsrooms may inadvertently amplify narratives that align with implicit biases. These biases can affect the perception of what constitutes a compelling or noteworthy story. For instance, stories that reinforce existing stereotypes might be seen as more newsworthy, while stories that challenge these biases might be deemed less important. This unintentional amplification of biased narratives can perpetuate harmful stereotypes and contribute to a skewed media landscape.

Neglect of Diverse Perspectives:

Implicit biases can lead to the neglect of stories that offer diverse perspectives or challenge prevailing narratives. Newsrooms might inadvertently prioritize stories that resonate with their unconscious attitudes, leading to the exclusion of stories that provide a more balanced and nuanced understanding of events. This omission can result in an incomplete portrayal of reality and reinforce existing biases.

Influence on Editorial Decisions:

The editorial decisions made within newsrooms play a pivotal role in shaping public discourse. Implicit biases can unconsciously influence these decisions, affecting which stories are deemed newsworthy and which are not. This process occurs behind the scenes, often without deliberate intent, making it imperative to address these biases to ensure fair and accurate representation.

Mitigating Bias through Awareness:

Recognizing the influence of implicit biases is the first step toward mitigating their impact on story selection and prioritization. By acknowledging the potential for biases to shape editorial decisions, news organizations can implement measures to counteract these effects. This might involve creating transparent guidelines for story selection, encouraging diverse perspectives, and offering training to enhance awareness of unconscious biases.

Striving for Balanced Coverage:

Newsrooms that actively strive for balanced coverage are better positioned to address the impact of implicit biases. By consciously seeking out stories that offer a variety of perspectives and experiences, news organizations can mitigate the unintentional amplification of biased narratives.

This commitment to balanced coverage contributes to a more accurate and nuanced portrayal of events.

Championing Inclusive Journalism:

Inclusive journalism requires newsrooms to critically assess their story selection and prioritization processes. By championing diversity, equity, and inclusion, news organizations can challenge implicit biases and ensure that a broad spectrum of stories, viewpoints, and voices are represented in their coverage. This commitment enhances journalistic integrity and fosters a more informed and empathetic public discourse.

In conclusion, the impact of implicit biases on story selection and prioritization is a complex phenomenon that underscores the need for increased awareness, transparency, and diversity within newsrooms. By acknowledging the potential for biases to shape editorial decisions, news organizations can work toward more equitable and unbiased reporting practices that reflect the diverse tapestry of human experiences.

Framing and Perception of Racial Groups

Beyond story selection, implicit biases can seep into the framing and portrayal of racial groups within news narratives. The framing of a story—

how it is presented, the language used, and the context provided—can subtly shape public perception. This section explores how implicit biases can influence the framing of stories involving racial issues, affecting how readers and viewers interpret and understand these events. It underscores the importance of critically analyzing framing choices to identify and counteract biases that may perpetuate harmful stereotypes.

The framing of a news story encompasses how the information is presented, including the language used, the context provided, and the overall narrative structure. While news reporting aims to convey information objectively, the framing of a story can subtly influence how readers and viewers perceive the events being reported. Implicit biases can inadvertently shape the framing of stories, particularly those involving racial issues, which can impact public perception and understanding.

Shaping Public Perception:

Implicit biases have the potential to influence how news stories are framed, which in turn affects how the audience interprets and understands the events described. The framing of a story can shape whether readers or viewers perceive an event as isolated or representative of broader trends, whether they view it sympathetically or critically, and whether they attribute the event to individual actions or systemic issues.

Influence on Language and Tone:

The language used in news reporting can carry significant connotations and implications. Implicit biases can unconsciously lead to the use of language that reinforces stereotypes or perpetuates biases. For instance, certain terms or phrases may inadvertently convey a negative bias toward certain racial groups or unintentionally perpetuate harmful stereotypes.

Context and Emphasis:

The context provided in a news story can greatly influence the audience's understanding of the events. Implicit biases can influence decisions about which aspects of a story to emphasize and which to downplay. This choice of emphasis can affect whether readers or viewers view an event as an isolated incident or as part of a larger pattern of issues.

Analyzing Framing Choices:

Critically analyzing framing choices is essential to identifying and countering the impact of implicit biases. News organizations need to be aware of how the framing of a story can be influenced by unconscious attitudes and beliefs. By examining the framing choices made during the editorial process, newsrooms can assess whether biases have influenced how the story is presented to the audience.

Addressing Unintended Biases:

Awareness of the potential for implicit biases to shape framing choices is crucial for addressing unintended biases in news reporting. Newsrooms can implement measures to ensure that framing decisions are based on journalistic principles of accuracy, fairness, and objectivity. This might involve seeking diverse perspectives, using language that avoids perpetuating stereotypes, and providing contextual information that presents a comprehensive view of the events.

Enhancing Media Literacy:

Media literacy plays a significant role in helping the audience critically engage with news content and recognize biased framing. Educating the public about how framing choices can influence perception equips individuals with the tools to identify and question biased narratives. Media literacy empowers readers and viewers to consume news more discerningly and to recognize when implicit biases might be at play.

Promoting Balanced and Inclusive Framing:

News organizations that prioritize balanced and inclusive framing contribute to more accurate and unbiased reporting. By actively seeking out diverse perspectives, considering the implications of language choices, and providing comprehensive context, newsrooms can counteract the potential influence of implicit biases on framing. This commitment to balanced framing ensures that news stories accurately reflect the complexities of the events being reported.

In conclusion, the framing of news stories holds the power to shape public perception and understanding. Implicit biases can unintentionally seep into framing choices, affecting the portrayal of racial groups and perpetuating harmful stereotypes. By recognizing the influence of biases on framing and taking proactive steps to counteract their impact, news organizations can uphold the principles of ethical and unbiased journalism.

Recognizing and Addressing Implicit Bias

Understanding the presence of implicit bias within newsrooms is the first step toward mitigating its impact on reporting. This section emphasizes the necessity of introspection and self-awareness among journalists, editors, and other media professionals. By acknowledging the potential for unconscious biases to affect their work, newsroom personnel can engage in ongoing efforts to identify and counteract these biases.

Implementing diversity and inclusion training is one approach to address implicit bias. Such training helps individuals recognize their own biases and equips them with strategies to make more impartial decisions. Newsrooms can also adopt editorial guidelines that prioritize accuracy, fairness, and balanced representation, with a particular focus on stories related to race and identity.

Furthermore, fostering a culture of open dialogue and accountability within newsrooms is essential. This includes encouraging candid discussions about biases, sharing best practices for unbiased reporting, and holding one another accountable for fair and accurate representation. By creating an environment that values self-reflection and growth, news organizations can work toward dismantling the impact of implicit bias in their reporting.

In conclusion, implicit biases have a subtle yet profound influence on news reporting, shaping story selection, framing, and the portrayal of racial groups. By recognizing the presence of these biases and taking active steps to mitigate their impact, newsrooms can move towards more accurate, equitable, and responsible journalism.

This section serves as a call to action for news organizations to embrace transparency, introspection, and continuous learning in the pursuit of unbiased reporting.

Consequences for Marginalized Communities

Biased news reporting has real-world consequences, particularly for marginalized communities. Negative portrayals can contribute to stigmatization, discrimination, and unequal treatment. This section examines how biased reporting exacerbates systemic inequalities and perpetuates a cycle of disadvantage for already marginalized groups. By spotlighting the impact of biased reporting on individuals' lives, it underscores the urgency of addressing this issue.

The Ripple Effect of Negative Portrayals

The consequences of biased news reporting extend far beyond the confines of media coverage, often spilling over into the lives of marginalized communities. This section delves into the tangible effects of negative portrayals on these communities, highlighting how biased reporting can exacerbate existing inequalities and perpetuate systemic disadvantages.

Biased news reporting doesn't exist in isolation—it has a ripple effect that can reach far beyond the realm of media. This section explores the broader consequences of negative portrayals in news coverage, revealing how these portrayals can have tangible and lasting impacts on marginalized communities.

Amplifying Stereotypes and Stigmatization:

Negative portrayals in the media can amplify harmful stereotypes and contribute to the stigmatization of certain racial groups. When biased reporting reinforces existing biases and stereotypes, it can lead to increased prejudice and discrimination against these communities. People may internalize these negative portrayals, affecting how they perceive and interact with members of these groups.

Reinforcing Systemic Inequalities:

Biased reporting doesn't exist in a vacuum—it interacts with and reinforces existing systemic inequalities. Negative portrayals can perpetuate the cycle of disadvantage that marginalized communities already face. By perpetuating stereotypes and biases, biased reporting can contribute to unequal treatment, limited opportunities, and a lack of representation for these communities.

Impact on Mental and Emotional Well-being:

Negative media portrayals can have a detrimental impact on the mental and emotional well-being of individuals within marginalized communities. Constant exposure to biased and stigmatizing narratives can lead to feelings of isolation, lower self-esteem, and a sense of hopelessness. This can contribute to the overall negative experiences of these individuals and exacerbate the challenges they face.

Influence on Policy and Decision-Making:

Media plays a significant role in shaping public opinion, which in turn can influence policy decisions and public discourse. Negative portrayals in the media can contribute to an environment where policies that disproportionately affect marginalized communities are endorsed or implemented. Biased reporting can hinder the implementation of equitable policies by perpetuating stereotypes that may inform decision-making.

Reduced Opportunities and Representation:

Biased media portrayals can impact how members of marginalized communities are perceived by the broader society. This can lead to reduced opportunities in areas such as education, employment, and housing. Additionally, biased reporting can contribute to a lack of diverse representation in various fields and positions of power, perpetuating the underrepresentation of these communities.

Weakening Social Cohesion:

Negative portrayals in the media can erode social cohesion and trust among different racial and ethnic groups. Biased reporting can contribute to divisions, misunderstandings, and hostility between communities. This weakened social cohesion can hinder efforts to build inclusive and diverse societies.

Amplifying Activism and Advocacy:

On the flip side, negative portrayals can also galvanize activism and advocacy within marginalized communities. When individuals and communities are consistently portrayed in a negative light, it can ignite a desire for change. Activists and advocates may rally together to challenge biased narratives, demand accurate representation, and address the systemic issues perpetuated by media bias.

Countering the Ripple Effect:

Understanding the ripple effect of negative portrayals underscores the urgency of countering biased reporting. By recognizing the far-reaching consequences of biased media coverage, news organizations can prioritize accurate and balanced reporting that avoids perpetuating harmful stereotypes. Promoting diverse and inclusive narratives can help mitigate the negative impact on marginalized communities and contribute to a more equitable society.

In conclusion, the ripple effect of biased reporting goes beyond media representation—it intersects with systemic inequalities, mental well-being, policy decisions, and social cohesion. The consequences of negative portrayals are real and can perpetuate disadvantage for marginalized communities. Recognizing this impact highlights the importance of ethical, responsible, and unbiased journalism.

Stigmatization and Reinforcement of Stereotypes

Biased news reporting can reinforce harmful stereotypes and stigmatize marginalized communities. When media consistently portrays certain racial groups in a negative light, it contributes to the creation of a skewed narrative that emphasizes criminality, poverty, or other negative attributes. This section explores how these portrayals can shape public perceptions and contribute to the broader societal stigmatization of marginalized communities.

Negative Emphasis on Certain Traits:

Biased news reporting tends to emphasize specific negative traits or incidents within marginalized communities while neglecting their diverse experiences and positive contributions. This selective portrayal can create an unbalanced and distorted view of these communities, perpetuating misconceptions and misrepresentations.

Perpetuation of Stereotypes:

The media's persistent portrayal of certain racial groups in a negative light reinforces harmful stereotypes that have deep historical roots. These stereotypes simplify complex identities and histories, reducing communities to a single narrative. As a result, audiences may internalize and perpetuate these stereotypes, contributing to a cycle of stigmatization.

Amplifying Limited Perspectives:

Biased reporting tends to amplify perspectives that align with preconceived notions, resulting in an overemphasis on crime, poverty, or other challenges within marginalized communities. This one-sided narrative fails to capture the full scope of these groups' experiences, overlooking their cultural richness, achievements, and resilience.

Shaping Public Perception:

The portrayal of marginalized communities as consistently negative can shape how the public perceives and interacts with these groups. When media consistently highlights negative attributes, it influences public attitudes, leading to misconceptions, bias, and even discrimination. These perceptions can affect various aspects of life, from personal interactions to policy decisions.

Contributing to Self-Fulfilling Prophecies:

Biased media portrayals can contribute to self-fulfilling prophecies, where individuals from marginalized communities are treated according to the stereotypes perpetuated by the media. This can lead to limited opportunities, reduced access to resources, and unequal treatment, ultimately reinforcing the very narratives that biased reporting creates.

Impact on Policy and Decision-Making:

The stigmatization perpetuated by biased reporting can influence policy decisions and resource allocation. When media consistently frames certain communities as problematic, policymakers may be more inclined to implement punitive measures rather than addressing underlying structural issues. This approach can further exacerbate systemic inequalities.

Societal Stigmatization and Its Consequences:

The portrayal of marginalized communities as inherently negative can contribute to broader societal stigmatization. This societal stigmatization goes beyond media consumption; it influences social interactions, employment opportunities, educational experiences, and more. This cycle of stigmatization can hinder individuals' ability to fully participate in society and access equal opportunities.

Challenging Biased Portrayals for Change:

Recognizing the impact of biased portrayals on stigmatization underscores the importance of challenging these narratives. Promoting accurate and inclusive representation in media requires conscious efforts to counteract harmful stereotypes and to offer a more comprehensive perspective. By advocating for authentic storytelling that highlights the complexities and strengths of marginalized communities, society can work towards dismantling stigmatization and fostering understanding.

In essence, the reinforcement of stereotypes and stigmatization through biased news reporting has far-reaching consequences that extend beyond media consumption. It shapes public perceptions, contributes to systemic discrimination, and affects policy decisions. Recognizing the power of media to perpetuate stigmatization emphasizes the need for responsible reporting that showcases diverse and authentic narratives, ultimately fostering empathy, understanding, and social change.

Impact on Equal Treatment and Opportunities

Media representation has the power to influence how individuals are treated within various societal contexts. Biased reporting can contribute to unequal treatment by fostering discriminatory attitudes among individuals, institutions, and even law enforcement. This section examines how negative portrayals can affect interactions in areas such as education, employment, housing, and criminal justice. It sheds light on how media biases can contribute to a cycle of disadvantage, limiting opportunities and perpetuating inequality.

Discriminatory Attitudes and Behavior:

Biased reporting that consistently portrays certain racial groups negatively can foster discriminatory attitudes among individuals. These attitudes can manifest in various forms of unequal treatment, from microaggressions in daily interactions to systemic discrimination in institutions and policies.

Educational Disparities:

Media bias can influence how educators perceive and interact with students from marginalized communities. Biased portrayals can contribute to the stereotyping of students, leading to lowered expectations and reduced access to quality education. This can result in unequal educational opportunities and hinder academic success.

Employment Barriers:

Negative media portrayals can impact how employers view job applicants from certain racial backgrounds. Biased narratives can perpetuate stereotypes that influence hiring decisions, limiting job opportunities and career advancement for individuals from marginalized communities.

Housing Inequities:

Media biases can influence housing discrimination, affecting where individuals from different racial backgrounds can live. Biased portrayals can shape perceptions of certain neighborhoods, contributing to redlining, gentrification, and unequal access to safe and affordable housing.

Criminal Justice Disparities:

Biased media portrayals can perpetuate stereotypes about criminality within specific racial groups. These biases can influence law enforcement practices, contributing to racial profiling, unfair treatment, and disproportionate rates of arrests and incarceration.

Limited Access to Resources:

Media biases that contribute to unequal treatment can also limit access to resources such as healthcare, social services, and community programs. Negative portrayals can lead to underfunding of services for marginalized communities, further perpetuating disparities.

Cycle of Disadvantage:

The impact of biased reporting on unequal treatment and limited opportunities can contribute to a cycle of disadvantage. Individuals who are consistently treated unfairly based on media-driven biases may face obstacles that prevent them from accessing resources, achieving upward mobility, and breaking free from systemic inequalities.

Systemic Inequalities and Biased Reporting:

Biased media reporting contributes to the reinforcement of systemic inequalities. By perpetuating negative narratives, media biases become intertwined with existing disparities, making it challenging for individuals to overcome obstacles and achieve equal treatment.

Promoting Equal Treatment and Opportunities:

Recognizing the relationship between media bias and unequal treatment underscores the urgency of promoting accurate and inclusive representation. By challenging harmful stereotypes and advocating for fair treatment, society can work towards dismantling systemic barriers and creating equal opportunities for all individuals, regardless of their racial background.

In essence, the impact of biased news reporting on equal treatment and opportunities is a complex and multifaceted issue. Media biases can foster discriminatory attitudes, contribute to disparities in education and employment, perpetuate housing and criminal justice inequities, and limit access to resources. By acknowledging these connections, society can strive for more just and equitable treatment for all individuals, regardless of their racial identity.

Reinforcing Systemic Inequalities

The consequences of biased reporting are intertwined with larger systemic inequalities. Biased media coverage can perpetuate existing power dynamics and reinforce the marginalization of certain communities. This section delves into how biased reporting becomes part of a larger narrative that justifies and sustains structural inequities. By contributing to the perpetuation of these inequalities, media biases hinder efforts to achieve a more just and equitable society.

Perpetuating Power Dynamics:

Biased media reporting can contribute to the preservation of existing power dynamics within society. When certain racial groups are consistently portrayed negatively, these portrayals reinforce stereotypes and narratives that have historically justified unequal treatment and discrimination.

Normalization of Inequity:

Biased reporting can normalize systemic inequities by framing them as inherent or justifiable. When media narratives consistently emphasize negative aspects of marginalized communities, they contribute to the acceptance of disparities as normal and unavoidable.

Impact on Public Policy:

Media biases can influence public perceptions, which, in turn, affect policy decisions. Biased reporting can shape how the public views certain issues, leading to policies that perpetuate inequalities rather than address their root causes.

Lack of Accountability:

Biased media coverage can divert attention away from the structural factors that contribute to systemic inequalities. By placing blame on individuals or specific incidents, media biases may overlook the larger systemic issues that sustain disparities.

Erosion of Empathy and Solidarity:

When media consistently portrays certain communities in a negative light, it can erode empathy and solidarity among different groups. Instead of recognizing shared struggles and working towards collective solutions, biased reporting can foster division and perpetuate stereotypes.

Reinforcement of Marginalization:

Media biases can further marginalize already disadvantaged communities by reinforcing negative narratives about their experiences. This can hinder efforts to address systemic barriers and prevent individuals from accessing opportunities to overcome their disadvantages.

Cultural and Structural Bias:

Biased reporting often reflects the cultural and structural biases embedded within media institutions. These biases influence not only the stories that are chosen for coverage but also the perspectives and framing used to present these stories.

Challenging Structural Inequities:

Addressing biased reporting requires acknowledging its role in reinforcing systemic inequalities. By recognizing how media narratives contribute to the perpetuation of structural disparities, society can take steps to challenge and disrupt these patterns.

A Call for Systemic Change:

To truly address the issue of biased reporting, a systemic approach is necessary. This includes promoting diversity within newsrooms, holding media organizations accountable for accurate and inclusive representation, and advocating for policies that dismantle the root causes of systemic inequalities.

In summary, biased reporting does not exist in isolation—it becomes part of a larger narrative that reinforces systemic inequities. By normalizing disparities, influencing public perceptions, and perpetuating negative stereotypes, media biases hinder efforts to achieve a more just and equitable society. Recognizing the interconnectedness of biased reporting with systemic inequalities is a crucial step towards transformative change.

Amplifying Discrimination and Exclusion

Biased reporting can amplify discrimination and exclusion by framing certain communities as inherently problematic or unworthy. This framing can have profound psychological and emotional impacts on individuals within these communities, fostering feelings of exclusion, shame, and self-doubt. This section explores how biased reporting can contribute to the erosion of self-esteem and a sense of belonging among marginalized individuals.

Biased reporting has the potential to magnify the harmful effects of discrimination and exclusion by perpetuating narratives that frame certain communities as inherently problematic or unworthy. This framing can deeply affect the psychological and emotional well-being of individuals within these marginalized communities, fostering feelings of exclusion, shame, and self-doubt.

Creation of Negative Stereotypes:

Biased reporting often relies on negative stereotypes that reinforce discriminatory attitudes. These stereotypes can further contribute to the marginalization of already disadvantaged communities, perpetuating a cycle of exclusion and disadvantage.

Psychological Impact:

The consistent portrayal of certain communities in a negative light can have a profound psychological impact on individuals belonging to those communities. It can lead to internalized feelings of inferiority, insecurity, and self-doubt, as individuals are bombarded with messages that suggest their worth is diminished.

Erosion of Self-Esteem:

Negative media portrayals can erode the self-esteem of individuals who see their identities reflected in these narratives. The constant exposure to biased reporting can create feelings of inadequacy and contribute to a diminished sense of self-worth.

Isolation and Alienation:

Biased reporting can create a sense of isolation and alienation among individuals who belong to marginalized communities. When media consistently reinforces negative perceptions, individuals may feel disconnected from the broader society and struggle to find a sense of belonging.

Undermining Collective Identity:

Media biases that emphasize problems within certain communities can undermine the sense of collective identity and pride that individuals within those communities may feel. This can weaken community cohesion and prevent individuals from seeking support from their own communities.

Impact on Mental Health:

The emotional toll of biased reporting can contribute to mental health challenges among individuals who are targeted by negative narratives. Feelings of anxiety, depression, and stress can result from the ongoing exposure to media portrayals that diminish one's worth.

Reinforcement of Discrimination:

Biased media reporting not only reflects existing discrimination but can also contribute to its reinforcement. Negative portrayals can be internalized by the broader society, leading to discriminatory behavior and attitudes.

Media as a Source of Validation:

Media plays a significant role in validating individuals' identities and experiences. Biased reporting denies individuals the validation and recognition they deserve, impacting their ability to feel seen and heard.

A Call for Inclusive Representation:

Addressing the amplification of discrimination and exclusion through biased reporting requires a concerted effort to promote inclusive representation in media. Accurate and diverse portrayals of marginalized communities can counteract the damaging effects of biased narratives and help individuals reclaim their sense of identity and belonging.

In conclusion, biased reporting can intensify the impact of discrimination and exclusion by perpetuating negative narratives that erode self-esteem, create feelings of isolation, and undermine collective identity. The consequences are far-reaching, affecting the mental and emotional well-being of individuals within marginalized communities. Recognizing the harmful effects of biased reporting is essential to fostering a media landscape that promotes inclusivity, respect, and a sense of dignity for all individuals, regardless of their background.

Demand for Ethical and Inclusive Reporting

The consequences of biased reporting underscore the ethical imperative for news organizations to prioritize accuracy, fairness, and inclusivity. By spotlighting the real-world impacts of media biases on marginalized communities, this section emphasizes the need for responsible reporting that accurately represents the diversity and complexity of human experiences. It calls for a commitment to challenging stereotypes, dispelling myths, and providing a more nuanced and empathetic understanding of marginalized communities.

The far-reaching consequences of biased reporting underscore the urgent need for news organizations to prioritize ethical and inclusive reporting practices. The real-world impacts of media biases on marginalized communities reveal the profound responsibility that journalism holds in shaping public perceptions and societal dynamics. This section highlights the imperative for news organizations to adopt practices that prioritize accuracy, fairness, and inclusivity.

Recognizing Ethical Obligations:

Media outlets have a fundamental ethical obligation to provide accurate and unbiased information to their audiences. Biased reporting not only breaches this obligation but can also perpetuate harm and inequality. This section emphasizes that responsible journalism extends beyond the delivery of news—it requires a commitment to understanding the impact of reporting on individuals and communities.

Promoting Empathy and Understanding:

The call for ethical and inclusive reporting stems from the understanding that media has the power to shape public opinion and influence societal attitudes. By accurately representing the diversity and complexity of human experiences, news organizations can contribute to a more empathetic and informed society. This is particularly crucial in countering the harmful effects of biased narratives.

Challenging Stereotypes and Myths:

Ethical reporting involves challenging stereotypes and dispelling myths that perpetuate discrimination. News organizations have a duty to critically examine the narratives they present and ensure that they do not reinforce harmful biases. This section emphasizes the importance of journalists as gatekeepers of information who can shape narratives in a way that reflects the truth and promotes understanding.

Fostering Inclusive Dialogue:

Inclusive reporting creates space for diverse voices and perspectives, fostering meaningful dialogue around issues that impact marginalized communities. This section highlights the role of news organizations in amplifying underrepresented voices, providing a platform for nuanced discussions, and challenging the status quo.

Promoting Transparency and Accountability:

News organizations must be transparent about their editorial processes and decision-making. By openly acknowledging potential biases and taking steps to mitigate them, news organizations can build trust with their audiences and demonstrate a commitment to responsible reporting.

Educating Journalists and Audiences:

Educating journalists and audiences about the potential pitfalls of biased reporting is essential. News organizations should provide training to journalists on recognizing and addressing biases, and audiences should be equipped with the skills to critically assess media content.

An Essential Shift in Mindset:

Ultimately, the demand for ethical and inclusive reporting necessitates a shift in the mindset of news organizations. It calls for a departure from sensationalism, bias, and harmful narratives toward a commitment to truth, accuracy, and the promotion of diverse voices. This section emphasizes that responsible reporting is not only a professional duty but also a means to contribute to a more just and equitable society.

In conclusion, the consequences of biased reporting highlight the ethical imperative for news organizations to prioritize accuracy, fairness, and inclusivity. By doing so, journalism can fulfill its role as a catalyst for positive change, promoting empathy, challenging stereotypes, and fostering a more informed and equitable society.

In conclusion, biased news reporting has wide-ranging consequences for marginalized communities, perpetuating stigma, reinforcing stereotypes, and exacerbating systemic inequalities. By understanding the tangible effects of biased reporting, news organizations can be motivated to adopt ethical reporting practices that contribute to a more just and equitable society.

This section serves as a call to action for media professionals to recognize their role in shaping public perceptions and to work towards dismantling the harmful impact of biased reporting on marginalized communities.

Ethics in Journalism and Unbiased Reporting

Ethical journalism is grounded in principles of accuracy, fairness, and objectivity. However, achieving unbiased reporting is a complex endeavor. This section delves into the ethical considerations that journalists and news organizations must grapple with in their pursuit of accurate and unbiased news coverage. It explores the challenges of balancing objectivity with the responsibility to challenge harmful narratives and provide a holistic view of events.

Media Literacy and Combating Bias

Media literacy is a crucial tool for audiences to critically engage with news content. This section explores the role of media literacy in recognizing and challenging biased reporting. It discusses how individuals can develop skills to identify bias, question narratives, and seek out diverse perspectives. By empowering audiences to be discerning consumers of news, media literacy can serve as a countermeasure against the perpetuation of bias.

Navigating the Ethical Landscape

Ethics serve as the guiding compass for journalism, shaping the ways in which news stories are researched, presented, and disseminated. Unbiased reporting, in particular, is a central tenet of ethical journalism. This section explores the intricate relationship between ethics and unbiased reporting, delving into the considerations that journalists and news organizations confront as they strive to uphold their ethical responsibilities while providing accurate and comprehensive news coverage.

Ethics form the foundation of journalism, providing the ethical framework that governs the decisions made in every stage of the news reporting process. Among these principles, unbiased reporting stands as a cornerstone of ethical journalism. This section delves into the complex interplay between ethics and unbiased reporting, examining the challenges and considerations that journalists and news organizations grapple with as they endeavor to uphold their ethical responsibilities while delivering accurate and comprehensive news coverage.

The Importance of Unbiased Reporting:

Unbiased reporting is rooted in the commitment to presenting information without favoritism, distortion, or undue influence. Ethical journalism holds that the truth should be conveyed in a fair, objective, and balanced manner. This section emphasizes that unbiased reporting is not a mere stylistic choice—it is an ethical imperative that ensures the integrity of news content.

Striving for Objectivity:

Objectivity is a cornerstone of unbiased reporting. Journalists aim to present facts and perspectives without injecting personal opinions or biases. This section explores the challenges of maintaining objectivity in a world where personal biases and societal influences can subtly infiltrate reporting, affecting story selection, framing, and tone.

Balancing Multiple Perspectives:

Ethical journalism demands that news stories reflect a range of perspectives to provide a comprehensive and accurate picture. This section delves into the complexity of balancing multiple viewpoints, even when those viewpoints may challenge prevailing narratives or biases.

Transparency and Accountability:

Transparency and accountability are essential components of ethical journalism. This section examines how news organizations can enhance transparency by disclosing potential conflicts of interest, acknowledging biases, and providing audiences with insight into the editorial decision-making process.

Challenges of Sensationalism and Clickbait:

In the digital age, the pursuit of high audience engagement can sometimes conflict with the principles of unbiased reporting. Sensationalism and clickbait can compromise ethical standards, leading to the prioritization of attention-grabbing headlines over accurate and balanced reporting. This section explores the ethical challenges posed by sensationalism and clickbait and underscores the importance of maintaining journalistic integrity.

Navigating Complex and Controversial Issues:

Unbiased reporting becomes particularly challenging when covering complex or controversial topics. This section delves into the ethical considerations journalists face when reporting on issues that are emotionally charged or involve deeply rooted biases.

The Role of Editorial Judgment:

Editorial judgment plays a pivotal role in unbiased reporting. This section examines how editors and journalists must make informed decisions about story selection, framing, and tone while upholding ethical principles.

Promoting Inclusive and Diverse Coverage:

Ethical journalism necessitates a commitment to inclusive and diverse coverage that reflects the breadth of human experiences. This section explores how news organizations can actively seek out underrepresented voices and perspectives to ensure that their reporting is comprehensive and representative.

Accountability to the Public:

Ultimately, ethical journalism is accountable to the public it serves. This section emphasizes that news organizations have a responsibility to provide accurate, unbiased, and truthful information that empowers audiences to make informed decisions and engage critically with the world around them.

In conclusion, navigating the ethical landscape of unbiased reporting requires a delicate balancing act between the principles of ethical journalism and the complexities of news reporting. By upholding the ethical imperative of unbiased reporting, news organizations can foster trust, credibility, and a more informed society.

The Pursuit of Objectivity

Objectivity is often heralded as a cornerstone of journalistic integrity. However, achieving true objectivity can be challenging, as journalists are inherently influenced by their own perspectives, backgrounds, and biases. This section examines the tension between the pursuit of objectivity and the recognition that complete neutrality is an elusive goal. It delves into how journalists can navigate their personal biases while still striving to present news stories in a balanced and fair manner.

Objectivity is a fundamental principle in journalism, representing the commitment to present information without personal bias or subjective influence. It embodies the idea that news stories should provide an accurate reflection of events and perspectives, allowing audiences to form their own judgments. However, the notion of achieving absolute objectivity is complex, as journalists are human beings with their own experiences, beliefs, and viewpoints. This section delves into the multifaceted nature of the pursuit of objectivity, exploring the challenges, nuances, and ethical considerations that arise as journalists strive to uphold this foundational principle while acknowledging their own inherent biases.

Recognizing Journalistic Biases:

While journalists endeavor to be impartial conveyors of information, the reality is that everyone possesses biases. These biases can stem from personal experiences, cultural backgrounds, and societal influences. This section acknowledges that journalists, like any individuals, are not immune to these influences and biases, which can subtly shape their reporting decisions.

In the intricate world of journalism, where the dissemination of information holds immense power, the pursuit of objectivity is a noble aspiration. However, it is a pursuit that takes place on the terrain of human minds, minds that are inherently shaped by a multitude of influences, perspectives, and biases. This section delves into the essential notion of recognizing journalistic biases, an understanding that forms the foundation for ethical and responsible reporting.

At the heart of journalism lies the intention to be impartial and fair, to present information without coloring it with personal beliefs or subjective inclinations. Yet, the complexity of human nature reminds us that absolute neutrality is a challenging ideal to attain. Every individual, including journalists, carries within themselves a tapestry of biases that have been woven over years through a myriad of life experiences.

Personal biases are often the product of these experiences—interactions with various individuals, exposure to different cultures, and immersion in diverse environments. These experiences etch impressions on the canvas of the mind, shaping perceptions and attitudes. Journalists are not immune to these influences; they are active participants in society, engaged in the same social interactions that contribute to the formation of biases. This section recognizes the inherent human nature of journalists, acknowledging that they, like anyone else, carry with them a range of biases that can subtly infiltrate their reporting decisions.

The tapestry of biases includes cultural backgrounds as well. The values, norms, and belief systems ingrained within a particular culture can inadvertently find their way into the narratives journalists create. The lens through which they view the world is often tinted by the cultural shades they have absorbed. As a result, certain stories may resonate more deeply, certain angles may seem more relevant, and certain voices may be inadvertently marginalized. This section contemplates the intricate interplay between cultural influences and reporting, highlighting the need for self-awareness and vigilance in recognizing these biases.

Beyond the personal and cultural, there are also societal influences that contribute to biases.

Society, with its own systemic structures and power dynamics, shapes the ways individuals perceive the world. Journalists, operating within this societal framework, are exposed to prevailing narratives and dominant discourses. These influences can seep into their reporting, subtly shaping the stories they choose to tell and the perspectives they choose to amplify.

Recognizing journalistic biases is not about casting blame or judgment; it is about acknowledging the complexity of the human mind and the multifaceted factors that contribute to the formation of biases. It is a call to self-awareness, an invitation to introspection, and a reminder that even in the pursuit of objectivity, the shadows of biases may cast themselves upon the canvas of reporting. By recognizing these biases, journalists can navigate their reporting landscape with greater sensitivity, striving to present stories that are grounded in truth, context, and fairness. In doing so, they honor the inherent complexity of human perspectives while upholding the principles of responsible journalism.

Navigating Personal Biases:

The pursuit of objectivity requires journalists to navigate their personal biases with awareness and care. This section explores strategies journalists can employ to identify and mitigate their biases, such as critically evaluating their own assumptions, seeking diverse perspectives, and subjecting their reporting to rigorous fact-checking and verification.

In the realm of journalism, where the presentation of information shapes public perceptions and influences societal discourse, the pursuit of objectivity stands as an essential tenet. However, this pursuit is not a straightforward path; it winds through the intricate landscapes of human minds, which are naturally colored by personal biases. This section embarks on an exploration of the art of navigating personal biases—a journey that requires journalists to tread with awareness, introspection, and a commitment to truth.

Personal biases are the echoes of our experiences, perceptions, and cultural backgrounds. They are the imprints left by our interactions with the world, shaping the way we view events, people, and issues. Journalism, while aspiring to be a beacon of impartiality, unfolds within the tapestry of these biases. Recognizing this inherent truth is the first step toward navigating personal biases effectively.

One strategy that journalists can employ in this endeavor is the critical evaluation of assumptions. Assumptions often serve as the silent architects of our biases. They are the unexamined beliefs that color our interpretations and guide our choices. By consciously examining these assumptions, journalists can uncover hidden biases and challenge preconceived notions. This section delves into the significance of questioning assumptions and the profound impact it can have on the accuracy and fairness of reporting.

Seeking diverse perspectives emerges as another invaluable strategy in the navigation of biases. Journalism, as a mirror to society, should reflect the richness of human experiences and viewpoints. Engaging with a diverse array of voices, backgrounds, and narratives can broaden journalists' horizons and shed light on blind spots that biases may create. This section explores the importance of creating a mosaic of perspectives and amplifying voices that might otherwise be marginalized.

Rigorous fact-checking and verification stand as pillars of responsible journalism and as potent tools in mitigating biases. This section delves into how subjecting reporting to meticulous scrutiny ensures that biases do not creep into the fabric of information presented. Verification not only upholds the integrity of reporting but also acts as a counterbalance to biases that may have unintentionally influenced the storytelling process.

The journey of navigating personal biases is not one of erasure; rather, it is an odyssey of self-awareness and intentionality. By acknowledging biases and actively working to counteract their influence, journalists align themselves with the ethical essence of journalism—truth-seeking, fairness, and accuracy. The navigation of biases is an ongoing process, a commitment to continuously refine the craft of storytelling by reflecting on personal perspectives, seeking diverse voices, and subjecting reporting to the unforgiving scrutiny of truth. In this pursuit, journalists uphold the principles that underpin the journalistic endeavor, all while embracing the complexities of human subjectivity.

Balancing Perspectives:

True objectivity entails presenting a variety of viewpoints and perspectives on a given topic. However, this can be challenging when some viewpoints are based on misinformation or promote harmful ideologies. This section delves into the ethical dilemmas journalists face when deciding how to balance the inclusion of diverse perspectives while ensuring that inaccurate or harmful information does not gain undue prominence.

In the dynamic realm of journalism, the pursuit of objectivity stands as a beacon guiding the way to comprehensive and fair reporting. At its heart lies the crucial practice of balancing perspectives—a delicate art that involves presenting a range of viewpoints on a given topic, allowing readers and viewers to form their own informed judgments. Yet, within this pursuit of balance, journalists are confronted with a complex ethical conundrum— one that revolves around the inclusion of viewpoints that may be rooted in misinformation or that propagate harmful ideologies. This section delves into the multifaceted landscape of this ethical dilemma, exploring the intricacies of balancing perspectives while upholding the principles of accuracy, integrity, and societal responsibility.

At its core, the endeavor to balance perspectives seeks to create a comprehensive narrative that reflects the diversity of opinions and viewpoints that exist within a society. This is crucial for fostering informed public discourse and enabling individuals to make their own judgments based on a well-rounded understanding of the issues at hand. However, this task becomes nuanced when certain perspectives are tainted by misinformation, disinformation, or harmful ideologies that can perpetuate division, hate, or perpetuate societal inequalities.

The ethical dilemma arises from the tension between the journalistic duty to provide a platform for diverse voices and the responsibility to avoid amplifying false or harmful information.

Journalism holds the power to shape public opinion and influence societal discourse, making the choices made in the presentation of perspectives inherently impactful. This section delves into the ethical considerations that journalists grapple with—weighing the principles of transparency, inclusivity, and accuracy against the potential harm that misguided or malicious perspectives can inflict.

Navigating this ethical tightrope requires a delicate balancing act that involves rigorous fact-checking, critical evaluation of sources, and discernment in deciding which perspectives warrant inclusion. It also demands a keen understanding of the societal context in which these perspectives are situated—a context that informs whether the inclusion of certain viewpoints may inadvertently legitimize harmful ideologies or amplify misleading information. This section explores the importance of journalistic discernment and the role it plays in shaping the media landscape.

Ultimately, the practice of balancing perspectives in journalism serves as a reflection of a commitment to truth and fairness. It is a call to wield the power of media responsibly, with a steadfast dedication to informing the public while safeguarding against the dissemination of harmful falsehoods. As this section deepens its exploration, it sheds light on the ethical considerations that journalists must grapple with when navigating the ever-evolving landscape of perspectives—a landscape that requires a delicate equilibrium between inclusivity and the imperative to prevent the perpetuation of misinformation or harm. In striving to achieve this equilibrium, journalists contribute to the foundation of an informed and engaged society—a society that can confidently form opinions while safeguarding against the spread of falsehoods that threaten the integrity of public discourse.

Context and Framing:

Objectivity extends beyond the mere presentation of facts—it also involves providing context and framing that accurately represent the complexity of a story. This section examines how journalists can use contextual information to enhance understanding while avoiding the pitfalls of inadvertently introducing bias through framing choices.

Within the realm of journalism, the pursuit of objectivity extends far beyond the surface-level presentation of facts. It encompasses a deeper commitment to providing comprehensive and nuanced coverage that goes beyond the mere enumeration of events. This commitment is epitomized by the vital practice of contextualizing information and framing stories in a way that accurately captures the intricate tapestry of reality. This section embarks on a profound exploration of this integral aspect of journalistic integrity—context and framing—unveiling its significance, complexities, and potential impact on the public's perception and understanding of news stories.

At the core of the endeavor to provide context and framing lies a recognition that news stories are not isolated incidents. They are threads woven into the fabric of a larger narrative, influenced by historical, cultural, social, and political factors that contribute to their meaning and significance. This section delves into the ways in which journalists can leverage contextual information to enrich the audience's comprehension of the news, enabling them to grasp the deeper implications and connections that lie beneath the surface.

Yet, as this section navigates the terrain of context and framing, it also delves into the ethical tightrope that journalists tread. The choices made in framing a story—how it is presented, the language used, and the emphasis placed—can subtly shape the audience's interpretation and understanding. While framing is a tool that enhances clarity and coherence, it can also inadvertently introduce bias if not executed with precision and care.

The exploration of context and framing within this section raises essential questions about how journalists can strike a balance between providing a comprehensive narrative and avoiding the potential pitfalls of bias introduction. It probes into the ways in which context can illuminate the broader significance of events while also empowering audiences to critically evaluate the information presented. Through in-depth analysis, this section underscores the responsibility that journalists hold in navigating the intricate dance between contextual enrichment and the avoidance of undue influence.

Furthermore, the concept of framing gains prominence as this section scrutinizes its implications on news stories. The choice of words, tone, and emphasis can shape how an audience perceives a given situation. It is a delicate dance between clarity and the potential to unintentionally skew perspectives. This section examines the ethical considerations journalists face as they grapple with framing choices and the potential consequences these choices might have on the public's interpretation.

In essence, the exploration of context and framing within this section encapsulates the multifaceted nature of journalistic storytelling. It illuminates the ways in which journalists must navigate the intricate web of information and perspective to provide accurate, comprehensive, and fair coverage. This exploration serves as a reminder that objectivity extends beyond the surface and into the realm of depth, understanding, and responsible presentation. It is a journey that journalists embark upon with a commitment to unraveling the complexities of stories while safeguarding against the introduction of unintended biases.

Subjectivity in Editorial Decisions:

Editorial decisions, such as story selection and headline choices, inevitably involve a degree of subjectivity. This section delves into how journalists can exercise editorial judgment while still adhering to the principles of objectivity and providing comprehensive coverage.

Within the realm of journalism, where the intricate dance between facts and narrative takes place, the role of subjectivity in editorial decisions emerges as a pivotal factor. Inevitably, decisions such as selecting which stories to cover and crafting impactful headlines entail a certain degree of subjectivity. This section is dedicated to navigating the nuanced path of how journalists can wield their editorial judgment while maintaining a steadfast commitment to the principles of objectivity and the delivery of all-encompassing coverage.

Story selection, a cornerstone of editorial work, requires a delicate balance between personal perspective and the responsibility to represent a diverse array of voices and perspectives. It is through these choices that journalists bring the world's events to their audiences. As this section delves into the intricacies of story selection, it explores the conscious and subconscious factors that influence these decisions. By understanding and acknowledging these influences, journalists can strive to ensure that their selections reflect a comprehensive and balanced representation of the world's complexities.

In the realm of headline creation, subjectivity holds the brush that paints the first strokes of a reader's perception. The selection of words, the emphasis placed on certain aspects, and the framing of the headline all contribute to how a story is perceived. This section immerses itself in the art of crafting headlines that encapsulate the essence of a story without compromising the principles of objectivity. It delves into the techniques that enable journalists to wield their editorial creativity while avoiding the pitfalls of bias or sensationalism.

The inherent subjectivity in editorial decisions, however, does not equate to an abandonment of the pursuit of objectivity. This section guides journalists in navigating this delicate equilibrium, where personal perspectives coexist with the duty to present news stories with accuracy and fairness. It underscores the importance of transparency—of making the audience aware of the potential subjectivity in editorial choices—thereby inviting readers and viewers into the process of news creation.

Ethical considerations permeate this discussion, highlighting the need for journalists to actively reflect on their own perspectives, biases, and intentions when making editorial decisions. By fostering self-awareness and engaging in continuous self-examination, journalists can minimize the impact of their subjectivity on their work while striving for the ideals of responsible, impartial journalism.

In essence, this section's exploration of subjectivity in editorial decisions is an invitation to embrace the complexities of journalism while upholding the principles that underpin the profession. It serves as a reminder that subjectivity need not be an obstacle to objectivity; rather, it can be a tool that enriches news coverage, amplifies diverse voices, and reflects the intricate mosaic of the world we seek to represent.

Story Selection and Its Nuances:

When it comes to the selection of stories for coverage, the process is imbued with both conscious and subconscious factors that shape these decisions. This section delves into these factors, shedding light on the interplay between editorial judgment and personal perspectives.

Often, journalists bring their experiences, values, and preconceptions to the table, influencing the stories they believe are worth sharing with the audience.

The section proceeds to explore how these influences can sometimes lead to unintentional biases. These biases might manifest as a preference for certain types of stories over others, inadvertently marginalizing particular perspectives or communities. By diving into this nuanced exploration, the section aims to equip journalists with an understanding of how personal subjectivity can find its way into the selection process.

To elaborate further, it examines the role of newsroom culture in story selection. The values and priorities of a news organization can influence what stories get the green light. Editorial meetings, where discussions about potential stories take place, can also be influenced by factors such as the urgency of breaking news, resource availability, and public interest. Delving into this aspect, the section paints a holistic picture of the dynamics that drive story selection.

By acknowledging these nuances, journalists can become more mindful of the potential impact of their subjectivity on the news they present. This understanding empowers them to critically assess their decision-making processes, strive for balance, and ensure that stories from diverse perspectives receive fair consideration. Ultimately, this exploration serves as a guide for navigating the complex landscape of story selection while upholding the ideals of responsible journalism.

In conclusion, the pursuit of objectivity is a noble endeavor in journalism, but it is one that requires constant self-awareness, ethical reflection, and a commitment to fairness. Journalists must navigate the intricate landscape of their own biases while striving to present news stories that are accurate, balanced, and contextualized.

Chapter 9: Media Literacy and Critical Thinking

Importance of Media Literacy in Understanding Racial Dynamics

In an era inundated with media, media literacy holds paramount importance. It equips individuals with the tools to navigate the complex and often biased portrayal of racial dynamics in various media forms. By honing media literacy skills, individuals gain the capacity to critically assess, analyze, and contextualize media content related to race. This, in turn, leads to a more nuanced understanding of racial issues, fostering empathy, dispelling stereotypes, and promoting accurate representations.

Deconstructing Stereotypes and Biases

This aspect of media literacy involves the skill to recognize and deconstruct stereotypes and biases present in media portrayals of race. By examining underlying assumptions, coded language, and visual cues, individuals can unveil the manipulation of emotions and opinions often woven into media narratives. Deconstructing stereotypes and biases allows for a more accurate and balanced comprehension of racial dynamics, fostering open dialogue and dispelling misconceptions.

Unveiling Structural Inequities

Media literacy empowers individuals to navigate beyond the surface of media narratives, delving into the structural inequities that influence how racial dynamics are portrayed. By critically analyzing the representation of power dynamics, socioeconomic factors, and historical contexts, individuals can discern the ways in which media reflects and perpetuates systemic inequalities. This understanding enables them to engage in informed conversations and advocate for change.

Recognizing Representation Gaps

A vital facet of media literacy is the ability to recognize representation gaps in media content. This involves identifying underrepresentation or misrepresentation of racial and ethnic groups. By scrutinizing narratives, individuals can pinpoint instances of tokenism, whitewashing, and cultural appropriation. Recognizing representation gaps fuels a demand for media that authentically represents the diversity of society, promoting inclusivity and challenging biased narratives.

Promoting Active Engagement

Media literacy encourages active rather than passive engagement with media content. It equips individuals with the skills to critically assess sources, discern credible information from sensationalism, and cross-reference data. Through active engagement, individuals not only gain a more comprehensive understanding of racial dynamics but also contribute to shaping media narratives and fostering informed conversations about race.

Empowering Informed Citizenship

Media literacy is a cornerstone of informed citizenship, particularly regarding racial dynamics. By critically analyzing media content, individuals can engage meaningfully in discussions about race, challenge discriminatory practices, and advocate for equitable change. Informed citizens play a vital role in dismantling biases, fostering empathy, and championing accurate and responsible media representations, thereby contributing to a more inclusive and just society.

In summary, the "Importance of Media Literacy in Understanding Racial Dynamics" underscores how media literacy skills empower individuals to engage critically with media portrayals of race. By deconstructing stereotypes, recognizing structural inequities, identifying representation gaps, actively engaging with media, and becoming informed citizens, individuals contribute to a more accurate, inclusive, and empathetic media landscape.

Teaching Critical Media Consumption Skills

In an age where media inundates every aspect of daily life, teaching critical media consumption skills has become an essential component of education. This skill set equips individuals, especially the younger generation, with the ability to navigate the vast array of media messages, discern reliable sources, and evaluate the accuracy and biases present in media content. By imparting these skills, educators empower students to engage thoughtfully with media representations of race, fostering a generation that is not only informed but also capable of challenging stereotypes and advocating for inclusive media narratives.

Recognizing Bias and Perspective

At the heart of critical media consumption lies the ability to recognize bias and perspective in media content. This skill enables individuals to identify not only overt biases but also subtle nuances that shape the portrayal of racial dynamics. By considering the background and motivations of creators, viewers can dissect the potential influences that impact media representation. This recognition empowers individuals to approach media content with a discerning eye, fostering a more nuanced understanding of racial issues and promoting open dialogue.

Analyzing Framing and Language

Media messages are often shaped by framing and language choices that influence the audience's perception of racial dynamics. Teaching individuals to analyze these elements equips them with the tools to decipher how narratives are constructed and how meaning is conveyed. By dissecting the use of specific terminology, visual cues, and narrative structures, individuals can unveil underlying biases and narratives that may perpetuate stereotypes. This skill encourages critical engagement with media, fostering a more accurate understanding of racial complexities.

Engaging in Cross-Reference and Verification

Critical media consumption involves cross-referencing and verifying information across multiple sources. In the digital age, misinformation spreads easily, and racial dynamics can be misrepresented. By teaching individuals to fact-check and corroborate information, educators empower them to discern credible sources from unreliable ones. This skill mitigates the risk of perpetuating inaccurate narratives and equips individuals to engage in informed discussions about race based on reliable information.

Understanding Media Production Processes

Educating individuals about the production processes behind media content offers insight into how biases and perspectives can be embedded. By delving into how media is created, individuals gain an understanding of the editorial decisions, narrative choices, and visual representations that influence the final product. This knowledge encourages critical analysis of media narratives and prompts individuals to question the factors that shape representations of race.

Promoting Media Literacy Advocacy

Teaching critical media consumption skills extends beyond individual empowerment—it also fosters media literacy advocacy. Educators can inspire students to become advocates for accurate and inclusive media representation. By instilling a sense of responsibility to challenge biases, call out misrepresentations, and demand equitable narratives, educators cultivate a generation that actively participates in shaping the media landscape to reflect the diversity and complexity of racial dynamics.

Building Resilience Against Manipulation

In an era of clickbait, sensationalism, and information overload, teaching critical media consumption skills builds resilience against media manipulation. Individuals armed with these skills can recognize manipulative tactics, resist the allure of sensational headlines, and prioritize accuracy and context. This resilience not only safeguards against falling victim to misinformation but also encourages active engagement with media content that promotes understanding and empathy toward racial issues.

In conclusion, "Teaching Critical Media Consumption Skills" highlights the importance of imparting these skills to learners of all ages. By fostering the ability to recognize bias, analyze framing, engage in cross-reference, understand production processes, and advocate for responsible media representation, educators lay the foundation for individuals to navigate the media landscape thoughtfully. These skills empower individuals to challenge stereotypes, promote accurate narratives, and contribute to a more informed and inclusive societal discourse surrounding race.

Case Studies of Successful Media Literacy Programs

1. "Media Literacy in the Digital Age" Initiative

One notable case study is the "Media Literacy in the Digital Age" initiative implemented in a diverse urban school district. The program integrated media literacy education into various subjects, teaching students how to critically assess online content, identify biases, and understand the impact of digital media on perceptions of race. By incorporating real-world examples and engaging discussions, students developed skills to navigate the complexities of media representation and became advocates for responsible online behavior.

2. "Media and Representation" University Course

A university case study focuses on a media studies course titled "Media and Representation." This course delved into the intricacies of media production, representation, and biases. Students analyzed historical and contemporary media content through a critical lens, discussing how racial dynamics were portrayed and shaped. The course also encouraged students to create their own media projects that challenged stereotypes and promoted diverse narratives, fostering a deep understanding of media's role in shaping societal views on race.

3. "Media Literacy for Social Change" Community Workshop

A community-based initiative, the "Media Literacy for Social Change" workshop targeted adults and community leaders. Participants learned to deconstruct media messages, identify stereotypes, and challenge biased narratives. The workshop included interactive activities, guest speakers, and collaborative projects that addressed local racial issues. As a result, participants became media literacy advocates within their communities, spreading awareness and fostering dialogue on accurate media representation.

4. "Youth Voices in Media" Youth Empowerment Program

The "Youth Voices in Media" program engaged young people in creating their own media content to counter stereotypes. Participants received training in video production, storytelling, and media analysis. Through personal narratives and documentaries, they explored racial experiences, shared diverse perspectives, and debunked misconceptions. The program not only enhanced media literacy skills but also empowered participants to take an active role in shaping media narratives.

5. "Media Literacy Across Generations" Intergenerational Workshop Series

This innovative case study involved intergenerational workshops that brought together diverse age groups to discuss media representation. Grandparents, parents, and children engaged in open conversations about how racial dynamics were depicted in media throughout their lifetimes. By comparing historical and contemporary portrayals, participants gained insights into evolving media trends and biases. The workshop series fostered empathy and understanding across generations.

6. "Critical Viewing Club" High School Extracurricular Activity

The "Critical Viewing Club" was an extracurricular activity in a high school that promoted media literacy through guided discussions and film screenings. Students selected films and TV shows that touched on racial themes and engaged in thoughtful analysis. The club provided a safe space for students to express their opinions, challenge assumptions, and expand their perspectives on media representation. The impact of the club extended beyond its meetings, as participants encouraged peers to think critically about media content.

7. "Media Literacy and Civic Engagement" Summer Camp

A summer camp focused on media literacy and civic engagement provided students with an immersive learning experience. Through workshops, interactive activities, and collaborative projects, participants explored the connection between media consumption, civic responsibilities, and racial understanding. The camp culminated in students creating media campaigns addressing local social issues, using their newfound skills to promote positive change in their communities.

In conclusion, these case studies highlight the effectiveness of various media literacy programs in fostering a deeper understanding of racial dynamics in media representation. From school initiatives to community workshops, these programs equip participants with critical thinking skills to navigate the complex media landscape, challenge biases, and promote accurate and inclusive narratives surrounding race.

Chapter 10: Shaping a More Inclusive Future

Policy Recommendations for Balanced Media Representation

1. Establishing Media Diversity Standards

One of the key policy recommendations for achieving balanced media representation is the establishment of media diversity standards. Regulatory bodies and industry associations can collaborate to set guidelines that ensure fair and accurate portrayal of various racial, ethnic, and cultural groups. These standards could encompass representation both in front of and behind the camera, encouraging media outlets to reflect the diversity of their audiences in their content creation and production teams.

2. Incentives for Inclusive Content Creation

To incentivize media organizations to produce more inclusive content, policymakers can introduce initiatives that offer tax breaks, grants, or other financial incentives to those who prioritize diversity and accurate representation. These incentives could be tied to specific diversity targets, encouraging media producers to actively seek out stories that reflect a range of racial and cultural experiences.

3. Mandatory Implicit Bias Training

Media professionals play a pivotal role in shaping content that reflects societal values. Mandatory implicit bias training for journalists, editors, producers, and other media personnel can raise awareness about potential biases and provide tools to mitigate them. This training could encompass recognizing and challenging biases in news reporting, content creation, and decision-making processes.

4. Diversity in Media Ownership

Policy recommendations could also focus on promoting diversity in media ownership. Encouraging a more diverse range of individuals and groups to own media outlets can lead to more varied perspectives being represented in the media landscape. Tax incentives, grants, or support for underrepresented entrepreneurs could contribute to breaking down barriers to entry and expanding the ownership base.

5. Media Literacy Integration in Education

To foster media literacy from a young age, policymakers can integrate media literacy education into school curricula. By teaching students how to critically analyze media content, understand biases, and interpret representations of race, schools can contribute to a more informed and discerning media audience. Media literacy education could also encompass the responsible consumption of digital media and online content.

6. Public Funding for Diverse Media Projects

Allocating public funds to support diverse media projects can encourage the creation of content that reflects a wide range of perspectives. Policy recommendations could include grants or subsidies for media organizations that produce content that challenges stereotypes and promotes accurate portrayals of racial and cultural diversity.

7. Collaboration with Industry Stakeholders

Policy recommendations should involve collaboration with industry stakeholders, including media organizations, advocacy groups, and academia. Establishing regular dialogues and partnerships can lead to the development of comprehensive strategies for achieving balanced media representation. Industry self-regulation and voluntary initiatives could also be encouraged to complement policy efforts.

In conclusion, these policy recommendations present a roadmap for shaping a more inclusive future in media representation. By focusing on standards, incentives, training, ownership diversity, education, public funding, and collaboration, policymakers can work toward a media landscape that authentically reflects the diversity of society and contributes to a more equitable and accurate portrayal of racial dynamics.

Political Initiatives to Address Racial Disparities

Political initiatives aimed at addressing racial disparities are crucial for creating a more just and equitable society. These initiatives encompass a range of policies and actions that target systemic racism, unequal opportunities, and social injustices that disproportionately affect racial and ethnic minority communities. By acknowledging historical and contemporary inequalities, political leaders can work toward implementing measures that promote equality, inclusivity, and social cohesion.

1. Criminal Justice Reform

One of the central areas where racial disparities persist is within the criminal justice system. Political initiatives in this realm include comprehensive criminal justice reform measures that focus on ending racial profiling, reducing excessive sentencing, and reevaluating the use of cash bail. These initiatives also aim to address the overrepresentation of racial minorities in prisons and ensure fair treatment throughout the criminal justice process.

2. Educational Equity

Political initiatives targeting educational equity seek to eliminate the achievement gap that exists between students of different racial backgrounds. These initiatives could involve increasing funding for schools in disadvantaged neighborhoods, expanding access to quality early childhood education, and implementing programs that provide additional support to students who face barriers to learning.

3. Affordable Housing and Redlining Remediation

To address housing disparities that stem from historical practices such as redlining, political initiatives may involve creating affordable housing programs, expanding housing vouchers, and implementing policies that prevent gentrification. Remediation efforts could include providing restitution and support to communities that were disproportionately affected by discriminatory housing practices.

4. Economic Opportunity and Wealth Redistribution

Political initiatives aimed at economic equity focus on narrowing the wealth gap between racial groups. This could involve implementing policies that promote minority-owned businesses, increasing the minimum wage, expanding access to affordable healthcare and childcare, and offering targeted financial support to historically marginalized communities.

5. Voting Rights and Representation

Ensuring equal voting rights and representation for all racial and ethnic groups is another critical aspect of political initiatives. This includes fighting against voter suppression, gerrymandering, and discriminatory voting laws. Initiatives could also focus on increasing representation of racial minorities in elected offices at all levels of government.

6. Health Equity and Access

Health disparities are prevalent in marginalized communities, and political initiatives in this area aim to provide equal access to healthcare services and address the social determinants of health. Initiatives could include expanding Medicaid, increasing funding for community health centers, and implementing policies that address environmental justice and the impact of pollution on minority communities.

7. Cultural Competency Training for Public Officials

To ensure that public officials are equipped to address racial disparities, political initiatives may involve requiring cultural competency training for government employees and law enforcement officers. This training aims to foster an understanding of different cultures and experiences, leading to more empathetic and effective policies.

8. Data Collection and Analysis

Comprehensive data collection and analysis are essential for understanding the extent of racial disparities and monitoring progress toward equity. Political initiatives could involve establishing data collection mechanisms that track disparities in various sectors, such as education, employment, healthcare, and criminal justice. This data can inform evidence-based policymaking.

In conclusion, political initiatives play a pivotal role in addressing racial disparities and promoting social justice. By focusing on criminal justice reform, educational equity, affordable housing, economic opportunity, voting rights, health equity, cultural competency, and data collection, policymakers can work toward dismantling systemic racism and creating a more inclusive society for all racial and ethnic groups.

Collaborative Efforts for a More Inclusive Media Landscape

Creating a more inclusive media landscape requires collaborative efforts from various stakeholders, including media organizations, content creators, advocacy groups, and the public. By working together, these groups can contribute to the production of diverse and representative content that reflects the full spectrum of human experiences and dismantles harmful stereotypes. Collaborative initiatives aim to reshape media narratives, challenge biases, and foster a sense of belonging for underrepresented communities.

1. Media Partnerships and Diversity Initiatives

Media organizations can collaborate with diversity-focused initiatives and advocacy groups to increase representation in storytelling and production. These partnerships can involve hiring diverse creators, consultants, and executives, as well as providing platforms for underrepresented voices. By embracing a commitment to diversity, media companies can amplify marginalized narratives and perspectives.

2. Community Engagement and Co-Creation

Collaborative efforts can involve engaging with communities to co-create content that accurately represents their experiences. By involving individuals from marginalized backgrounds in the storytelling process, media creators can ensure that narratives are authentic and respectful. Community engagement also helps build trust and empowers communities to share their stories on their own terms.

3. Mentorship and Training Programs

Establishing mentorship and training programs can help aspiring content creators from diverse backgrounds gain the skills and opportunities they need to succeed in the industry. Media organizations can partner with educational institutions and industry professionals to provide mentorship, workshops, and internships that support emerging talent.

4. Intersectional Advocacy and Alliances

Collaborative efforts can also extend to intersectional advocacy, where different social justice movements come together to address shared challenges. By recognizing the interconnectedness of issues related to race, gender, sexuality, and more, advocacy groups can leverage their collective power to demand change from media organizations and policymakers.

5. Public Engagement and Media Literacy

The public plays a vital role in shaping the media landscape through their consumption choices and demand for diverse content. Collaborative initiatives can involve media literacy campaigns that empower audiences to critically engage with media, recognize biases, and demand accurate representation. By educating the public, these efforts contribute to a more informed and discerning audience.

6. Industry Standards and Accountability

Collaboration can lead to the establishment of industry-wide standards and guidelines for responsible and inclusive media content. By holding media organizations accountable for their portrayal of marginalized communities, stakeholders can drive systemic change and encourage the adoption of ethical practices.

7. Funding and Support for Independent Creators

Collaborative efforts can also involve providing funding and support for independent content creators from underrepresented backgrounds. By investing in diverse voices, organizations and individuals can ensure that a wider range of perspectives are represented in the media landscape.

8. Global Partnerships for Cultural Exchange

Collaboration can extend beyond borders through global partnerships that facilitate cultural exchange and international representation. Media creators from different countries can work together to share stories, challenge stereotypes, and foster a deeper understanding of diverse cultures.

In conclusion, collaborative efforts are essential for shaping a more inclusive media landscape. By forming partnerships, engaging with communities, providing mentorship, advocating for intersectional change, promoting media literacy, establishing industry standards, supporting independent creators, and fostering global partnerships, stakeholders can collectively contribute to a media environment that reflects the richness and diversity of our global society.

Chapter 11: Case Studies from Around the World

Region-Specific Analysis of Race, Politics, and Media

In this chapter, we delve into a series of region-specific case studies that examine the intricate relationship between race, politics, and media. These case studies shed light on how different parts of the world grapple with issues of representation, bias, and the role of media in shaping public perceptions of race.

1. Case Study: Media and Race in North America

The media landscape in North America, particularly the United States and Canada, has been shaped by a complex history of racial tensions, inequalities, and social movements. This case study explores how media portrayals of racial minorities have evolved over time, from harmful stereotypes to more inclusive narratives. It examines the impact of influential racial justice movements, such as the civil rights movement, on media representation and discusses ongoing challenges in achieving balanced coverage.

This case study delves into the dynamic interplay between media portrayals of racial minorities and the historical context in which these portrayals have evolved.

Historical Context and Racial Dynamics

The historical roots of race and media in North America stretch back to colonization, slavery, and the systemic oppression of Indigenous, Black, and other minority communities. Media has played a pivotal role in shaping perceptions and reinforcing hierarchies that have contributed to racial discrimination and inequality.

Evolution of Media Portrayals

This case study examines the evolution of media portrayals of racial minorities. It traces the trajectory from the era of overt racial stereotypes, where media reinforced harmful biases, to more recent shifts towards inclusive narratives. The civil rights movement of the 1960s marked a pivotal turning point, catalyzing a broader recognition of the need for fair and accurate representation.

Influence of Racial Justice Movements

The civil rights movement, alongside subsequent movements for Indigenous rights, Black liberation, and other marginalized communities, significantly influenced media portrayals. The case study explores how these movements pressured media organizations to reconsider their coverage, leading to greater visibility and diverse perspectives.

Challenges and Ongoing Biases

Despite progress, challenges persist. This case study delves into the subtle and overt biases that still shape media coverage. Stereotypes, tokenism, and underrepresentation continue to affect how racial minorities are depicted. The rise of digital media has introduced new avenues for both progressive and regressive narratives, creating a complex media landscape.

Balancing Representation and Responsibility

The case study examines the delicate balance between representation and responsible reporting. Media outlets face the challenge of reflecting the diversity of their audiences while avoiding harmful tokenism or shallow portrayals. The push for authentic and nuanced representation is often met with resistance, highlighting the tension between media's commercial interests and their societal responsibilities.

Impact on Public Perception and Policy

Media has a profound impact on public perception and policy. Biased or inaccurate portrayals can shape public attitudes, perpetuate stereotypes, and influence political decisions. This case study analyzes how media narratives have affected societal attitudes towards issues such as criminal justice, immigration, and affirmative action.

Empowerment through Representation

The case study delves into how media representation has empowered marginalized communities. By providing platforms for their voices and stories, media has contributed to mobilization, community building, and awareness of systemic injustices. Representation has the power to challenge mainstream narratives and redefine the discourse around race.

Digital Age Challenges and Opportunities

The digital age has brought both challenges and opportunities. Social media platforms have democratized content creation, allowing marginalized voices to be heard. However, these platforms also amplify echo chambers and can perpetuate harmful narratives. This case study explores how social media has both diversified and polarized media discourse.

Conclusion

The case study on media and race in North America encapsulates a journey through history, progress, and ongoing struggles. It underscores the profound impact media has on shaping perceptions, influencing policy, and facilitating societal change. From harmful stereotypes to empowering narratives, media plays a pivotal role in the complex journey towards racial equity and justice in the region.

2. Case Study: Race and the Media in Europe

Europe is a diverse continent with a history of colonialism, migration, and multiculturalism. This case study delves into how media in various European countries address issues of race and ethnicity. It examines the portrayal of immigrant communities, the rise of far-right movements, and efforts by media organizations to promote diversity and challenge stereotypes. The case study highlights the nuances of media representation in different European contexts and explores the role of media in shaping debates around immigration and cultural integration.

Europe stands as a complex tapestry of cultures, histories, and identities, a continent marked by its colonial past, waves of migration, and evolving notions of multiculturalism. This case study delves into the intricate relationship between media and issues of race and ethnicity across various European countries.

Historical Legacies and Cultural Diversity

Europe's history is marked by colonialism, imperialism, and a legacy of interactions with diverse cultures through trade, conquest, and migration. This case study explores how these historical legacies have contributed to the continent's diverse racial and ethnic landscape.

Media and Immigrant Communities

This case study examines how media in Europe portray immigrant communities. It delves into the portrayal of immigrants and their descendants in both mainstream and alternative media outlets. It analyzes how media narratives reflect the challenges and contributions of these communities and how they intersect with broader debates on cultural integration, identity, and belonging.

Rise of Far-Right Movements and Xenophobia

The case study delves into the influence of far-right movements and xenophobic ideologies on media representation. It explores how some media outlets have amplified anti-immigrant sentiments, perpetuating harmful stereotypes and contributing to the polarization of public discourse. It also examines the role of media in legitimizing or challenging far-right narratives.

Media Initiatives for Diversity and Inclusion

This case study explores the efforts made by media organizations in Europe to promote diversity and challenge stereotypes. It examines initiatives that aim to amplify marginalized voices, provide platforms for intercultural dialogue, and counteract discriminatory narratives. These initiatives are essential in creating a more inclusive and equitable media landscape.

Intersectionality and Marginalization

The case study delves into the intersectionality of race with other identities, such as gender, religion, and socioeconomic status. It examines how media portrayal of individuals at these intersections influences public perception and policy debates. It also highlights the importance of recognizing and addressing the unique challenges faced by individuals with intersecting identities.

Media's Role in Immigration Debates

The case study analyzes how media shapes debates around immigration and cultural integration in Europe. It examines how media narratives can influence public opinion, policy decisions, and societal attitudes towards migrants and refugees. It also explores the role of media in challenging stereotypes and fostering informed discussions on immigration-related issues.

Representation and Identity Politics

This case study explores the ways media representation intersects with identity politics in Europe. It delves into the representation of minority politicians, activists, and cultural figures in media narratives. It examines how media can empower marginalized communities by providing role models and challenging prevailing stereotypes.

Challenges of Cultural Sensitivity

The case study discusses the challenges media faces in addressing cultural sensitivity. It examines instances where media coverage has perpetuated stereotypes or failed to accurately represent diverse communities. It also explores the role of media literacy in fostering critical engagement with these representations.

Conclusion

The case study on race and the media in Europe illuminates the diverse ways in which media both reflects and shapes societal attitudes towards race and ethnicity. It underscores the complexity of media's role in a continent marked by historical legacies, ongoing debates around immigration, and efforts to promote diversity and inclusion. From challenging stereotypes to amplifying marginalized voices, media has a vital role in shaping Europe's evolving discourse on race and identity.

3. Case Study: Media and Indigenous Peoples in Latin America

Indigenous communities in Latin America have often been marginalized and overlooked by mainstream media. This case study focuses on how media in the region have historically represented Indigenous peoples, their cultures, and their struggles for recognition and rights. It examines the role of Indigenous media outlets in amplifying their own narratives and challenges the colonial legacy of media representation. The case study highlights the importance of accurate and respectful portrayals of Indigenous communities to foster understanding and social change.

Latin America is a region rich in cultural diversity, shaped by the legacies of Indigenous civilizations, colonization, and contemporary struggles for recognition and rights. This case study delves into the complex relationship between media and Indigenous communities, highlighting their historical marginalization and ongoing efforts to shape their own narratives.

Colonial Legacy and Marginalization

This case study explores the historical context of media representation of Indigenous peoples in Latin America, rooted in the colonial legacy that perpetuated stereotypes, erasure, and cultural appropriation. It examines how this legacy has contributed to the marginalization and invisibility of Indigenous voices in mainstream media.

Representation and Identity

The case study delves into the portrayal of Indigenous identities in media narratives. It examines how Indigenous cultures, languages, and traditions have been both romanticized and exoticized by mainstream media. It also highlights instances where media perpetuated harmful stereotypes, contributing to the broader social and cultural challenges faced by Indigenous communities.

Media as a Tool of Empowerment

This case study showcases how Indigenous communities are utilizing media outlets to amplify their own narratives. It explores the emergence of Indigenous media platforms, including radio stations, television programs, and online platforms, that provide spaces for Indigenous voices to be heard. It examines how these outlets are crucial in challenging the dominant narrative and reclaiming their cultural heritage.

Cultural Preservation and Revitalization

The case study examines how Indigenous media serves as a tool for cultural preservation and revitalization. It delves into the ways Indigenous communities use media to document oral histories, traditional practices, and ecological knowledge. It also explores how media contributes to intergenerational knowledge transfer and the assertion of cultural identity.

Challenging the Colonial Gaze

This case study confronts the colonial gaze in media representation of Indigenous peoples. It examines how media outlets are challenging the traditional narrative by offering alternative perspectives that counteract stereotypes and portray Indigenous communities as dynamic, resilient, and multifaceted.

Media Literacy and Indigenous Representation

The case study explores the role of media literacy in promoting a more nuanced understanding of Indigenous representation. It examines how media literacy initiatives can empower audiences to critically engage with media content, question stereotypes, and recognize the importance of respectful and accurate portrayals.

Cultural Appropriation and Ethical Reporting

This case study delves into the challenges of avoiding cultural appropriation in media representation. It examines instances where media outlets have exploited Indigenous cultures for profit or sensationalism, and it highlights the ethical responsibilities of media professionals in reporting on Indigenous issues.

Indigenous Media's Impact on Social Change

The case study analyzes the impact of Indigenous media on social change within Indigenous communities and broader society. It examines how media campaigns and initiatives have led to increased awareness of Indigenous rights, cultural heritage, and social justice issues. It also explores the potential for media to influence policy changes and challenge discriminatory practices.

Conclusion

The case study on media and Indigenous peoples in Latin America underscores the significance of media as a vehicle for empowerment, cultural preservation, and challenging the colonial legacy. It emphasizes the vital role that media, both mainstream and Indigenous, play in shaping perceptions, advocating for rights, and fostering understanding between Indigenous and non-Indigenous populations. By amplifying Indigenous voices and narratives, media can contribute to a more inclusive and equitable society that values and respects the cultural diversity of the region.

4. Case Study: Media, Race, and Post-Apartheid South Africa

South Africa's transition from apartheid to democracy brought significant changes to the media landscape. This case study delves into how media in post-apartheid South Africa have grappled with issues of race, reconciliation, and nation-building. It examines efforts to promote diversity in newsrooms, the challenges of balancing freedom of expression with responsible reporting, and the ongoing struggle to address historical inequalities in media ownership and representation.

The story of South Africa's transformation from a racially segregated society under apartheid to a multicultural democracy is intimately intertwined with the evolution of its media landscape. This case study delves into the complex relationship between media, race, and the nation-building process in post-apartheid South Africa.

Apartheid's Legacy on Media Representation

This case study explores how the media landscape in South Africa was deeply influenced by the apartheid regime. It delves into how media played a role in reinforcing racial divisions, perpetuating stereotypes, and advancing the government's agenda of racial segregation. The study examines how the media contributed to shaping public perceptions of race during this tumultuous period.

Media as a Catalyst for Change

The transition from apartheid to democracy brought with it a shift in media dynamics. This case study examines how media outlets and journalists played a pivotal role in challenging the apartheid narrative and advocating for democratic reforms. It explores how media coverage of anti-apartheid movements, protests, and negotiations contributed to raising awareness and galvanizing public opinion against the discriminatory regime.

Challenges of Media Transformation

The case study delves into the challenges that emerged as South Africa sought to transform its media landscape after apartheid. It explores the efforts to promote diversity and inclusivity in newsrooms, reflecting the country's multicultural identity. It also examines the tension between the ideals of freedom of expression and the need for responsible reporting that respects human dignity and promotes social cohesion.

Media's Role in Reconciliation and Healing

This case study analyzes how media contributed to the process of reconciliation and healing in post-apartheid South Africa. It explores how media outlets engaged in truth and reconciliation initiatives, providing platforms for victims and perpetrators to share their stories and seek forgiveness. The study also examines the role of media in fostering dialogue and understanding between different racial and ethnic groups.

Addressing Historical Inequalities in Ownership

The case study highlights the ongoing struggle to address historical inequalities in media ownership and representation. It delves into efforts to promote a more equitable distribution of media ownership across racial lines, addressing the concentration of media power in the hands of a few. The study explores policies aimed at ensuring that diverse voices are represented and heard in the media landscape.

Media's Role in Nation-Building

The case study examines how media has contributed to the process of nation-building in post-apartheid South Africa. It explores how media outlets have navigated the challenges of representing a diverse nation while also confronting the legacies of apartheid. The study delves into the role of media in promoting a shared national identity and fostering social cohesion.

Media Literacy and Democratic Citizenship

This case study delves into the importance of media literacy in the context of post-apartheid South Africa. It examines how media literacy initiatives have empowered citizens to critically engage with media content, question biases, and navigate the complexities of a rapidly changing media landscape. The study emphasizes the role of media literacy in promoting informed and responsible democratic citizenship.

Conclusion

The case study on media, race, and post-apartheid South Africa underscores the transformative power of media in shaping social, political, and cultural dynamics. It highlights the pivotal role that media played in challenging apartheid, advocating for democratic reforms, and contributing to the processes of reconciliation and nation-building. The study also underscores the ongoing challenges of promoting diversity, responsible reporting, and media ownership in a country still grappling with the legacy of its divided past.

5. Case Study: Race, Politics, and Media in Asia

Asia is home to diverse racial and ethnic groups, each with its own history of media representation. This case study explores how media in various Asian countries address issues of race, identity, and politics. It examines the portrayal of minority groups, the role of media in exacerbating or mitigating ethnic tensions, and the challenges of navigating cultural diversity in a rapidly changing media landscape.

The vast and diverse continent of Asia is marked by a rich tapestry of racial, ethnic, and cultural identities. This case study delves into the intricate relationship between media, race, and politics in various Asian countries, shedding light on how media portrayals influence identity dynamics and political discourse.

Media Portrayals of Minority Groups

This case study explores how media in different Asian countries represent minority groups within their societies. It delves into how media outlets contribute to shaping public perceptions of these groups, often impacting their social status, access to opportunities, and interactions with the larger society. The study examines the role of media in either challenging stereotypes or perpetuating biases against minority communities.

Ethnic Tensions and Media Narratives

The case study examines how media can either exacerbate or mitigate ethnic tensions within Asian societies. It delves into instances where media coverage has contributed to fanning the flames of intergroup conflicts, as well as cases where media has acted as a platform for dialogue and understanding. The study analyzes how media narratives can shape public attitudes toward ethnic diversity and influence political landscapes.

Media's Role in Identity Politics

This case study explores how media intersects with identity politics in Asia. It delves into instances where media outlets align themselves with certain identity-based political agendas and how this influences public discourse. The study examines how media can contribute to the construction of collective identities and the ways in which these identities impact political alliances and policy decisions.

Cultural Diversity in a Changing Landscape

The case study delves into the challenges of navigating cultural diversity within a rapidly changing media landscape in Asia. It explores how media outlets grapple with representing the multifaceted identities of their audiences while also adapting to technological advancements and globalization. The study examines the tensions between preserving cultural heritage and embracing globalized media trends.

Media Literacy in Culturally Diverse Contexts

The case study highlights the importance of media literacy in culturally diverse Asian societies. It explores how media literacy initiatives have empowered individuals to critically analyze media messages, discern biases, and understand the complex interplay between media, race, and politics. The study emphasizes the role of media literacy in fostering informed citizenship and promoting respectful dialogue across ethnic lines.

Conclusion

The case study on race, politics, and media in Asia underscores the significance of media in shaping the dynamics of racial and ethnic identities in the region. It highlights the power of media to either reinforce or challenge stereotypes, exacerbate or mitigate ethnic tensions, and influence identity-based politics. The study also emphasizes the importance of media literacy in helping individuals navigate the complex media landscape of culturally diverse Asian societies and fostering meaningful intergroup dialogue.

6. Case Study: Indigenous Media and Cultural Revival in Oceania

In the Pacific Islands region, Indigenous communities have used media as a tool for cultural revival, activism, and self-expression. This case study examines the ways in which Indigenous media outlets have provided platforms for preserving traditional knowledge, challenging colonial narratives, and advocating for social and environmental justice. It highlights the role of media in strengthening Indigenous identities and fostering connections across the diverse cultures of Oceania.

The vast expanse of the Pacific Islands, collectively known as Oceania, is home to a rich tapestry of Indigenous cultures and communities. This case study delves into the transformative role of Indigenous media in the region, exploring how these platforms have become vehicles for cultural revival, social activism, and the reclamation of Indigenous voices.

Preserving Traditional Knowledge and Languages

This case study examines how Indigenous media outlets in Oceania have become custodians of traditional knowledge and languages. It delves into the ways in which radio, television, and digital platforms have been used to document oral histories, traditional practices, and stories that are integral to the identities of Indigenous communities. The study highlights how media has played a crucial role in ensuring the continuity of cultural heritage.

Challenging Colonial Narratives

The case study explores how Indigenous media outlets in Oceania have challenged colonial narratives and reasserted Indigenous perspectives. It examines instances where media has been used as a tool to counter stereotypes, debunk myths, and provide a counter-narrative to historical injustices. The study delves into the power of media in reshaping public perceptions and reframing discussions around Indigenous rights and autonomy.

Advocacy for Social and Environmental Justice

This case study delves into how Indigenous media in Oceania has become a platform for advocating social and environmental justice. It examines how media outlets have shed light on issues such as land rights, climate change, and resource exploitation, amplifying the voices of communities affected by these challenges. The study highlights the role of media in fostering cross-cultural solidarity and prompting action at local, regional, and international levels.

Strengthening Indigenous Identities

The case study explores how Indigenous media has played a pivotal role in strengthening Indigenous identities in Oceania. It delves into the ways in which media outlets have provided a space for self-expression, cultural affirmation, and the celebration of Indigenous arts and traditions. The study examines the impact of media in building a sense of pride and resilience within Indigenous communities.

Fostering Connections Across Diverse Cultures

This case study highlights the role of Indigenous media in fostering connections across the diverse cultures of Oceania. It examines how media has facilitated the exchange of stories, knowledge, and experiences among Indigenous communities spread across vast distances. The study explores how media has acted as a bridge that transcends geographical boundaries and reinforces a sense of shared heritage.

Media as a Tool for Empowerment

The case study underscores the transformative power of Indigenous media as a tool for empowerment. It delves into how media outlets have empowered Indigenous individuals and communities to have agency over their narratives, challenge systemic injustices, and participate in shaping their own destinies. The study emphasizes how Indigenous media has contributed to cultural revitalization and social change in the Pacific Islands region.

Conclusion

The case study on Indigenous media and cultural revival in Oceania illuminates the profound impact of media on Indigenous communities' efforts to preserve their cultural heritage, challenge colonial legacies, advocate for justice, and foster connections across diverse cultures. It highlights the critical role of media in empowering Indigenous voices and promoting cultural resilience in the face of social and environmental challenges.

7. Case Study: Media and Racial Conflict in the Middle East

The Middle East is a region characterized by complex political dynamics and diverse racial and ethnic identities. This case study delves into how media in the Middle East have navigated issues of race, sectarianism, and cultural diversity. It explores the role of media in perpetuating or mitigating conflicts along racial and ethnic lines and examines efforts to promote understanding and dialogue in a context often marked by polarization.

The Middle East is a region of intricate cultural tapestries, diverse ethnicities, and historical complexities. This case study delves into the complex interplay between media and racial conflict in the Middle East, examining how media narratives have both reflected and contributed to tensions and divisions along ethnic and religious lines.

Historical Context and Media Narratives

This case study explores the historical context in which media narratives have shaped perceptions of racial identities in the Middle East. It delves into how media outlets have historically portrayed different ethnic and religious groups, often influencing public opinion and political dynamics. The study examines instances where media narratives have deepened divisions and contributed to racial conflict.

Media and Political Agendas

The case study investigates how media in the Middle East has been utilized to further political agendas and exacerbate racial tensions. It examines the ways in which media outlets have sometimes prioritized sensationalism and polarization over objective reporting, leading to the perpetuation of stereotypes and the amplification of divisive narratives. The study delves into the role of media in fueling conflicts and hindering peaceful resolutions.

Racialized Media Representations

This case study delves into how media representations of racial and ethnic groups in the Middle East have been racialized and politicized. It examines how media narratives often frame certain groups as the "other," perpetuating biases and reinforcing social hierarchies. The study explores the impact of such representations on public attitudes, social interactions, and policies.

Social Media and the Amplification of Divisions

The case study explores the role of social media in amplifying racial divisions in the Middle East. It delves into how online platforms have provided a space for the rapid dissemination of inflammatory narratives, hate speech, and misinformation. The study examines the challenges of combating online radicalization and the potential for social media to either exacerbate conflicts or facilitate dialogue.

Media as a Catalyst for Change

This case study also examines instances where media in the Middle East has acted as a catalyst for positive change and reconciliation. It explores how media outlets have used their platforms to promote interfaith dialogue, challenge extremist narratives, and foster cross-cultural understanding. The study delves into the potential for media to counter racial conflict by amplifying voices advocating for peace and tolerance.

Ethical Considerations and Responsible Reporting

The case study delves into the ethical considerations that media professionals in the Middle East face when reporting on racial conflict. It examines the challenges of providing objective and balanced coverage in an environment characterized by deep-rooted historical grievances and ongoing political disputes. The study explores the responsibilities of media outlets to uphold ethical standards while navigating complex narratives.

Conclusion

The case study on media and racial conflict in the Middle East sheds light on the intricate relationship between media narratives and racial tensions in the region. It highlights the ways in which media has both perpetuated divisions and acted as a potential catalyst for positive change. The study underscores the need for responsible reporting, ethical considerations, and the power of media in either exacerbating or alleviating racial conflicts in the Middle East.

8. Case Study: Media, Caste, and Identity in South Asia

Caste-based discrimination is a deeply entrenched issue in South Asian societies. This case study focuses on how media in countries like India have portrayed caste identities, challenges, and movements. It explores the role of media in challenging caste-based discrimination, amplifying marginalized voices, and promoting social justice. The case study also examines the complexities of media representation in a region marked by diverse caste and class dynamics.

Introduction

Caste-based discrimination is a deeply ingrained issue in South Asian societies, affecting millions of lives. This case study delves into the role of media in addressing caste identities, challenges, and movements in countries like India. It explores how media narratives shape perceptions, amplify marginalized voices, and contribute to the struggle for social justice.

Historical Context of Caste in South Asia

The historical legacy of the caste system is fundamental to understanding its impact on contemporary society. Media representations of caste have historically either perpetuated or challenged its existence, reflecting broader societal attitudes and beliefs.

Media Representations of Caste Identities

Media portrayals of caste identities have ranged from perpetuating stereotypes to highlighting stories of resilience and change. Understanding the nuances of these representations is essential for comprehending the complex relationship between media, identity, and social change.

Challenges and Opportunities in Media Representation

Media outlets grapple with the challenge of presenting caste-related issues accurately while avoiding perpetuating stereotypes. This section explores the difficulties faced by journalists in navigating sensitive topics and the potential for media to provide a platform for marginalized communities to share their experiences.

Media and Caste-based Movements

Media has played a significant role in amplifying the voices of caste-based movements advocating for equality. By highlighting protests, campaigns, and advocacy efforts, media coverage can shed light on the struggles of marginalized communities and garner public support for their cause.

Promoting Social Justice through Media

Media has the power to expose instances of caste-based violence, exploitation, and discrimination. By holding authorities accountable and raising awareness, media can contribute to fostering a more just society and inspiring collective action.

Media and Policy Discourse

Media's influence extends to policy discussions surrounding caste-based discrimination. By shaping public debates, media coverage can drive awareness about policy gaps and advocate for reforms that address systemic inequalities.

Intersectionality of Caste and Identity

The intersection of caste with other aspects of identity, such as gender, religion, and socioeconomic status, adds layers of complexity to media representation. This section explores how media can navigate these intersections to provide a more holistic understanding of individuals' experiences.

Conclusion: The case study underscores the pivotal role of media in addressing caste-based discrimination. By challenging stereotypes, amplifying marginalized voices, and advocating for policy reforms, media can contribute to dismantling the deeply rooted inequalities associated with the caste system in South Asia.

These region-specific case studies provide valuable insights into the ways in which race, politics, and media intersect and interact across different parts of the world. By examining the successes, challenges, and ongoing efforts in various regions, we gain a more comprehensive understanding of the global dynamics of media representation and its impact on society.

Diverse Cultural Contexts and Their Impact

Cultural Diversity in South Asia

The concept of caste varies across different countries and regions in South Asia. India, for instance, has a complex and hierarchical caste system, while other countries like Nepal have their own unique variations. Media representations must account for these differences to provide accurate and nuanced coverage.

Media's Role in Perpetuating Stereotypes

Media has at times perpetuated harmful stereotypes related to caste identities. Depicting certain castes as inferior or associating them with particular occupations can reinforce societal biases. This section explores how such stereotypes are disseminated through media and their impact on shaping public perceptions.

Challenging Stereotypes and Biases

Media also has the potential to challenge prevailing stereotypes and biases. By highlighting stories of individuals breaking caste barriers, achieving success, or advocating for change, media can counteract negative portrayals and contribute to reshaping societal attitudes.

Representation and Marginalized Voices

A critical aspect of media's role is providing a platform for marginalized voices within caste-affected communities. This involves not only sharing their stories but also ensuring their perspectives are accurately represented and not filtered through dominant narratives.

Caste and Media Ownership

Media ownership plays a significant role in shaping the content that is produced and disseminated. This section delves into how caste dynamics can influence media ownership, impacting the range of stories covered and the perspectives presented.

Media's Influence on Social Norms

Media narratives influence societal norms and behaviors. They can perpetuate discriminatory practices or contribute to challenging them. This section examines how media coverage can influence social norms related to caste interactions, marriage, education, and more.

Coverage of Caste-based Violence

Caste-based violence is a grim reality in many South Asian countries. Media has a responsibility to cover such incidents accurately and sensitively. This section explores how media's framing of caste-based violence can impact public discourse and the call for justice.

Portraying Caste and Social Mobility

Media's portrayal of social mobility within caste-affected communities reflects both individual stories and broader societal shifts. By showcasing instances of individuals breaking free from the constraints of caste-based discrimination, media can inspire hope and change.

Educational Role of Media

Media is a powerful educational tool. Documentaries, reports, and investigative journalism can raise awareness about caste-based discrimination, its historical roots, and its impact on society. This section discusses the potential for media to educate the public on these crucial issues.

Challenges in Reporting Caste Issues

Journalists face challenges when reporting on sensitive topics related to caste. This section examines issues such as access to information, fear of backlash, and the ethical considerations of balancing sensitivity with the responsibility to expose injustice.

Media's Influence on Policy

Media plays a role in shaping policy discussions around caste-based discrimination. By bringing attention to gaps in legislation, advocating for reforms, and highlighting instances of policy failure, media can contribute to policy changes that promote equality.

Caste and Digital Media

The rise of digital media has expanded the scope for discussions on caste-related issues. Social media platforms, podcasts, and online forums provide spaces for marginalized voices to be heard and stories to be shared.

Conclusion

The cultural diversity of South Asia brings with it a complex array of caste dynamics. Media's influence on shaping perceptions, challenging stereotypes, and advocating for change is immense. By navigating these complexities responsibly and sensitively, media can contribute to fostering a more inclusive and just society, where caste-based discrimination is challenged and dismantled.

Chapter 12: Conclusion

The journey through the intricacies of "Race, Politics, and the Media: Understanding Global Intersections" has illuminated the profound impact that media wields in shaping perceptions, influencing attitudes, and driving societal change. This comprehensive exploration of the interplay between race, gender, sexuality, and politics within media narratives underscores the necessity of a more nuanced and inclusive approach to storytelling.

As we reflect on the myriad topics traversed within this journey, several key takeaways emerge:

1. Media's Role in Shaping Reality

Media, as a powerful influencer, has the ability to construct and redefine reality through its portrayals of various identities, experiences, and social dynamics. The chapters of this book have revealed how media representation holds the potential to either reinforce harmful stereotypes or promote understanding, empathy, and inclusivity. The responsibility of media to accurately reflect the diversity of human experiences cannot be overstated.

2. Intersectionality and Inclusive Narratives

The concept of intersectionality has emerged as a central theme throughout this exploration. The intricate connections between race, gender, sexuality, and other aspects of identity highlight the complexity of lived experiences. This book has emphasized the importance of crafting narratives that reflect these intersections, as well as the necessity of amplifying voices that have historically been marginalized.

3. Media Literacy and Critical Thinking

One of the key tools for navigating the modern media landscape is media literacy. As the book has demonstrated, media literacy equips individuals with the skills to critically analyze, question, and interpret media content. This chapter has showcased how media literacy is not only essential for understanding media representation but also for dismantling biases and promoting more accurate portrayals.

4. Policy and Systemic Change

The chapters dedicated to policy recommendations and global case studies have highlighted the imperative for policy initiatives that foster balanced media representation. Addressing racial disparities in media requires systemic changes that prioritize diversity in newsrooms, challenge discriminatory practices, and hold media organizations accountable for responsible reporting.

5. Collaborative Efforts for Change

The examination of global movements for intersectional equality underscores the significance of collaboration and solidarity. In a world interconnected through media and technology, individuals and communities have the power to unite in challenging biased reporting, advocating for inclusive narratives, and holding media accountable for accurate representation.

6. Toward a More Inclusive Future

As we conclude this journey, it is evident that the path to a more inclusive media landscape is complex and multifaceted. It requires the active participation of media organizations, policymakers, activists, and individuals alike. By recognizing the influence of media on societal perceptions and valuing the importance of diverse and accurate representation, we take steps toward shaping a future where media narratives reflect the richness of human experiences.

In closing, "Race, Politics, and the Media: Understanding Global Intersections" invites readers to engage critically with media, challenge biases, and champion narratives that honor the complexity of identity. The book is a call to action, reminding us that our collective efforts are instrumental in creating a world where media is a force for positive change, inclusivity, and understanding.

With this conclusion, we complete our exploration of the intricate relationship between race, politics, and the media. However, the journey toward a more equitable media landscape continues, propelled by the shared commitment to fostering understanding, empathy, and social transformation.

Recap of Key Findings

1. Media's Profound Impact: The media holds significant power in shaping public perceptions and influencing societal attitudes. Our journey highlighted how media representation can either perpetuate harmful stereotypes or foster understanding and empathy toward intersectional identities.

2. Intersectionality Matters: The concept of intersectionality, which recognizes the interconnectedness of various aspects of identity, emerged as a central theme. We explored how individuals with intersecting identities often face unique challenges and how media can authentically represent these complexities.

3. Media Literacy as a Tool: Media literacy is essential for navigating the media landscape. By critically analyzing content, individuals can identify biases, challenge stereotypes, and contribute to a more informed and equitable media environment.

4. Policy for Change: The chapters on policy recommendations and global case studies underscored the need for systemic change. Efforts to promote diversity in newsrooms, challenge discriminatory practices, and advocate for balanced media representation are essential for lasting transformation.

5. Collaboration and Solidarity: Global movements for intersectional equality demonstrate the power of collaboration and solidarity. Media can amplify marginalized voices, and collective action can challenge biased reporting, promoting inclusive narratives on a global scale.

6. Toward an Inclusive Future: The conclusion of our journey emphasized the importance of valuing diverse and accurate representation. By recognizing the impact of media and committing to inclusive narratives, we can shape a future where media serves as a positive force for understanding and change.

7. Continuous Efforts: Our exploration is a reminder that the journey toward equitable media representation is ongoing. Through ongoing critical engagement, advocacy, and conscious media consumption, we contribute to a more inclusive and empathetic media landscape.

In summary, "Race, Politics, and the Media: Understanding Global Intersections" illuminated the complexities of media's influence on racial dynamics, intersectionality, and societal perceptions. By recognizing the power of media and working collaboratively, we have the opportunity to reshape narratives, challenge biases, and contribute to a more inclusive and equitable world.

Call to Action for Continued Research and Advocacy

The journey we've embarked upon in exploring "Race, Politics, and the Media: Understanding Global Intersections" serves as a catalyst for further action. The call to action is not just an endpoint but a beginning, as our understanding deepens and our commitment to change strengthens. As we conclude this exploration, we extend a resounding call to continue research and advocacy in the realm of media representation, racial dynamics, and intersectionality.

1. Continued Research: The landscape of media representation is dynamic and ever-evolving. There is a constant need for rigorous research that examines emerging trends, analyzes the impact of media on diverse communities, and investigates the effectiveness of various strategies aimed at promoting equitable representation. Academics, scholars, and researchers are encouraged to delve further into this field, unearthing new insights that can inform policy, media practices, and societal attitudes.

2. Amplification of Marginalized Voices: A core aspect of advocacy is giving voice to those who have been marginalized. As we move forward, let's uplift and amplify the stories and perspectives of individuals and communities that have historically been underrepresented or misrepresented. By centering their experiences, we reshape the narrative landscape, providing a platform for authentic voices to be heard.

3. Collaboration across Disciplines: The issues explored in this journey are multidimensional and interconnected. To achieve meaningful change, collaboration across disciplines is essential. Academics, activists, journalists, policymakers, artists, and communities must work together, leveraging their unique expertise to address the multifaceted challenges of media representation and racial dynamics.

4. Media Literacy Initiatives: Media literacy is a powerful tool for empowering individuals to critically engage with the media they consume. Educational institutions, community organizations, and media outlets should prioritize media literacy initiatives that equip people with the skills to recognize bias, challenge stereotypes, and navigate complex narratives.

5. Policy Advocacy: The policy recommendations outlined in this exploration provide a roadmap for legislative and institutional change. Advocacy efforts must continue to push for equitable media policies, diverse newsrooms, and accountability mechanisms that challenge discriminatory practices and promote balanced representation.

6. Ethical Responsibility: Media organizations hold a unique responsibility in shaping public discourse. Ethical journalism and responsible media practices are crucial to fostering an inclusive media environment. News outlets should commit to accurate, unbiased reporting that reflects the diverse realities of their audiences.

7. Inclusive Education: Educational curricula at all levels should incorporate discussions about media representation, intersectionality, and racial dynamics. By fostering understanding and critical thinking from an early age, we lay the foundation for future generations to engage thoughtfully with media content and contribute to positive change.

In conclusion, our exploration has shed light on the complex interplay between race, politics, and the media. It is now incumbent upon each of us, regardless of our roles and backgrounds, to heed the call to action. By continuing research, advocacy, collaboration, and education, we forge a path toward a media landscape that honors the richness of human diversity, challenges biases, and contributes to a more just and equitable world.

Recommended Books

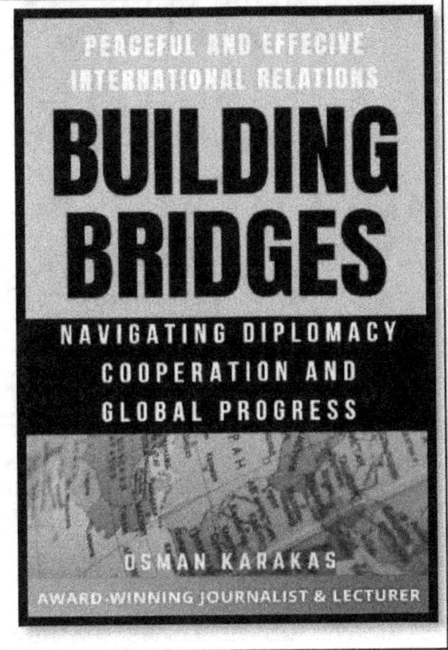

The collection of books is accessible for purchase on Amazon.com platform.